The Warrior Mentality

for

High School Teams

Copyright © 2024 The Warrior Mentality, LLC
Permission is granted to the user to reproduce this form for personal use. **No part of this book can be reproduced or sold for profit without prior written consent from the publisher.**

**The Warrior Mentality
For High School Teams**

ISBN   9798325358142

Cover photo credit:
Aldo Gonzalez & Stephen Williams

Disclaimer:
This book is not meant to be a substitute for direct advice from a medical or mental health provider.

About the Authors

Rachel Ocampo, Ph.D.
I grew-up as a small town kid in a big, Mexican American, football family in the U.S. Southwest. As a coach's kid and competitive athlete, I learned that sport has a tremendous impact on the lives of diverse young people. In my work as a licensed psychologist for youth and families in the Phoenix area, I have come to more fully appreciate the ways coaches and teams impact the overall development and wellness of my patients. In my current role as a Clinical Assistant Professor in the School of Counseling and Counseling Psychology at Arizona State University, I've had the opportunity to conduct sport psychology research and train fledgling mental health providers and consultants. During my time at ASU, I've noticed very few applied models that guide coaches' support and engagement of players with diverse experiences, abilities, identities, and cultural backgrounds. This led me to conduct a large-scale, cross-country, qualitative study surrounding the work of high school football coaches that informed my creation of The Warrior Mentality. The Warrior Mentality framework integrates cross-cultural worldviews, wisdom from coaches, psychological theory and research, and my own clinical insights into a new approach to engaging diverse athletes and teams.

Aaron Ocampo, M.S.
I'm honored that my youngest sister, Rachel, asked me to collaborate on this workbook for coaching high school teams. I grew up as the oldest son of a high school football coach, spending most of my afternoons on the field at my father's practices. Eventually, I played for him in high school and used football to fund my education at two universities in the U.S. Southwest. Upon graduation, I started my career doing the only thing that made sense to me, coaching high school football. Over the past 25 years, I have been working with high school athletes as a teacher, assistant, and head football and a track coach. During this time, I also earned my Masters of Science in Sports Administration from the University of New Mexico which has increased my ability to meet the needs of my players. Since 2012, I've served as the head football coach at a new school and program I helped to open in Southern New Mexico. Throughout my years of coaching, I have come to appreciate the need for frameworks and models to guide coaches in their work with diverse young people. I'm excited to be part of The Warrior Mentality and pass along the wisdom I've received from countless coaching mentors in this workbook.

Illustrator: Marianna Ocampo Hoogasian

Contents

Chapter 1: Identifying Your Purpose..10
1.1 Coach Activity: Clarify Personal and Collective Purpose...13
1.2 Coach Activity: Develop a Programmatic Mission Statement...14
1.3 Coach and Player Activity: Goal Setting..15
1.4 Coach Activity: Direct Action toward Goals..17
1.5 Coach Activity: Assess and Adjust Progress toward Goals..19
1.6 Coach Activity: Fuel Motivation toward Goals..21
1.7 Coach Activity: Finding a Coaching Job 23
1.8 Coach Activity: Hiring a Good Coach..25

Chapter 2: Acknowledging a Shared Destiny..26
2.1 Coach Activity: Assessing Shared Destiny in Coaching Staffs..33
2.2 Player Activity: Assessing Shared Destiny between Coaches and Players......................35
2.3 Player Activity: Assessing Shared Destiny Between Players...37
2.4 Parent Activity: Assessing Shared Destiny Between Coaches and Caregivers................40
2.5 Coach Activity: Leaning into Shared Destiny in Coaching Staffs....................................43
2.6 Coach Activity: Leaning into Shared Destiny in the Coach-Player Relationship.............46
2.7 Team Code...49
2.8 Player Leadership Councils 50
2.9 Player Activity: Leaning into Shared Destiny within Teams..51
2.10 Player Mentorship Program...54
2.11 Coach Activity: Leaning into Shared Destiny within the Coach-Parent Relationship....55
2.12 Program Activity: Roles and Responsibilities in the Program..59
2.13 Coach Activity: Holding Accountability and Operationalizing the Mission Statement..60
2.14 Coach Activity: Holding Accountability and Setting Clear Consequences....................63
2.15 Coach Activity: Being H.U.M.B.L.E..66
2.16 Coach Activity: Being O.P.E.N...67
2.17 Coach Activity: Filters and How We Communicate...68
2.18 Coach Activity: Filters and How We Receive Communication......................................70
2.19 Coach Activity: Communication B.A.S.I.C.S..72

Chapter 3: Recognizing Risks and Building on Resilience...73
3.1 Coach Activity: Identifying Risks and Resources..79
3.2 Coach Activity: Supporting the Physical and Mental Health of Differently Abled Players 82
3.3 Coach Activity: Supporting the Physical and Mental Health of High Talent Athletes....92
3.4 Coach Activity: Supporting the Physical and Mental Health of LGBTQ+ Players.......101
3.5 Coach Activity: Supporting the Physical and Mental Health of Players Living in Poverty.............110
3.6 Coach Activity: Supporting the Physical and Mental Health of Players Living in High Violence....118
3.7 Coach Activity: Supporting Immigrant, Ethnic, and Racial Minority Athletes..............124
3.8 Coach Activity: Helping a Team Cope with Grief and Loss...132
3.9 Coach Activity: Supporting Your Own Mental Health in Coaching...............................142

Appendices: Player Leadership Council Lesson Plans..156
A. Forming Leadership Platoons..157
B. Instagram, SnapChat, Tiktok, Twitter, etc..160
C. Approaches to Leadership..163
D. Troubleshooting Leadership Issues with Teammates...167
E. Goal Setting 172
F. Mental Health Issues and Getting Support..176
G. Communication Filters...180
H. Being H.U.M.B.L.E..187
I. Communication B.A.S.I.C.S...192
J. Diversity and Inclusion in Teams...195
K. Sport Psychology and Mental Performance...197
L. Navigating Injury...202
M. Looking toward the Future..205

"My coaching philosophy is to love every player like they were one of my own kids..."

-Alfred Ocampo

Introduction

Adolescence is a time of tremendous physical, cognitive, and socio-emotional growth. Physically, young people are navigating incredible changes across puberty. During puberty, young people's bodies develop under the influence of hormones and other processes (Rogol et al., 2002) to become almost unrecognizable over the course of a few short years. Cognitively, adolescents also undergo significant changes. Teens develop more complexity in their abilities to think abstractly, self-reflect, and form relationships due to improved functioning in their social brains (Blakemore, 2012). This, alongside other socio-emotional factors, can carry positive and negative implications for teens' psychological development.

Adolescents are influenced by socio-emotional tendencies during this time that shape the ways they see themselves, others, and the world. Due to a phenomenon called, imaginary audience, young people are extra attuned to the ways they are viewed by peers (Ryan & Kuczkowski, 1994). This can be beneficial to adolescent development in that teens spend most of their time with peers and are actively trying to foster relationships with them. If teens were not tuned into the ways they act in a relationship, they would have a hard time connecting. Unsurprisingly, however, being overly concerned with negative judgment from others can make teens more prone to embarrassment and negative psychological outcomes associated. Similarly, adolescence is also a time when young people have a hard time de-centering because they are developmentally egocentric (Schwartz, et al., 2008). Egocentrism is important for socio-emotional development because teens move toward maturity and self-sufficiency through tuning into and prioritizing their own needs. Despite this, teens who are unable to balance self-focus and appreciating the experiences and needs of others may struggle to form growth-fostering relationships across the lifespan.

Finally, adolescents often view themselves and their experiences as fundamentally different from others because of a phenomenon called personal fable (Elkind, 1981). In this, they believe that what happens to them will be different from what happens to others. Much like imaginary audience and egocentrism, personal fables can be both developmentally adaptive and maladaptive. On the one hand, it is crucial for adolescents to have a period of time in which they feel indestructible so that they have the courage to try new things and venture out on their own. On the other hand, personal fables can lead teens to make unsafe decisions that can threaten their immediate health and safety and impede long-term development (Alberts et al., 2007).

Personal fables, maturity in the reward center of the brain, and lagging of prefrontal cortex development creates the perfect storm for teens to engage in risky behaviors (Van Leijenhorst et al., 2010). Adolescents who believe they are impermeable to harm, who experience danger as thrilling in the brain, and who are unable to appreciate the long-term impacts of their decisions, will likely engage in unsafe behaviors. Unfortunately, according to the Centers for Disease Control and Prevention (CDC, 2023) the leading causes of death for adolescents around the world are traffic accidents, homicide, and suicide. Unsurprisingly, each of these are related to risk taking, challenges with inhibition, and the inability to see long-term consequences of immediate decision making.

In addition to the above considerations for physical, cognitive, and socio-emotional development in adolescence, Erikson's psychosocial theory also speaks to important identity processes occurring during this time. According to Erikson (1963), adolescence is a stage in which young people explore their identities. It is appropriate for adolescents to explore their gender, sexual, ethnic, and racial identities during this time and crucial to have caring and supportive adults surrounding them during the process. When teens are unable to form positive identities in any of these areas, they can experience detriment to psychological well-being as well as other outcomes (Meeus et al., 1999). One great way for teens to build relationships, try new things, and develop self-esteem is through joining clubs and sport teams (Slutzky & Simpkins, 2009). Young people who engage in sport can reap the physiological and psychological benefits in adolescence and across their lifetimes (Logan et al., 2020). Even in the context of great trials and tribulations, sport can be a positive source of stability. During the Covid-19 lockdowns, teens who were still able to engage in sport had better psychological outcomes in comparison to those who could not (Gonzalez-Valero et al., 2020).

The Warrior Mentality for High School Teams

In order for high school sport teams to be successful, coaches must attend to the physical, psychological, and socio-emotional development of young people. Coaches need to understand the contextual challenges faced by this new generation of players and how these impact mental health and performance. When coaches are able to do this, they not only increase players' satisfaction in programs and overall team cohesion, they also increase their capacity to win. Throughout this workbook, we offer coaches strategies to better support the holistic development of high school athletes using The Warrior Mentality (Ocampo, 2024). The Warrior Mentality is a new framework for coaching diverse teams that is based upon collectivistic worldviews, psychological theory and research, insights from clinical work, and advice from veteran coaches. This workbook is composed of three chapters, each covering a dimension of The Warrior Mentality framework. Each chapter will begin with an overview of the dimension as well as definitions of key concepts and activity descriptions. Concepts will be brought to life through recommendations, scripts, exercises, assessments, and worksheets that coaches can use to support the success of their teams. The workbook ends with Appendices A-M of lesson plans for coaches to teach key components of The Warrior Mentality to their athletes.

Chapter 1: Identifying Your Purpose describes the ways coaches can better understand their values and operationalize them into specific mission statements and team goals. This chapter also includes an activity that will help players reflect upon their own values and implement them on the team. This chapter closes with two exercises related to finding the right fit in a coaching job and recruiting good coaches. Chapter 2: Acknowledging a Shared Destiny explores how coaches can improve their relationships with other coaches, players, and players' caregivers by increasing: mutual investment, authenticity, accountability, humility, openness, and healthy communication. This chapter also includes assessments, ideas, and activities for supporting cohesion across every level of a program. Chapter 3: Recognizing Risks and Building on Resilience discusses the challenges and strengths of athletes from differing abilities, identities, experiences, and cultural backgrounds. Various recommendations and strategies will be presented to promote the positive health and development of individual athletes as well as the overall success of teams. This chapter closes with activities to help coaches support their own mental health needs in the profession.

If you would like to know more about The Warrior Mentality and its creation, we recommend that you review the flagship research book, *The Warrior Mentality: A New Framework for Coaching Diverse Teams*. If you or someone you know has interest in applying the framework to other developmental age groups, we recommend that you review the two other workbooks in this series (*The Warrior Mentality for Youth Teams* and *The Warrior Mentality for College Teams*). In the end, more resources and learning opportunities can be found on The Warrior Mentality social media pages. Feel free to connect with us if you would like to know more about implementing The Warrior Mentality in your program.

Chapter 1: Identifying Your Purpose

📖 Definitions:

In order to be a successful leader one must first identify their purpose in approaching the field of coaching. Many times our 'why's' are bound-up in values we've learned through important relationships with others. According to The Warrior Mentality (Ocampo, 2024) individuals exist within a shared destiny in which the actions of one influence the actions of another. Similarly, coaches have a special impact on their communities and thus have a responsibility to act in ways that benefit young people. Across age groups and competitive levels we have found that coaches' personal and interpersonal values come from adults in their own lives. Some coaches have caring and supportive parents and family members that instilled in them the importance of giving back. These coaches often see their position as an opportunity to positively shape the lives of young people. Other coaches who didn't have those same levels of support in the home, often found care and guidance with their own coaches growing-up. This second group became coaches because of their past experiences and a deep recognition that kids need adults to be there for them.

🔑 Key Concepts:

Identifying purpose helps coaches to: 1) Clarify Personal and Collective Purpose, 2) Develop a Programmatic Mission Statement, 3) Direct Action toward Goals, 4) Assess and Adjust Progress toward Goals, and 5) Fuel Motivation toward Goals.

1) <u>Clarify Personal and Collective Purpose</u>: Identifying personal and collective purposes for entering the coaching profession is the first step within The Warrior Mentality. Coaches' personal 'why's' could include: a love for their sport and a desire to stay connected to it, a pull to be the best in their field, or enjoying challenges and growing from them. Coaches' collective 'why's' could include: a desire to have a positive impact on future generations, a feeling of fulfillment in seeing others grow and progress, and deep satisfaction in relationships and feeling valued by others.

2) <u>Develop a Programmatic Mission Statement and Goals:</u> Once you have identified your particular 'why's,' you can develop programmatic mission statements. These might include phrases or axioms like: approaching the game with passion, being competitive in everything we do, having a growth-mindset, having a personal investment in programmatic success, holding each other accountable, growing together, and loving each other through it all. Once a mission statement is developed this can help clarify specific goals coaches may have for themselves, their coaching staffs, individual players, and the team as a whole.

Goals are usually reliant on a number of factors including: the demands of the situation; the abilities, challenges, and resources of individuals involved; and the mission and culture already established within a team. A head coach in a high competition school district, with players who are gifted athletically, and a coaching staff that is motivated and cohesive; may set a goal for winning a district and a state championship. Whereas, a head coach in the same district, who had to let some coaches go due to accountability issues, and whose high talent players graduated the previous year, may set goals for stabilizing and re-building.

3) <u>Direct Action toward Goals:</u> After you have a solid mission statement and goals, you can use these to direct action. For example, in the case of a high talent player showing up late to practice or not giving 100%, coaches can revisit and implement a team's mission statement to guide decision making. Some coaches in this case would have conversations with this player about the importance of showing up for themselves and for the team. Similarly, they would find ways to hold this player accountable, while also communicating care and compassion. Each of these approaches tie back to elements of their mission statements: growth-mindset, investment in programmatic success, holding accountability, and communicating care.

4) <u>Assess and Adjust Progress toward Goals:</u> When moving toward goals, you must continually assess your team's progress and make adjustments as needed. For example, a coach may decide to re-visit her team's mission statement and specific goals if she finds that the team is continually missing the mark. This coach may find that the goals she instituted at the beginning of the year (e.g. winning district and state) may be unattainable due to injuries or other issues that have arisen across the season. In this case, she may decide to de-emphasize one element of the mission statement (being competitive in everything we do) and bring forward others (approaching the game with passion, growing together, and loving each other through it all).

5) <u>Fuel Motivation toward Goals:</u> Finally, elements of your mission statement can fuel individual and programmatic investment and progress toward goals. For example, a coach may start to see that players' motivation is starting to wane after a couple of tough losses. This coach may decide to spend a whole practice re-visiting the mission statement of the team as a means to increase investment. He may work with fellow coaches to develop fun and challenging activities that remind players of their commitment to each other and love of the game. This team may go on to lose more games (depending on the difficulty of their schedule and other uncontrollables), but the kids are much more likely to put forward effort, leave the season satisfied, and come back next year.

Activities:

1.1 Coach Activity: Clarify Personal and Collective Purpose, is the first activity in this chapter and probably the most important. In this exercise, coaches will explore their own early relationships, the values they learned from loved ones, and the reasons they entered the coaching profession.

1.2 Coach Activity: Develop a Programmatic Mission Statement, is the second activity in this chapter. This exercise will help coaches translate their reasons for coaching into elements of a personalized programmatic mission statement.

1.3 Coach Activity: Goal Setting, is the third activity in this chapter. This exercise teaches coaches how to set P.U.R.P.O.S.E. driven goals within The Warrior Mentality. Goals attend to the mission of the team, their shared destiny, and specific risks and resiliencies of each player.

1.4 Coach Activity: Direct Action toward Goals, is the fourth activity in this chapter. This exercise will help coaches use their mission statements to determine the best course of action at the individual level for common struggles faced by coaches on staff and specific players.

1.5 Coach Activity: Assess and Adjust Progress toward Goals, is the fifth activity in this chapter. Coaches can use this exercise to assess programmatic movement toward goals using their mission statements. Coaches will make team level adjustments across different example scenarios.

1.6 Coach Activity: Fuel Motivation toward Goals, is the sixth activity in this chapter. This exercise provides opportunities for coaches to build motivation in themselves, their coaches, and players during times of great struggle. They will draw from their mission statements to fuel motivation across different example scenarios.

1.7 Coach Activity: Finding a Coaching Job is the seventh activity in this chapter. Coaches can use this exercise to understand what to look for in a coaching job that matches with their purpose, mission, and goals. Key questions will be posed that help coaches better prepare themselves for finding a position that can be lasting.

1.8 Coach Activity: Hiring a Good Coach is the eighth activity in this chapter. Head coaches, administrators, and athletic directors can use this exercise to help in hiring a coach that matches with their mission and goals for the program. Key questions will be posed regarding recruitment and interviewing.

1.1 Coach Activity: Clarify Personal and Collective Purpose

This activity will ask you questions about your purpose in entering the field of coaching and the important people who have guided you along the way.

Who were the most influential people in your life as a young person?

_____

_____

_____

Why were they so impactful to you?

_____

_____

_____

What values did you learn from these people growing-up?

_____

_____

_____

Identify specific reasons you entered the field of coaching?

Example: I care about young people and want to make them feel valued.

1. Reason: _____

2. Reason: _____

3. Reason: _____

4. Reason: _____

5. Reason: _____

1.2 Coach Activity: Develop a Programmatic Mission Statement

Use your above reasons for entering the coaching profession to formulate elements of a programmatic mission statement.

> **Example:** Reason: I care about young people and want to make them feel valued.
> Mission: We will care about each other on and off the field.

1. Reason: _____

   Mission: _____

2. Reason: _____

   Mission: _____

3. Reason: _____

   Mission: _____

4. Reason: _____

   Mission: _____

5. Reason: _____

   Mission: _____

Use your mission statements written above to come up with a complete team mission statement. This should be written as one paragraph.

_____

_____

_____

_____

1.3 Coach Activity: Goal Setting

Goals help individuals and teams clarify what they want to achieve and how they want to achieve it. Many times coaches have a hard time setting goals that are attainable and sustainable because they fail to connect goals with their mission, the shared destiny of the team, and the risks and resilience of each player. Below is an acronym that coaches can use to help them set goals within The Warrior Mentality.

 P.U.R.P.O.S.E. driven goals...

Prioritize the program's mission
Goals should prioritize the mission of the team. If the mission involves giving best efforts, goals should reflect that. <u>Example:</u> *"Each player will improve on their one-rep max across 3 lifts by the end of summer."*

Unite individuals within a shared destiny
Goals should unite the team within their shared destiny. Individual goals should benefit the team and collective goals should influence growth in the individual. <u>Example:</u> *"I will attend 90% or more of practices this season because my attendance makes me and the team better."*

Reflect risks and resilience
Goals should take into account the specific experiences, abilities, identities, and cultural backgrounds of each player. Growing-areas and obstacles should be considered as well as strengths and resources. <u>Example:</u> *"I will start a group chat with teammates in my position group and message them weekly during the season to remind them to attend practice and ask if they need anything from the group."*

(have) Plans
Goals need to be accompanied by plans to make them happen. Each goal should have an answer to these questions: Who is involved? What is expected? When will it be accomplished? Where will it be accomplished? Why is the goal important? How will the team achieve the goal? <u>Example:</u> **Who** = each athlete, **What** = improve their times in at least 1 race, **When** = by the end of the season, **Where** = in a sanctioned meet, **Why** = because individual improvement moves the team forward, **How** = each athlete will take care of their physical health (e.g. nutrition and sleep); attend practice, meetings, and weights; and listen to and implement feedback from coaches.

(are) Open to feedback
Goals and plans to meet them should be open to feedback, discussed, and mutually agreed upon within a team. If players do not feel like their wishes and desires are reflected in team goals, then they will have very little investment and motivation to achieve them. Example: A coach might spend some time at the preseason retreat to discuss P.U.R.P.O.S.E. driven goals with the coaching staff and team leaders. They would formulate mutually agreed upon goals for the team to pursue in the upcoming season as well as specific plans to achieve them.

See and celebrate progress
Goals should make room for seeing and celebrating progress. The most effective way to motivate people is to reinforce their behavior. When coaches appreciate players' movement toward goals and small victories, players grow in their desire to continue persisting. This is even more important when it is difficult to see progress amidst set-backs and struggles. Example: A volleyball coach might highlight improvements in a player's technique who has had some physical challenges this season, *"I see you, Jenny, getting that butt down and keeping those arms straight and strong! Keep gettin' it girl!"*

Evaluate progress and redirect action
Goal progress should be evaluated and redirected as needed. Many times teams fail at meeting goals because they are not flexible to the needs of the team and each player. Injury, illness, contextual stressors, familial struggles, grief and other issues may de-rail a team's movement toward goals. Coaches need to be able to adjust goals to accommodate these concerns to maintain players' motivations and encourage continued efforts. Example: If a couple starters become injured or unable to play and a team is no longer in the running for a championship, updated goals should be created to prepare new players for their starting positions. A coach might say, *"Even though we might not win a District Championship this year, we can re-focus on preparing our new starting five to be successful. Although you starting players won't be able to get in the game, you need to support the players who can and help them be confident in their new roles. You need to work with them in practice and outside of practice, giving them feedback and encouraging them. I know it may be frustrating and we will have some growing pains, but what we do now sets us up for the future. If we keep working hard now and preparing ourselves, we will have a shot at District and State in upcoming seasons."*

1.4 Coach Activity: Direct Action toward Goals

Utilize elements of your mission statement to decide the right course of action in the below scenarios at the *individual level*.

An athlete with physical challenges is struggling in practice and is not likely to play much on the team due to: their ability level, the composition of the team, and the difficulty of the schedule. You can see that they contribute to the team in other ways (e.g. player leadership and morale). You also appreciate that they really enjoy being part of the team and have built strong relationships with teammates. What would you do as a coach in this situation at the *individual level* that aligns with your mission statement and goals for the team?

I would emphasize individual player development, growth mindset, and personal investment in team progress as elements of the mission statement that could help in this situation. I would meet with the player individually and encourage them to keep trying. I would highlight the ways they have progressed throughout the season (on the field or in the weightroom). I would also find ways to shine light on their achievements in front of the team and have other players celebrate that player as well. I would find ways to highlight the ways this player moves the team forward outside of athletic contributions. I might consider involving them in leadership roles on the team to increase their investment and give them ways to feel successful.

You have a coach on staff that is not engaging with the athletes during practice. He stands in the back and is really quiet compared to other coaches. His body language also shows you that he doesn't seem to want to be at practice. The coach seems to check his watch often during practice, maybe to see how close we are to ending. When you hired this coach, he seemed really excited about the job and talked about wanting to help the team win a state championship. He is a skilled position coach, but his behavior in the past few weeks seems out of character. What would you do as a coach in this situation at the *individual level* that aligns with your mission statement and goals for the team?

_____
_____
_____
_____
_____
_____

One of your star players has 3 failing grades on their latest grade check. They have 3 until the end of the grading period which will determine eligibility for the 2nd half of the season. You know that sometimes he struggles to remember plays and kids on the team have joked about the player not being very smart. You also know that the teachers in his 3 failing classes tend to be less patient with student-athletes they have had in the past. What would you do as a coach in this situation at the *individual level* that aligns with your mission statement and goals for the team?

_____

_____

_____

_____

_____

_____

You have a coach on your staff with a daughter on the team that she rides very hard. The daughter is one of the best players on the team and a kid that really tries her best. You notice that the coach will yell at her daughter after she makes small mistakes during games and in practice. You can see that the daughter struggles with the added pressure that comes with her mom's yelling. You've made some passing comments and jokes about the coach laying off her daughter and you've also tried to give the daughter lots of positive feedback. This doesn't seem to be improving the situation. What would you do as a coach in this situation at the *individual level* that aligns with your mission statement and goals for the team?

_____

_____

_____

_____

_____

_____

1.5 Coach Activity: Assess and Adjust Progress toward Goals

Practice assessing your teams' progress toward goals in the below scenarios and decide the course of action you would take to stay on course or re-direct progress at the *programmatic level*.

Your team has just won a big game with your cross-town rivals. You and your players are feeling happy and proud of your achievement. You notice, however, that players have started to become lackadaisical in practices following the victory. You see them making many small mistakes due to lack of focus and over-confidence. What would you do as a coach in this situation at the *programmatic level* that aligns with your mission statement and goals for the team?

I would make sure that in my film sessions after the game that we are very diligent in pointing out the things that we need to improve on, even though we just won a big game. The team needs to understand that the main season goal isn't to beat the rival, but to improve over the course of the season and play our best. Part of our mission statement is to give our best effort. Championship teams are usually focused more on becoming their best team, rather than being better then another team. The best athletes and teams are always hungry to improve and don't base personal confidence on comparisons to other teams. The biggest question to ask is, "Will this practice effort and focus be good enough to win the championship?"

Your team has just finished 4 consecutive winning seasons at the 5A level. The enrollment of your school has increased to the point that you will be in the 6A division next year. The 6A division is much more competitive and your team will have one of the smallest enrollments instead of the biggest, like it was in the 5A division. On top of this, you will now be in the conference with the returning state champion from the year before. What would you do as a coach in this situation at the *programmatic level* that aligns with your mission statement and goals for the team?

_____
_____
_____
_____
_____

Your team has started the season decently and you've beaten the teams you were supposed to beat and lost to the teams that are ranked higher than you. Approaching the second month of the season, however, you've lost your top player and three other starters to injuries. It is unclear if they will be able to return for the latter part of the season. The kids stepping-up to fill their roles are lacking confidence and making mistakes they shouldn't be making. What would you do as a coach in this situation at the *programmatic level* that aligns with your mission statement and goals for the team?

_____

_____

_____

_____

_____

_____

You coach a team that is a perennial powerhouse. The 5 other schools in your district are also very good and you have big rivalries with them. Your district is an open enrollment district where kids can choose to go to any of the high schools. On top of this, players can transfer schools at any time during their high school careers and they only have to sit out 40% of the season before they will regain eligibility to play. You hear that some players are thinking of transferring to a different school in the upcoming season. What would you do as a coach in this situation at the *programmatic level* that aligns with your mission statement and goals for the team?

_____

_____

_____

_____

_____

_____

1.6 Coach Activity: Fuel Motivation toward Goals

Utilize the elements of your mission statement to determine ways to increase motivation at the *individual and* programmatic levels.

Your team has suffered the loss of one of your most charismatic and caring kids due to gun violence that happened in the middle of the season. Your kids are suffering, parents are concerned, and you are having trouble managing your own emotions related to the death. You want to make sure that the kids feel supported, but also understand that you have to prepare for subsequent games in the season. What could you do as a coach in this situation at the *individual and* programmatic levels that aligns with your mission statement and goals for the team?

There really is no good answer for a situation like this. You are dealing with the loss of a life in your team family. When something like this happens, competing in a meaningless game is not the priority. The best thing I can do as a coach is to make sure the grieving players are feeling supported. Part of our mission statement is to care about each other on and off the field. Players need to be the decision makers when it comes to how the team will address the upcoming schedule with practices and games. If the players don't feel they are up to competing, they shouldn't compete. If and when they are ready, they should be supported by the coaching staff at every step of the way. If I am having a hard time, I need to be okay with asking for help from fellow coaches and asking for help outside of the team. I may need to tap into spiritual support or even go to a counselor.

You are the new coach of a program that has been very successful. The previous coach was a local legend that just retired. She was very popular and had a great reputation for having well-coached, hard-nosed teams. As a coach, you feel that every decision you make is being questioned by your new players and parents. You constantly hear, "That isn't how Coach used to do it." As the season gets closer to starting, you feel that the team's confidence is not very high. What could you do as a coach in this situation at the *individual and* programmatic levels that aligns with your mission statement and goals for the team?

_____
_____
_____
_____
_____

One of your starters just lost her father to a long battle with cancer. The player has been expecting the worst with the situation, but the death just happened and she seems negatively impacted. She finds it hard to make it through practice and you see that when she is not feeling down she seems to be distracted and making more mistakes than she used to. You worry that if you take her off the starting line-up that could make her more upset, but you also don't want the team to suffer by keeping her in. What could you do as a coach in this situation at the *individual <u>and</u> programmatic levels* that aligns with your mission statement and goals for the team?

_____
_____
_____
_____

After winning the first game of the season, your team has lost four games in a row. The first two losses were close, but the last two teams beat you handily. Your team has started to have very little motivation to practice hard and you are now starting to have players miss practice all together. You have tried punishing the team for lack of motivation by making them do more endurance training, but that just seemed to make them angry and even less motivated to attend. What could you do as a coach in this situation at the *individual <u>and</u> programmatic levels* that aligns with your mission statement and goals for the team?

_____
_____
_____
_____

1.7 Coach Activity: Finding a Coaching Job

Finding a coaching job can be very stressful and time consuming, especially for coaches who do not have access to many mentors who can walk them through the process. This activity will be useful for coaches who are looking for more guidance on finding a position that is right for them. Please review and reflect upon the following questions.

🔑 Key questions to ask yourself if you are currently a head coach looking for another job:

- *Is the new opening a better situation than your current job?* Think about pay, prestige, flexibility, administrative support, etc.
- *Does the new school have a tradition of success?* Think about winning records as well as player outcomes, coach turnover, etc.
- *Are you and your family willing to move?* Think about closeness to family, job opportunities for your partner, your children's adjustment to a new home and school, etc.
- *Can you be more successful as a coach at the new job?* Reflect on what success means in this position in the short and long run.
- *Will applying for the new job hurt your standing with your current employer or team?* Remember that the names of the applicants may be announced in the media. You don't want to be penalized at your current position, especially if you don't get the new one.
- *Is the pressure to win at the new job going to be too much?* Think about your physical and mental health needs (now and into the future) as well as the impact of stress on your familial relationships.

🔑 Key questions to ask yourself if you are currently an assistant coach considering another position (either as a head coach or otherwise):

- *Are you and your family willing to move?* Think about closeness to family, job opportunities for your partner, your children's adjustment to a new home and school, etc.
- *Is the new position one that is going to help you grow as a coach?* Think about your short and long-term goals in coaching as well as the personality and cohesion of the coaching staff you hope to join.
- *Are you in a good situation as an assistant coach now, where you are challenged and have a good mentor?* Depending on the new position, you may have more or less access to mentors and growth opportunities compared to your current position.
- *Is the new job a place that has had previous success or does it struggle with turnover?* There are some jobs where it is very hard to win at a high level because of systemic difficulties and low cohesion. In these cases, it may be better to wait for another job to open. This may be difficult to hear because it is hard to pass on a head coaching position when you've been waiting on a job to open. In the end, you have to do what is right for yourself and your family. We just want to remind you that if you are unsuccessful in one of these programs it may negatively impact you in the long-run, looking for other coaching positions later.

- *Do you have a program, mission statement, or approach you hope to bring into the new position?* You will likely be asked this in your interviews and it would be a good idea to have this clarified within yourself before going on the job hunt. If you are reading this workbook, however, you are definitely off to a great start! The Warrior Mentality would be an excellent framework for you to learn and integrate within your next team.
- *Do you have assistant coaches in mind, if you get the job?* You will likely need to have an idea of who you will invite to join your coaching staff if you get offered the position. See *activity 1.9* for more guidance on hiring coaches.
- *Do you have enough experience to get the position?* Even if you don't, it is still a good idea to throw your name in the hat. Getting interview experience is really important as it helps you to practice talking about yourself, your goals as a coach, and your approach to players. You may not get this job, but you could leave a good impression that could help you down the road.

Key questions to ask potential programs for a head coach position:

- What is the pay?
- What is the assistant coaching pay?
- Why did the previous head coach leave? How long were they in the position?
- Can you hire your own assistant coaches?
- Are there openings to hire coaches as teachers at the school (if applicable)?
- What would your teaching position be (if applicable)?
- What would your duties be other than coaching your sport?
- Is there an athletic enhancement class where you can work with your athletes during the school day? Are assistant coaches able to be in that class also?
- What limitations do they have on off-season and summer programs/practices?
- Is there a booster club already established?
- What are the rules/limitations when it comes to fundraising?
- What expectations do they have of you as the head coach?

Key questions to ask potential programs for an assistant coach position:

- What is the pay?
- What is the time commitment year round?
- What would your teaching position be (if applicable)?
- What would your duties be other than coaching your sport?
- Is there an athletic enhancement class where you can work with your athletes during the school day?
- What expectations does the head coach have of you in this position?
- What opportunities are available to you for mentorship within the coaching staff?
- How cohesive is the coaching staff?
- What is the philosophy and approach of the head coach?

1.8 Coach Activity: Hiring a Good Coach

In order to have an effective program, your coaching staff must be highly cohesive and work well together. All coaches have to join behind a unified vision, philosophy, and approach for the team. The first step in achieving this goal is hiring the right people. Below are some considerations for head coaches and administrators to review during the hiring process.

 Green flags when it comes to hiring coaches:

- The applicant has a track record of working well with other coaches.
- The applicant has a track record of being a good teacher.
- The applicant describes wanting to coach because they care about kids and want to positively shape the lives of young people.
- The applicant shows flexibility, humility, and an openness to learn from other coaches.
- The applicant has evidenced consistency, reliability, and punctuality.
- The applicant has the energy and passion necessary to work with young people.

 Red flags when it comes to hiring coaches:

- The applicant has a poor track record of working well with other coaches.
- The applicant has a poor track record of being a good teacher.
- The applicant describes wanting to coach because they want to win a championship and does not mention caring about kids.
- The applicant only wants to coach because their child is coming into the program.
- The applicant only wants to coach if they can work on the varsity team.
- The applicant does not appear flexible, humble, or open to learning from other coaches.
- The applicant has not evidenced consistency, reliability, and punctuality.
- The applicant does not appear to have the energy and passion necessary to work with young people.

When interviewing new coaches, it is important to give them as much information about their assignments and expectations as possible. This will help in assessing their fit for the position and support their longevity in the program. Below are some areas to discuss with possible applicants:

- Mission statement and goals of the program
- Travel expectations
- Non-sport related roles/duties
- Coaching position assignments
- Practice and training locations and hours
- Practice plan expectations
- Scouting duties
- Game plan assignments
- Gameday roll/charting/decision making

For further ideas in hiring effective coaches, programs should ask applicants about their work with diverse players. Nearly any case example within this workbook could be used to assess applicants' knowledge and approach to work with diverse players.

Chapter 2: Acknowledging a Shared Destiny

 Definitions:

After identifying their purpose and using it to create a mission statement and goals, coaches can move on to acknowledging the shared destiny of their team. According to The Warrior Mentality (Ocampo, 2024), shared destiny is a concept foundational to group harmony and progress. Shared destiny prioritizes the interests of the many *and* the few. When individual players are struggling with injury or some emotional concern, their team members can feel the impact. Similarly, when a team wins a state championship each individual player can walk away feeling like they are on top of the world!

Many coaches have trouble with getting players to rely on one another and lean into their shared destiny. This is often due to the inherent vulnerability it takes to trust someone to be there for you when you need them. Often early negative experiences with caregivers being untrustworthy or unreliable leads people to have difficulties trusting others. Why would a player trust that their coach or their teammates will have their back if they have been burned by loved ones in the past?

Coaches also have challenges with leaning into shared destiny within their coaching staffs. Assistant coaches indicate that their head coach's approach to leadership can either help or hinder staff cohesion. Staff cohesion, inevitably, sets the tone for cohesion between players. When all coaches on staff feel valued, cared for, and respected they are much more likely to work hard for each other and for their players. In turn, when head coaches feel they can rely on their assistants to be present and positive for the team, they are much more willing to delegate and share power.

Lastly, coaches' relationships with players' caregivers also impact the shared destiny of programs. When coaches are open and communicative with caregivers, caregivers are more trusting and supportive of programs. When caregivers are absent or overbearing they negatively impact their children and frustrate coaches.

 Key Concepts:

The Warrior Mentality (Ocampo, 2024) highlights four avenues toward supporting cohesion and leaning into the shared destiny of the program: 1) Mutual Investment and Authenticity, 2) Holding Accountability, 3) Being Humble and Open, and 4) Healthy Communication.

1) <u>Mutual Investment and Authenticity</u>: In positive and well-functioning relationships each person makes emotional (and sometimes instrumental) investments in the other. Coaches spend countless hours investing in their programs to further the development of their players as athletes and as young people. Similarly, players on teams expend blood, sweat, and tears to move the team forward and make their coaches proud.

In this process, each team member brings their authentic selves into the relationship. Coaches and players do this by being genuine with each other and true to themselves on the team. Authenticity is challenging, however, because it involves showing parts of ourselves that we don't often share with others. These are our vulnerabilities and struggles that we hide for fear of not being accepted. True authenticity can become even more challenging for male dominated teams or individuals with marginalized identities.

Adolescent boys have often been socialized to hide weakness and be unaccepting of others' vulnerabilities. Because of this, they may struggle to fully invest in teams, hear and implement growth-fostering feedback, and open themselves to the full range of socio-emotional benefits a team can offer. In the same way, gender and sexual minority players may stay closeted and hide their authentic selves to avoid being bullied, ostracized, or even assaulted.

According to psychological research on the development of healthy relationships (and healthy people), there is consensus surrounding the importance of people having relationships in which they feel seen, appreciated, and valued. In sport psychology research, players and coaches who can develop these types of relationships in teams feel more satisfied, self-efficacious, and motivated. They also experience less anxiety, perform better, and are more apt to persist on the team and in future sports.

Within this chapter, coaches can find multiple assessments for measuring mutual investment and authenticity across: coaching staffs, players' relationships with coaches, players' relationships with each other, and coaches' relationships with caregivers. Scores on these assessments will shed insight into the ways coaches can help improve cohesion within their teams. Later, several activities will be presented that contain strategies and ideas to support relationships across these levels.

2) <u>Holding Accountability:</u> In cohesive and well-functioning teams, each member is mutually invested, authentic, and able to hold one another accountable. Holding accountability also relies on setting and living-up to expectations one has formed in the context of a relationship. On teams the commitment coaches and players have to one another is often measured by their ability to live-up to their mission statements. If a team has "caring for each other on and off the field" as an element of their mission statement, coaches should hold themselves and their players accountable to times when this does and does not happen.

It is important for coaches to return to their mission statement operationalizations and provide clear examples of what "caring for each other" and other elements of the mission statement mean and look like. Similarly, it is crucial that coaches explain the ways in which they will hold accountability when expectations and commitments are not met. Finally, coaches must ensure that they are holding all members of the team equally accountable to the mission statement of the team. If a high talent player is given more slack than other players, ripples of resentment will surely permeate the team.

Within this chapter, coaches will be guided through activities to clarify and operationalize their mission statements and set consequences for meeting, exceeding, and failing to meet the standard.

3) <u>Being Humble and Open:</u> In cohesive and well-functioning teams, each member is able to approach their roles and responsibilities with humility and openness. Within the shared destiny of the team, each member realizes that they have personal shortcomings and room to grow. The beauty of being part of a team is that individual members have access to a group of caring people who are invested in bettering each other. A member only needs to be cognizant of their growth areas and open to receiving and implementing feedback to achieve this goal. Unfortunately, this is easier said than done.

It is hard for coaches to humble themselves and be open to feedback from each other because there are emotional and economic investments they make in this profession. No coach wants to hear that they need to change their approach because they really care about their players and feel that they are already trying their best. Similarly, coaches may take critical feedback as threatening to their identity as a coach, a profession in which they've invested years of energy, time, and effort. Assistant coaches receiving critical feedback from head coaches may feel even more uneasy because their livelihoods and future career goals may be on the line. In the same way, assistant coaches may fear critiquing head coaches due to these same fears.

It is hard for players to humble themselves and be open to receiving feedback from each other because they, too, have invested physically and emotionally into their programs. Adolescent players could have even more struggles with being open to feedback because they are developmentally more attuned to negative judgment from peers and possible embarrassment.

In addition, it may be hard for players to humble themselves and be open to hearing and implementing feedback from coaches due to unconscious psychological processes within this relationship. Players may begin to see coaches as stand-in caregivers and be more sensitive to negative feedback because they view it as a threat to this relationship. This may happen more frequently and intensely with players who experience strain or abandonment in early or current parental relationships.

Across these situations, it is important for coaches and teams to adopt and normalize humility and openness to feedback. Coaches must push past their emotional discomfort in this area to create a context in which they model these values within the team. Over time players will recognize that acknowledging emotions and learning from them, makes them and the team stronger. Within this chapter, coaches will be introduced to two acronyms they can use to help each member of the program to be more H.U.M.B.L.E. and O.P.E.N.

4) <u>Healthy Communication</u>: In cohesive and well-functioning teams, coaches, players, and caregivers engage in healthy communication. Each member of a program understands that the words they use and how they use them matters. Knowing this, each member must ensure they speak from a place of respect and intention.

   Each person has their own relational expectations, worldviews, values, emotions, and developmental considerations that they bring into communication. When one member of a program talks to another member their words and tone are filtered through each persons' history and experience.

   For example, an assistant coach may yell at a high school player in front of their position group because he has had a bad day and that is the pattern he's learned from coaches growing-up. The player, then, may become angry and defensive because he has experienced absent or punishing caregivers and is more developmentally apt to experience embarrassment. Similarly, a head coach might use humor to indirectly admonish an assistant coach for a mistake because she has been burned by direct communication in the past. This assistant coach, in turn, may view the head coach as being disrespectful and think the jokes are made at her expense.

   Additionally, a young coach may be overly accommodating to a player's parents because he fears that having firmer boundaries will create more problems than the alternative. Parents in this case, may start to question this coach's confidence and competence to lead the team because they miss the head coach who recently retired. Finally, a player may avoid giving a teammate feedback because she worries it will evoke anger and threaten their relationship. The player who doesn't get the feedback will notice changes in their teammate's behavior toward them. They may question why their teammate is not passing the ball to them as often as they used to and come up with an explanation that is likely worse than the real reason.

   To mitigate misunderstandings, members of a program must reflect upon their own histories and experiences and how these filter communication. They must also strive to respect and attend to others' filters and modulate their message accordingly. When coaches and players take the time to reflect they create distance between themselves and maladaptive patterns. This distance allows them to move toward control and intentionality in communication. In this chapter of the workbook, activities will be presented that help coaches and players better understand the ways in which they give and receive communication as well as some B.A.S.I.C.S. to improve as communicators.

Activities:

2.1 Coach Activity: Assessing Shared Destiny in Coaching Staffs is the first activity in this chapter. In this exercise coaches can assess coaching staff cohesion and receive feedback on ways to increase mutual investment and authenticity within their coaching staffs.

2.2 Player Activity: Assessing Shared Destiny Between Coaches and Players is the second activity in this chapter. In this exercise coaches can assess the quality of coach-player relationships within the team. Coaches can have players fill this out for the head coach and/or position coaches and receive feedback on ways to increase mutual investment and authenticity within these relationships.

2.3 Player Activity: Assessing Shared Destiny Between Players is the third activity in this chapter. In this exercise coaches can assess the quality of team cohesion amongst players. Feedback on ways to increase mutual investment and authenticity within players' relationships with one another will be given.

2.4 Parent Activity: Assessing Shared Destiny Between Coaches and Caregivers is the fourth activity in this chapter. In this exercise coaches can assess the quality of relationships they have with players' parents. Feedback on ways to increase mutual investment and authenticity within coaches' relationships with parents will be given. Depending on the state of the team, personality of caregivers involved, and other contextual factors, it may not be advisable to use this assessment within programs.

2.5 Coach Activity: Leaning into Shared Destiny in Coaching Staffs is the fifth worksheet in this chapter. This worksheet includes considerations and strategies for increasing coaching staff cohesion in programs. Ideas will be given for in-season and out-of-season activities that foster positive relationships between coaches (e.g. ideas for attending coaches clinics together and holding regular meetings about personal and professional development).

2.6 Coach Activity: Leaning into Shared Destiny in the Coach-Player Relationship is the sixth worksheet in this chapter. This worksheet includes considerations and strategies for building positive relationships between coaches and their players. Ideas will be given for in-season and out-of-season activities to increase coach-player cohesion (e.g. holding a coach-player retreat and instituting a Player Leadership Council).

2.7 Team Code is the seventh worksheet in this chapter. This worksheet can be used by players to determine a code they can aspire to for their season. The Team Code is structured by: what the team stands for, how they want to practice, and how they want to play. It is recommended that leaders on the team create the code during the off-season (maybe at the retreat), explain the code to their teammates at the start of the season, obtain signatures from all players, and post the code in the team locker room and/or meeting room.

2.8 Player Leadership Council is the eighth worksheet in this chapter. This worksheet describes the roles and responsibilities of council members and what they can expect in taking-on this position. It also includes a list of topics that could be covered in their weekly meetings. In Appendices A-M of this workbook you can find lesson plans for implementing each topic area listed. Coaches can have players review and sign this worksheet prior to joining the council at the start of the season.

2.9 Player Activity: Leaning into Shared Destiny within Teams is the ninth worksheet in this chapter. This worksheet includes considerations and strategies for fostering positive relationships between players. Ideas will be provided for in-season and out-of-season activities to increase team cohesion (e.g. "The Rock Challenge" and instituting a Mentorship Program).

2.10 Player Mentorship Program is the tenth worksheet in this chapter. This worksheet describes the roles and responsibilities of Mentors and Mentees and what they can expect in their commitment to the Mentorship Program. Coaches can have players review and sign this worksheet prior to becoming a Mentor or Mentee.

2.11 Coach Activity: Leaning into Shared Destiny within the Coach-Parent Relationship is the eleventh worksheet in this chapter. This worksheet includes considerations and strategies for fostering healthy relationships between coaches and players' caregivers. Ideas will be given for in-season and out-of-season activities to increase cohesion with players' caregivers (e.g. preseason parent meetings and Booster Club initiatives).

2.12 Program Activity: Roles and Responsibilities in the Program is the twelfth worksheet in this chapter. This worksheet is a table used to explain how coaches, players, and caregivers work together to address the physiological and psychological needs of each athlete while attending to the needs of the team. Coaches can use this worksheet in preseason meetings with coaches, players, and parents to explain and clarify expectations within the program.

2.13 Coach Activity: Holding Accountability and Operationalizing the Mission Statement is the thirteenth activity in this chapter. In this exercise coaches will practice operationalizing elements of their mission statements to clarify what each looks like and does not look like in the context of the team. Coaches can share this worksheet with their staff and players to communicate standards to which each team member will be held accountable.

2.14 Coach Activity: Holding Accountability and Setting Clear Consequences is the fourteenth activity in this chapter. In this exercise coaches will practice setting clear consequences for when members of the team fail to meet, meet, or exceed behavioral expectations. Coaches can use this exercise to track individual players and coaches' contributions to the program. Coaches can also refer to these records when making tough decisions about an individuals' future involvement in the program.

2.15 Coach Activity: Being H.U.M.B.L.E. is the fifteenth activity in this chapter. In this worksheet coaches can use the acronym H.U.M.B.L.E. to determine ways to effectively accept, process, and implement feedback.

2.16 Coach Activity: Being O.P.E.N. is the sixteenth activity in this chapter. In this worksheet coaches can use the acronym O.P.E.N. to determine ways to improve their understanding of and relationship with emotions.

2.17 Coach Activity: Filters and How We Communicate is the seventeenth activity in this chapter. In this worksheet (2.17 and 2.17a) coaches can reflect upon their past experiences and relationships and how these filter the ways they communicate with others. Coaches can use this worksheet to help them clear away obstructions to effective communication.

2.18 Coach Activity: Filters and How We Receive Communication is the eighteenth activity in this chapter. In this worksheet (2.18 and 2.18a) coaches can reflect upon their past experiences and relationships and how these filter the ways they receive communication from others. Coaches can use this worksheet to help them clear away blockages and better absorb messages as they are given.

2.19 Coach Activity: Communication B.A.S.I.C.S. is the nineteenth activity in this chapter. In this worksheet coaches can learn useful approaches to communication through the acronym, B.A.S.I.C.S. Coaches can use this worksheet to help themselves practice healthy communication within and beyond the program.

2.1 Coach Activity: Assessing Shared Destiny in Coaching Staffs

Please reflect upon the following questions as a way to assess levels of coaching staff cohesion on your team. Please be as truthful as possible, your answers to these questions will help determine areas of strength and areas of growth to improve the program. Rate your answers on a scale of 0-4 (0=strongly disagree, 1=disagree, 2=neutral, 3=agree, 4=strongly agree).

1. I am able to share my personal concerns with other coaches on staff. ____
2. I am able to share my professional concerns with other coaches on staff. ____
3. I feel that the coaching staff has my back when I need them personally. ____
4. I feel that the coaching staff has my back when I need them professionally. ____
5. I feel that I am able to be a resource for other coaches on staff, personally. ____
6. I feel that I am able to be a resource for other coaches on staff, professionally. ____
7. I feel that I am listened to and respected on the coaching staff. ____
8. I feel coaches accept me and my cultural background (e.g. race/ethnicity, religion). ____
9. I feel coaches accept me and my different identities (e.g. gender, sexual orientation.). ____
10. I feel that my ideas are considered seriously and often implemented within the team. ____
11. If I make a mistake, I feel that my coaching staff will be patient and supportive. ____
12. If I have a personal or professional accomplishment, the coaching staff celebrates me. ____
13. I enjoy spending time with my coaching staff outside of work. ____

14. Please list some ideas for increasing positive relationships within the coaching staff:
_____
_____
_____

15. Please list some ideas for improving the overall program:
_____
_____
_____

2.1 Assessment Score Analysis:

<u>High Scorers (mostly 3's and 4's):</u> You are likely part of a highly cohesive coaching staff in which you feel valued personally and professionally. You are likely to have high levels of investment in your relationships with other coaches on staff and feel comfortable to be yourself around them. You likely feel confident that if you share a professional or personal concern with your fellow coaches it will be considered and you will be supported. Similarly, you feel that you can contribute to the team and that your contribution is respected and valued. Even though you have high levels of cohesion on the staff, it is recommended that you pay attention to your responses on individual items. You may have noticed a pattern in which you feel more comfortable with the coaching staff on a personal level, but professionally there may be some areas to further grow (or vice versa).

<u>Mid Level Scorers (mostly 2's):</u> You are likely part of a coaching staff that may not be struggling, but definitely isn't succeeding as far as cohesion. At times you may feel valued personally but not professionally (or vice versa), or maybe you feel neutral in both areas. You are likely to invest less in relationships with coaches in whom you feel invest less in you. You are also comfortable to be yourself around those coaches who you trust the most on staff. You likely feel a bit shaky about sharing professional or personal concerns with your fellow coaches, especially in cases where you are not confident you will be supported. Similarly, you may feel that you can contribute to the team but your contribution is not always respected, valued, or implemented. If you are a coach in this range it is recommended that you pay attention to your responses on individual items and identify areas that need further development. It would be useful to share your responses with your head coach and others on staff to spark a discussion that will hopefully bring everyone closer.

<u>Low Scorers (mostly 0's and 1's):</u> You are likely part of a minimally cohesive coaching staff in which you feel undervalued personally and professionally. You probably have low levels of investment in your relationships with other coaches on staff and feel uncomfortable to be yourself around them. You likely do not feel confident in sharing a professional or personal concern with your fellow coaches because you fear they will be unconsidered or used against you. Similarly, you feel that you can't contribute to the team because your contribution won't be respected and valued. If you are a coach in this range it is recommended that you reflect again on your purpose or 'why's' in approaching the profession (Chapter 1). If you feel that you are unable to pursue your purpose and mission within this program, then it may be time to look into other avenues that will allow you to do so. Staying in a position that hurts your mental health (and subsequent physical health) may not be worth it to you at this time in your career. Conversely, if you feel that you are able to stick it out and believe that you can pursue other areas of purpose, it may be worth it for you to stay and fight the good fight. It is possible to turn programs around, but change can only happen when coaches take a hard look at themselves and find ways to do things differently.

2.2 Player Activity: Assessing Shared Destiny Between Coaches and Players

Please answer the questions below with your true thoughts about the relationships you have with your coaches. Your scores will be reviewed by coaches to help them understand ways they can better support you and the team as a whole. Your coaches may have you fill out a separate list of questions for your position coach and your head coach so that they can understand differences in each relationship. Rate your answers on a scale of 0-4 (0=strongly disagree, 1=disagree, 2=neutral, 3=agree, 4=strongly agree).

1. I am able to share my family or friendship problems with my coaches. ____
2. I am able to share my academic issues with my coaches. ____
3. I am able to tell coaches when I need help in my sport. ____
4. My coach accepts me and my cultural background (e.g. race/ethnicity, religion). ____
5. My coach accepts me and my different identities (e.g. gender, etc.). ____
6. My coaches have my back when I need them. ____
7. My coaches see me as an asset to the team. ____
8. My coaches listen to me and take my suggestions. ____
9. If I make a mistake, my coaches will be patient and supportive. ____
10. If I accomplish something in (or outside of) my sport, my coaches celebrate me. ____
11. I enjoy spending time with my coaches. ____
12. My coaches enjoy spending time with me. ____

13. Please list some ideas for increasing positive relationships between players and coaches:

_____
_____
_____

14. Please list some ideas for improving the overall program:

_____
_____
_____

2.2 Assessment Score Analysis:

<u>High Scorers (mostly 3's and 4's):</u> They likely feel valued by you as coaches. They have high levels of investment in their relationships with you and feel comfortable to be themselves around you. They are likely confident enough in your relationship with them to share personal, academic, and sport related problems with you. They trust that you will be patient and support them. Similarly, they feel that they can contribute to the team and that their contribution is respected and valued. Even more importantly, they likely enjoy spending time with you and feel that you like them as a person. Even though players in this range have high levels of cohesion in relationships with coaches, it is recommended that coaches interpret scores with a grain of salt. Players may have over-inflated their scores because they fear telling the truth, getting into trouble, or making coaches feel bad or angry. In cases where coaches have concerns about players not answering truthfully, it may be advisable to have the assessments be anonymous and taken without coaches present. Additionally, having players take assessments on their own or without other teammates in close proximity would be helpful in decreasing other interferences to validity.

<u>Mid Level Scorers (mostly 2's):</u> They likely feel inconsistently valued by you as coaches. They are likely to invest in their relationships with you to the level in which they feel you invest in them. At times they may feel comfortable to be themselves around you, while at other times they do not. They may be confident enough in your relationship with them to share some academic challenges or sport related problems, but may hold back personal issues (e.g. family or friend related). They may trust that you will be patient and support them academically and on the field, but wonder if you can help them with other socio-emotional concerns. Similarly, they wonder about their contribution to the team and may feel less confident as a player. They might enjoy spending time with you as a coach, but still wonder if you like them as a person. It is recommended that coaches interpret scores in this range (and other ranges) with a grain of salt due to developmental considerations with work in this age group. Adolescence can be a tumultuous time in young people's lives in which one day they feel great, and the next day their world may feel like it is falling apart. Your immediate interactions with a player before they take this assessment may have a big impact on their answers on this assessment. If you yelled at them in practice for making a mistake earlier in the day, this could negatively impact their scores.

<u>Low Scorers (mostly 0's and 1's):</u> They likely feel undervalued by you as a coach. They invest little in their relationships with you because they do not feel that you invest in them. Most often they feel uncomfortable to be themselves around you, maybe because they fear being negatively judged. They also may hold back academic challenges, sport related problems, and personal issues because they do not feel confident that you can (or would be willing to) help them. Similarly, they may worry about their contribution to the team and feel less confident as a player. They likely do not enjoy spending time with you as a coach, and don't feel you like them as a person. Coaches with players scoring in this range should consider multiple factors moving forward. While teens struggle with socio-emotional concerns that could cloud their ability to accurately judge relationships with coaches (contributing to lower scores on this assessment), it is still recommended that coaches take players' responses very seriously. Coaches should reflect upon the ways they interact with players and the direct and indirect messages they send them through their communication. Coaches need to also understand that coaching is not a one-sizes-fit-all enterprise. You can raise your voice with one kid with little to no negative impact, while doing the same for another will cause you to lose that kid for a game or season.

2.3 Player Activity: Assessing Shared Destiny Between Players

Please answer the questions below with your true thoughts about the relationships you have with your teammates. Your scores will be reviewed by coaches to help them understand ways they can better support you and the team as a whole. Rate your answers on a scale of 0-4 (0=strongly disagree, 1=disagree, 2=neutral, 3=agree, 4=strongly agree).

1. I am able to share my family or friendship problems with my teammates. ____
2. I am able to share my academic issues with my teammates. ____
3. I am able to tell teammates when I need help on the field, court, etc. ____
4. My teammates accept me and my cultural background (e.g. race/ethnicity). ____
5. My teammates accept me and my different identities (e.g. gender, etc.). ____
6. My teammates have my back when I need them. ____
7. My teammates see me as an asset to the team. ____
8. My teammates listen to me and take my suggestions on the field, court, etc. ____
9. If I make a mistake, my teammates will be patient and supportive. ____
10. If I accomplish something in (or outside of) my sport, my teammates celebrate me. ____
11. I enjoy spending time with my teammates. ____
12. My teammates enjoy spending time with me. ____

13. Please list some ideas for increasing positive relationships between players:

    _____
    _____
    _____

14. Please list some ideas for improving the overall program:

    _____
    _____
    _____

2.3 Assessment Score Analysis:

High Scorers (mostly 3's and 4's): They likely feel valued by their teammates. They are likely to have high levels of investment in their relationships with teammates and feel comfortable to be themselves around them. They are likely confident enough in their relationships with teammates to share personal, academic, and sport related problems with them because they trust that teammates will be patient and support them. Similarly, they feel that they can contribute to the team and that their contribution is respected and valued. Even more importantly, they likely enjoy spending time with their teammates and feel that they are well liked as a person. Even though players in this range have high levels of cohesion in relationships within the team, it is recommended that coaches interpret scores with a grain of salt. Players may have over-inflated their scores because they fear telling the truth, getting into trouble, or making teammates feel bad or angry. In cases where coaches have concerns about players not answering truthfully, it may be advisable to have the assessments be anonymous and taken without coaches present. Additionally, having players take assessments on their own or without other teammates in close proximity would be helpful in decreasing other interferences to validity.

Mid Level Scorers (mostly 2's) They likely feel inconsistently valued by their teammates. They are likely to invest in their relationships with other players to the level in which they feel teammates invest in them. At times they may feel comfortable to be themselves around teammates, while at other times they do not. They may be confident enough in their relationships within the team to share some academic challenges or sport related problems, but may hold back personal issues (e.g. family or friend related). They may trust that teammates will be patient and support them academically and on the field, but wonder if teammates can help them with other socio-emotional concerns. Similarly, they may wonder about their contribution to the team and feel less confident as a player. They might enjoy spending time with some teammates but not others and wonder if they are well liked on the team. It is recommended that coaches interpret scores in this range (and other ranges) with a grain of salt due to developmental considerations in coaching this age group. Adolescence can be a tumultuous time in young people's lives in which one day they feel great, and the next day their world may feel like it is falling apart. Teens' interactions with one another earlier in the week (or day) could very well impact their responses on this questionnaire in the positive or negative direction. Either way, responses should be taken seriously and coaches should tune into individual item answers to determine ways they can positively impact team cohesion.

Low Scorers (mostly 0's and 1's): They likely feel undervalued by the team. They invest little in their relationships with teammates because they do not feel teammates invest in them. Most often they feel uncomfortable to be themselves around the team, maybe because they fear being negatively judged. They also may hold back academic challenges, sport related problems, and personal issues (e.g. family or friend related) because they do not feel confident that teammates can (or would be willing to) help them. Similarly, they may worry about their contribution to the team and feel less confident as a player. They likely do not enjoy spending time with teammates outside of practice, and don't feel teammates like them as a person. Coaches with players scoring in this range should consider multiple factors moving forward. While teens struggle with socio-emotional concerns that could cloud their ability to accurately judge relationships with their teammates (contributing to lower scores on this assessment), it is still recommended that coaches take players' responses very seriously. Coaches should reflect upon the ways players interact with each other, the quality of the relationships coaches have with individual players, and the relationships coaches have with one another on staff. The quality of coaching staff cohesion has a tendency to trickle down to coaches' relationships with players and players' relationships with one another. If there is tension between coaches, that has a negative impact on coaches' relationships with players. When players feel undervalued by coaches, they may invest less in the team and their relationships with teammates suffer. Players who don't care about each other, or the success of the team, perform suboptimally. Suboptimal performance frustrates coaches and coaches' frustration leads to further tension within the staff. This dangerous, downward cycle can cause negative impact for adolescent players' developmental and socio-emotional health. Adolescence is a time in which young people invest more energy in their peer relationships than they do at any other period across the lifespan. They are highly tuned into the ways they are perceived by peers and the quality of relationships they build with them. When players feel invested and valued by team members, that carries huge implications for their self-esteem and psychological adjustment in high school and years after. Unfortunately, the same can be said in the opposite direction.

2.4 Parent Activity: Assessing Shared Destiny Between Coaches and Caregivers

Please reflect upon the following questions as a way to assess the quality of relationships you have with coaches on your child's team. Rate your answers on a scale of 0-4 (0=strongly disagree, 1=disagree, 2=neutral, 3=agree, 4=strongly agree).

1. I am able to share my or my child's personal concerns (e.g. familial issues, child's academic or emotional concerns) with coaches on staff. ____
2. I am able to share my concerns about the team with coaches on staff (e.g. child's playing time, child's position). ____
3. Coaches accept me and my child's cultural background and identities (e.g. race/ethnicity, religion, family composition, etc.). ____
4. The coaching staff is personally invested in my child's socio-emotional health and development. ____
5. The coaching staff has my child's athletic interests in mind now and into their future as an athlete. ____
6. I am able to be a resource for coaches on staff (e.g. volunteering for booster club events). ____
7. My child is listened to and respected by the coaching staff. ____
8. I am listened to and respected by the coaching staff. ____
9. I enjoy spending time with the coaching staff. ____
10. I enjoy spending time with fellow team parents. ____

11. Please list some ideas for increasing positive relationships between coaches and parents:

_____
_____
_____

12. Please list some ideas for increasing positive relationships between team parents:

_____
_____
_____

13. Please list some ideas for improving the overall program:

_____
_____
_____

2.4 Assessment Score Analysis:

<u>High Scorers (mostly 3's and 4's):</u> Players' caregivers likely feel that they and their children are valued by the coaching staff. They are likely to have high levels of investment in the program and are comfortable and willing to share challenges they or their children have with coaches. Caregivers in this range feel confident that if they share personal issues or possible concerns they have with the team, they will be listened to and considered. Caregivers may also actively seek out support from coaches in these programs who they view as advocates for the best interests of their children. Since caregivers view their relationships with coaches in these programs as highly positive they are willing to put in more time and effort into the team. These caregivers are likely to be helpful on booster club initiatives and be understanding when coaches make decisions for the greater good of the team (even if that means less playing time for their particular child). Although you have high levels of cohesion with caregivers in these programs, it is recommended that you pay attention to individual item responses. You may notice a pattern in which caregivers feel more comfortable or confident with the coaching staff in some areas and not others. It will also be important to take answers with a grain of salt as some caregivers' responses may be inflated due to their fears of angering coaches and threatening their child's chances of success on the team.

<u>Mid Level Scorers (mostly 2's):</u> Players' caregivers likely feel that they and their children are inconsistently valued by the coaching staff. They may have mid level investment in the program because they question coaches' investment in their child. Caregivers in this range are wary about sharing personal issues or possible concerns they have with the team with coaches because they are not confident that they will be listened to or considered. Caregivers are not likely to seek out support from coaches in these programs because they may not view coaches as advocates for the best interests of their child. Since caregivers view their relationships with coaches in these programs as tenuous they are not always willing to invest time and effort into the team (beyond the needs of their individual child). These caregivers are likely to be frustrated when coaches make decisions for the greater good of the team, especially when that means less playing time for their particular child. It is recommended that you pay attention to individual item responses for these scorers. You may notice a pattern in which caregivers feel more comfortable or confident with the coaching staff in some areas and not others. It will also be important to identify growth and strength areas to address before, during, and after the season with these caregivers. Just giving caregivers this assessment and implementing some of their suggestions will go far to increase their positive relationships with coaches.

<u>Low Scorers (mostly 0's and 1's):</u> Players' caregivers likely feel that they and their children are undervalued by the coaching staff. They have low levels of investment in the program because they do not believe coaches invest in their child. Caregivers in this range are unlikely to share personal issues or possible concerns they have with the team with coaches because they don't believe that they will be listened to or considered. Caregivers won't seek out support from coaches in these programs because they do not view coaches as advocates for the best interests of their child. Since caregivers view their relationships with coaches in these programs as negative, they are not willing to invest time and effort into the team (beyond the needs of their individual child). These caregivers are likely to be angered when coaches make decisions for the greater good of the team, especially when that means less playing time for their particular child.

Although some caregivers in this range may be more passive in their discontent with coaches, other caregivers may actively and inappropriately share their frustrations causing uneasiness and instability within programs. Caregivers may use harsh language and speak badly about coaches in person and online as a means to express their anger, which likely causes embarrassment for their child. In worst case scenarios, some of these caregivers may even attempt to get coaches fired because of their discontent.

If caregivers score low on this assessment and low scores are noted on the player and assistant coaches' questionnaires, it will be crucial for head coaches to take stock of their coaching style and approach to communication on the team. Coaches should reflect upon the ways they effectively or ineffectively engaged with their fellow coaches, players, and players' caregivers. Head coaches who respect and value their assistant coaches increase these coaches' investment in the program. Players who feel their head coach and assistant coaches care about them, try harder and build stronger relationships with their teammates. Caregivers who see that coaches consistently care about their child (and the other children on the team) are more likely to invest time and effort into the program. Subsequently, mutual investment across levels can result in head coaches feeling increased energy, passion, and satisfaction in their role.

In the unlikely event that parental scores are low but coaching and player scores are high, it will be important for coaches to take caregivers' scores with a grain of salt. Coaches can make good faith efforts to build positive relationships with caregivers and communicate consistent care to their children, *but* caregivers may still be left feeling dissatisfied. If caregivers are still unable to join with you on the superordinate goal of developing their child (as an athlete and young person), then it may be time to refocus efforts. Coaches need to remember that caregiver conflict cannot always be avoided and you can't make everyone happy 100% of the time. If coaches are confident that they are doing right by their players and acting in ways that are consistent with their programmatic mission and goals, that should be good enough. It is unfortunate for coaches and kids in these scenarios because at times this contributes to caregivers pulling kids away from teams. Coaches should do their best to positively influence individual players in these cases for as long as they have them, because kids *will* remember the lessons and care coaches expressed to them well beyond their time in high school.

2.5 Coach Activity: Leaning into Shared Destiny in Coaching Staffs

Ideas for the Off-Season:

Spending Time Together. A great way to build staff cohesion is to spend time together across multiple sport and non-sport related contexts. When coaches take a trip to a clinic or other high school together they set aside the distractions of everyday life, invest in their relationships, and further the success of the team. When coaches spend time in non-sport related activities like hikes and trips to an amusement park, they see different sides of each other and create shared positive memories. Similarly, when coaches and their loved ones come together for dinners or BBQ's, they meet and build relationships with the most important people in each other's lives.

- Most often coaches attend coaching clinics together as a means of learning new approaches to advance their teams' progress toward goals. In the same way, a coaching staff can visit a different high school program and talk shop with those coaches to gain ideas for doing things better in their own programs.
- In preparation for visiting another high school or clinic, coaches can collectively draft a list of questions that they would want answered (e.g. different plays to add to the playbook).
- After attending a clinic or visiting another high school, coaches can share their biggest takeaways and ideas for applying these to the program (e.g. new strategies for endurance training).
- While professional development is key on these trips, coaches should remember to engage in fun, non-sport related, activities to make the most of their time together (e.g. going to a comedy club, doing an escape room, or spending time in nature).
- If your program does not have the resources to attend a clinic, you might consider *hosting* a mini clinic and inviting coaching staff from other programs to attend. If you have middle schools or youth sport programs in your community that would benefit from attending this clinic it would be useful to invite them as well. At the mini clinic, each coach on your staff can present a topic of their interest that is also relevant to the needs of the program this season.
- Reading and completing activities within this workbook as a coaching staff, would also be a great way for coaches to spend time together and improve the trajectory of the team.
- Along these same lines, coaches can host staff and family BBQ's or potlucks prior to or after the season. Coaches should invite their partners and children as a way to recognize and appreciate the investments that coaches and their families make in being part of the team.

Setting Goals and Asking for Support. Another great way to increase staff cohesion is to build-in time together to discuss personal and professional goals in the off-season. In this, coaches communicate to each other their personal and professional needs as well as ways they can support one another. Coaches who feel they can share their desires, concerns, and needs and be supported are more satisfied in their roles and invested in the team. Additionally, these coaches are also more able to hear and attend to the concerns of their fellow coaches.

- Prior to the season, have a staff meeting in which the head coach shares personal and professional goals they have for the year. Head coaches should review happenings in their lives that may positively or negatively influence their movement toward goals (e.g. the Head coach's wife has been diagnosed with breast cancer and they need to spend more time caregiving and stabilizing their family). Head coaches can also share ways they need support from assistant coaches to achieve their goals this season (e.g. asking assistant coaches to take-on more active roles in the day to day processes of the team).
- In the same way, head coaches can have separate meetings with each assistant coach to discuss their short and long-term personal and professional goals. This meeting should include reviewing happenings in the assistant coaches' personal lives that may positively or negatively influence their movement toward goals (e.g. having a baby, moving homes, financial issues). Head coaches can ask assistant coaches how they can best support their goals this season (e.g. ensuring coverage for times when the assistant coach will be absent).
- After the season coaches can have individual meetings, again, to discuss their progress toward personal and professional goals and what they would like to work on next season. Coaches can review other ways to support each other moving forward.
- If there are communication issues or coaches are having a hard time getting along, it may be useful to use the assessment in this workbook to further explore the situation and find avenues toward improvement (e.g. see activity 2.1).

Ideas for the In-Season:

Implementing Support. In order to build coaching staff cohesion, coaches must make good on the commitments they made to supporting each other during the season. If head coaches indicated that they needed more flexibility in their attendance of practice because of familial concerns, then they should expect assistant coaches will be there to pick-up the slack. If an assistant coach expressed a desire to move into a head coaching position in the distal future, then they should expect that their current head coach will involve them in more administrative tasks related to running a successful program.

- During the season, coaches can consistently hold meetings to check-in with each other on personal and professional goals and happenings that could impact the team. Coaches should discuss ways to support each other and make adjustments to keep the team moving toward their mission.

- Coaches can also regularly review film of games and discuss successful and unsuccessful moments during the season. Coaches should share ways they can assist each other and their players in making adjustments for subsequent weeks of the season.
- During the season, coaches can also hold regular depth chart meetings in which they discuss individual players' strengths and needs (both sport and non-sport related). Coaches can share strategies for supporting players and make a plan to implement these in the subsequent weeks of the season (e.g. coaches commit to having more caring conversations with a player who is struggling with his parents' divorce).
- At the programmatic level, head coaches should also implement policies that would positively impact the entire team throughout a season. An example of this would be adjusting and/or limiting practice and meeting times. If coaches and players are spending unnecessary amounts of time in practices and meetings, their chances of feeling frustrated and burnt-out are high. Further, coaches and players who spend inordinate amounts of time in their sport may experience strain in their outside relationships and resent their roles on the team. Head coaches who can set policies to support work-life balance within their teams will increase coaches and players' overall investment in the program and make their own lives a whole lot easier.

2.6 Coach Activity: Leaning into Shared Destiny in the Coach-Player Relationship

Ideas for the Off-Season:

Going on Retreat. A great way to build mutual investment and authenticity in the coach-player relationship is to spend time together in the off-season. When coaches and players do this as a team, it can also work to increase cohesion between players. Spending time in activities like retreats or camps, helps coaches and players get to know one another on a personal level. Coaches can also use these opportunities to communicate to players that they are valued as people, apart from their athletic contributions to the team. In addition, camps and retreats can be used to strengthen coaches' and players' relationships with one another through shared investment in planning for the season. Below are some considerations and ideas for holding a Leader Retreat or Senior Retreat with players:

- Consider having the retreat happen on a camping trip or in another location that minimizes outside distractions. When players and coaches are away from everyday life they are more able to focus on each other and the team.
- Consider making the most of meal time and having the coaches serve the players. For many families food is a way to communicate love and care. Having coaches feed players, lets players know that they are valued and cared for within the team.
- Consider making the most out of free-time with athletes by playing fun games. Coaches should play non-sport related games with players (e.g. charades) to help with: getting players and coaches more comfortable with each other, decreasing inherent power differentials between coaches and players, and creating opportunities for coaches and players to join together on shared goals.
- Another great activity to be done at the team retreat to strengthen the player-coach relationship would be to hold individual meetings with players to discuss their personal, academic, and athletic goals for the season. In this, players can communicate any challenges they may encounter in achieving their goals as well as ways coaches and the team can support them. Players who feel they can share their desires, concerns, and needs with coaches are more satisfied and invested in the team. Additionally, these players are also more able to hear and attend to the concerns of their fellow teammates. *It may be more feasible for position coaches to hold these individual meetings with their players in larger sport teams like football. Further, this would provide useful opportunities for position coaches to bond with their particular players.*
- After the season coaches can have individual meetings with players, again, to discuss their progress toward goals and what they would like to work on next season. Coaches can also review other ways to support players moving forward.
- As far as activities to address programmatic concerns and goals, coaches could consider splitting players and coaches into small groups to discuss the team's strengths and weaknesses for the upcoming season. These small groups will return to the large group to share what they discussed.

- The small groups can then re-convene to brainstorm ways they can build upon strengths and mitigate weaknesses in the upcoming season. These small groups will return to the large group to share what they discussed, creating a master list of strategies moving forward.
- During the retreat, would be a good time to discuss the mission of the team and ways you all will hold each other accountable to that mission more effectively. You can use activities in this workbook to help structure that discussion.
- On retreat coaches could encourage players to come up with their own "Team Code" for this particular season (see activity 2.7). Within this code, they should include: what they want the team to stand for, how they want to practice, and how they want to play. All team members and coaches should sign this code at the start of the season and it should be posted in the meeting room and/or locker room.
- If you notice players having challenges getting along with each other, the retreat may be a good time to use assessments from this workbook to further explore the situation and determine better ways to support players' relationships with one another and coaches (see activities 2.2 and 2.3).
- Toward the end of the retreat, coaches should consider integrating a "Warm and Fuzzy" activity. In this, each member of the team (including coaches) will be called to the middle of the circle and the rest of the team (including coaches) will share positive elements of this person's character. When done in a ceremonial way around a campfire at night, players seem to be more emotionally engaged and able to remember the activity later. This type of activity is integral to building strong ties within the program because players and coaches get to hear and more deeply appreciate how much they are valued and cared for by the team.

Ideas for the In-Season:

Implementing Support. In order to build and maintain strong player-coach relationships, coaches must make good on their commitments to players during the season. If players expressed academic concerns, they should expect that coaches will be asking about grades and possibly talking with teachers. Similarly, if players noted that they may be struggling due to financial strain in the family, they should expect that coaches will advocate for them to have access to what they need on and off the field. Below are more considerations for improving the player-coach relationship during the season:

- During the season, coaches should consistently hold small group and/or individual meetings to check-in with their players. These check-ins should cover progress toward the team mission and goals as well as happenings in players' lives that carry impact for them and the team. Coaches and players should discuss ways to support one another and make adjustments to keep the team moving forward.
- Coaches can also regularly review film of games and discuss successful and unsuccessful moments during the season with players. Within these film reviews, the players and coaches should share ways they can assist each other in making adjustments for subsequent weeks of the season.

- Finally, the most useful programmatic initiative for supporting player-coach relationships would be assembling a Player Leadership Council. Players can be chosen by coaches for the council or they can be appointed by other players via a team vote. Coaches can hold meetings with the council weekly during the season and less frequently during the off-season. In addition to receiving some structured leadership training (see activity 2.8 and Appendices A-M), players on the council would be tasked with representing teammates' interests in the program. Council members would share feedback surrounding player concerns and give suggestions on how to improve the overall functioning of the program in their meetings with the coaching staff. It will then be up to coaches to seriously consider and implement this feedback, respecting and recognizing players' experiences, insights, and contributions. Members of the Player Leadership Council could also act as mentors to individual underclassmen on the team. See activities 2.9 and 2.10 for more details on implementing a Mentorship Program.

2.7 Team Code

What do we stand for?

1.
2.
3.

How do we practice?

1.
2.
3.

How do we play?

1.
2.
3.

<u>Team Signatures</u>

2.8 Player Leadership Councils

Roles & Responsibilities as a Council Member:

- Act in a way that is consistent with the Mission and Goals of the team
- Be a role model for your teammates on the field, in the classroom, and in the community
- Check-in with teammates regularly regarding issues or concerns
- Attend council meetings weekly with the coaching staff and other council members
- Share teammates concerns in council meetings and provide feedback to coaches about making the team better
- Complete assignments or homework given to you by coaches related to the topics covered each week (e.g. readings, reflections)
- If unable to successfully fulfill roles and responsibilities as a Council Member, I will notify coaches ASAP so that they can intervene, support, and/or find another teammate able to serve on the council.

Some topics to be covered on the Player Leadership Council this year:

A. Forming Leadership Platoons
B. Instagram, SnapChat, Tiktok, Twitter, etc.
C. Approaches to Leadership
D. Troubleshooting Leadership Issues with Teammates
E. Goal Setting
F. Mental Health Issues and Getting Support
G. Communication Filters
H. Being H.U.M.B.L.E.
I. Communication B.A.S.I.C.S.
J. Diversity and Inclusion in Teams
K. Sport Psychology and Mental Performance
L. Navigating Injury
M. Looking toward the Future

By signing below, I agree to the Roles & Responsibilities of being a Council Member:

_____   _____
                Name   Date

2.9 Player Activity: Leaning into Shared Destiny within Teams

Ideas for the Off-Season:

Pushing Limits. A great way to build cohesion, mutual investment, and authenticity within teams is to create a context in which players push their physical and psychological limits and rely on one another to achieve a goal. In contexts such as these, players cannot complete a task without the encouragement and support of their teammates. "The Rock Challenge" is an activity that coaches have used prior to the start of a season to push players' limits and get them working together to achieve a goal. Below is a thorough description of "The Rock Challenge" and considerations for implementing it in teams:

"The Rock Challenge" is done on a hike that takes the team to the top of a mountain. At the beginning of the hike, players choose a rock (between 15 to 30 lbs in weight) that they will carry with them for the duration of the excursion. Coaches should give a briefing after players choose their rock about what it symbolizes and what will be expected of them in the activity. They could say:

"The rock is a symbol of all of the things that you will have to overcome in order to be successful in the season and life. Many of us live easier lives than generations before us. It is important for us to do something that makes us push our limits. The rock challenge makes us face a challenge to show what we are made of. Each of you will have to carry your rock to the top of the mountain without letting it down. The beauty of being on a team, however, is that you won't have to do it alone. You will hike alongside a teammate that will help you get through this. They will also be carrying their rock, so there will also be times that they need encouragement from you. During this hike, you will have to complete different exercises or mini challenges along the way. You may get angry on the hike and want to give-up. You may see other guys having easier times than you or harder. In these moments, it is important to keep going. Life is a series of adversities that make us stronger. Obstacles are put in our path to show us what we're made of. They happen for us, not to us. The Rock Challenge, today, is your opportunity to be a hero."

When the team gets to the top of the mountain (or the end of the hike) the coaches will take the rocks from the players and stack them off to the side. While coaches do this, they can explain their role on the team and the commitment they have to players. Coaches can say,

"As coaches we are taking the rocks from you. We do this as a symbol to show you that we are also here to help you on your journey. As coaches we work with each of you to help you push past the things that hold you back in life. We've been in your shoes, we carry our burdens through life–same as you. We know you can get through the tough times because we did. Us coaches choose to be with you on this team. We choose to be with you today and all throughout the season to help you carry your rocks and overcome adversity. In the same way, you all have chosen to do the same for your teammates.

We will rest here for a few minutes before heading back down the mountain. However, the hike is not finished. All of us will take turns carrying a 'team rock' down the mountain. This rock represents what the team will need to overcome during the season. We will take this rock with us to every game as a reminder of what we have already overcome and what we still face together. You can look at the rock and know that you are not alone. You can look at the guy next to you and trust he's got your back. When you see that rock at the game, you can return to this moment and remember what you are capable of. Remember how you feel at this moment. Look down the mountain from where you came. You did it! Your partner did it! We did it together!"

Ideas for mini challenges to do on the hike:

1. Have players do sit-ups while holding their rock.
2. Have players do squats while holding their rock.
3. Have players maintain a squat while holding a rock for 20-30 second intervals.
4. Have players do other exercises with or without their rocks (e.g. push-ups, bear crawls, lunges, sprints, army crawls).
5. Have players switch rocks with their partners for short stints of the hike.
6. Have players give their rocks to their partners (and vice versa) for short stints of the hike. You can emphasize, *"Sometimes we have to carry more to help our teammates get through tough moments. Other times, we need our teammates to carry more for us."*

Below are some ideas to make "The Rock Challenge" more successful:

- Start early in the morning so you see the sun rise at the end of the hike. Not only is sunrise a great symbol of starting a new day, it will also allow you to complete physical tasks before it gets too hot (especially if done in the summer).
- Have coaches accompany the players on the hike who will provide lots of positive encouragement, reminding players that they can do this for themselves and for the team.
- *You might consider having chalk or markers available for players to write a word(s) on their rock that represent the personal challenges they will face in the season. This will strengthen the mental connection between the rock and the burden it symbolizes. For example, a player could write the word 'fear' on the rock if they have multiple worries for the season. Another player may write the word 'sadness' if they have suffered a loss recently that they feel will make it harder to get through the season.*
- Encourage players to sing chants and songs during the hike. These can be very useful in distracting players from their physical and psychological discomfort as well as reminding them that they are not alone in this endeavor. These same chants and songs can be sung before and during games throughout the season as a way for players to access the memory of "The Rock Challenge" and how they overcame adversity as a team.
- Give team leaders a chance to talk during breaks. These will likely be your upperclassmen who have endured "The Rock Challenge" before. Prior to the hike, let these leaders know that they will be called upon to offer extra support and words of encouragement on breaks.
- Have players bring a backpack with water to drink, as the hike can be long. Coaches should also bring extra drinks, snacks, and first aid supplies in case they are needed.

- Make sure the players remain in pairs during the hike to prevent individuals from falling behind and becoming discouraged.

- *Have coaches document what the players have accomplished during the hike through pictures and video. You can display a group picture in the locker room or meeting room and consider having a wall dedicated to "The Rock Challenge" group pictures from each season. You might also have the 'team rock' be on display next to the pictures. Some coaches may also choose to post video and pictures via the team's social media.*

Ideas for the In-Season:

Implementing Support. In order to foster positive relationships between players, coaches must create opportunities for players to support one another throughout the season and reinforce times in which they see players caring for each other. Additionally, coaches must also hold players accountable when they are not supporting each other or acting in ways that are uncaring. Below are considerations for implementing a Mentorship Program to improve team cohesion during the season:

- A Mentorship Program would include matching upperclassmen with underclassmen on the team for the duration of the season (see worksheet 2.10).
- These pairs would meet weekly throughout the season to discuss personal, academic, and sport related issues that may arise for underclassmen.
- Upperclassmen would offer advice, feedback, and support on navigating these concerns and report back to the coach if issues arise that are beyond their ability to help. Having a Mentorship Program in a high school sport team has the potential to be very beneficial for young people in this developmental time period. Many times, teens are hesitant to share concerns with adults and rely more on peers for support. Additionally, teens spend much more time with peers than they do with adults so having a built-in partnership that extends beyond the field can be invaluable.
- Upperclassmen who are the mentors should have bi-weekly meetings with coaches to discuss how their mentee is adjusting to the team and bring-up any instances in which they may need guidance in working with their mentee.
- If a coach has implemented a Player Leadership Council in the team, they may consider using these leaders as mentors for underclassmen (see worksheets 2.6 and 2.8).
- When the Player Leadership Council meets with coaches to discuss team concerns, they can also discuss concerns that arise with their mentees.
- Part of the structured leadership training on the council could also surround ways to be a good mentor to younger players on the team.
- Finally, it will be crucial for coaches to fully clarify the roles of mentors and mentees on the team. Mentors should keep mentees' concerns private and only share them with coaches or other mentors during Player Leadership Council meetings. They would share these concerns when seeking consultation on better supporting their mentees. If mentees feel that their concerns will just be shared with everyone on the team, they will likely lose trust in their mentors and fail to disclose serious issues that could arise across the season. Mentees should also understand that in the case of serious issues their mentor will be reaching out for extra help from coaches to determine the best way to support them.

2.10 Player Mentorship Program

Roles & Responsibilities as a Mentor:

- Act in a way that is consistent with the Mission and Goals of the team
- Be a role model for your teammates on the field, in the classroom, and in the community
- Check-in with your Mentee weekly during the season to discuss their personal, academic, and sport related issues or concerns
- Attend Mentorship meetings bi-weekly with the coaching staff and other Mentors
- Share Mentees concerns in Mentorship meetings that you feel unable to support on your own (e.g. Mentee is having familial, relationship, academic, and/or mental health issues).
- Only share Mentees concerns within Mentorship meetings or individual meetings with coaches. Respect your Mentees privacy and DO NOT share their concerns with others (unless there is an emergency in which you need immediate help).
- If unable to successfully fulfill roles and responsibilities as a Mentor, you must notify coaches ASAP so that they can intervene, support, and/or find another teammate able to serve as a Mentor.

By signing below, I agree to the Roles & Responsibilities of being a Mentor:

_____   _____

Name   **Date**

Roles & Responsibilities as a Mentee:

- Act in a way that is consistent with the Mission and Goals of the team
- Be a role model for your teammates on the field, in the classroom, and in the community
- Check-in with your Mentor weekly during the season to discuss your personal, academic, and sport related issues or concerns
- Your Mentor will be meeting with other Mentors and the coaching staff to discuss ways they can better support you on the team.
- Mentors and coaches value your privacy and they have agreed to NOT share your concerns with others (apart from Mentors and coaches) unless there is an emergency in which you need immediate help.
- If you feel uncomfortable with your Mentor or that your Mentor is not able to successfully fulfill their roles and responsibilities, you must notify coaches ASAP so that they can intervene, support, and/or find another teammate able to serve as your Mentor.
- Your role in the Mentorship Program is completely voluntary and you can discontinue participation at any time.
- If you agree to be a Mentee in the program, you will likely be called to serve as a Mentor in later seasons.

By signing below, I agree to the Roles & Responsibilities of being a Mentee:

_____   _____

Name   **Date**

2.11 Coach Activity: Leaning into Shared Destiny within the Coach-Parent Relationship

Ideas for the Off-Season & In-Season:

Parent Meetings. A great way to positively influence the coach-parent relationship is to hold parent meetings prior to the start of the season. This provides an opportunity for coaches to discuss the roles and responsibilities of coaches, players, and parents as well as logistics concerning the upcoming season. Coaches could hold an all-parent meeting as well as smaller meetings for caregivers of incoming 8th graders or those interested in serving on booster clubs. Below are considerations for holding parent meetings:

- Prior to the start of the season, coaches should hold all-parent meetings in which all parents and caregivers (e.g. grandparents, adult siblings, aunts/uncles) are expected to attend. In this meeting coaches would first introduce themselves and their roles on the team, then, discuss the mission and goals of the program. After presenting the mission and goals, coaches can discuss the ways these are operationalized and describe the behaviors that are expected out of each coach and player. Coaches should share how they will hold themselves and players accountable to their commitments to the team and discuss positive and negative consequences when team members exceed, meet, or are unable to meet these standards. Coaches can use worksheets 2.13 and 2.14 to help structure this discussion.
- Later, coaches should describe how players, coaches, and parents will work together throughout the season using worksheet 2.12 to describe players, coaches, and caregivers' roles and responsibilities in the program. Individual athletes' physical and psychological needs are discussed as well as upholding the overall mission and goals of the team. Coaches might consider using this explanation,

"Now that we are on the same page as far as the mission and goals of the program, we can move on to discussing the roles and responsibilities of players, coaches, and caregivers within the program. Firstly, players are responsible to take care of their own physical health and safety needs. They need to make sure they are eating and sleeping right as well as not engaging in unsafe behaviors in or out of their sport. Coaches in this area are also responsible for each player's physical safety and athletic development on the team. We will do our best to ensure that we physically prepare players to be successful in the program and mitigate injury to the best of our ability. As caregivers you are also tasked with keeping your children physically safe and healthy. Making sure your child gets enough to eat and sleep as well as making sure they don't make risky and dangerous choices in the community would be good examples of this. If you find it difficult to meet your athlete's needs in this area for whatever reason, please know that you can reach out to coaches for support and we will do our best to advocate and get you connected with assistance.

Secondly, players need to take care of their own psychological and socio-emotional health. They need to feel confident in us as adults to reach out for help when they are emotionally struggling so that we can assist them. We never want a kid to feel that they have nowhere to turn or no one to rely on. When this happens, kids are at risk of finding other ways to feel better that can cause further pain and suffering to themselves, their families, and the team. Coaches are also tasked with ensuring that kids feel confident, cared for, and valued. We, as coaches, care about your child's emotional health and character development much more than their athletic contributions and performance. Our job is to help all players develop a sense of confidence that they can use to overcome adversity and pursue goals throughout their lives. As caregivers, you are crucial to your child's psychological development and wellness. You do this in showing-up for them, being patient and supportive, as well as holding them accountable. Just being here today shows that you care for your child and are already doing these things. We appreciate you and value the investments you make in your child and the team. If you have a concern about your child's emotional health, please feel free to reach out to the coaching staff so we can work together to support them.

The last area is players', coaches', and caregivers' roles and responsibilities to the team. We've already discussed our specific mission statement and goals as well as how we will hold ourselves accountable to them. Here, we want to emphasize that although we strive to meet an individual athlete's physical and psychological health and development needs, we must understand that the team is also a priority. Players need to understand that no one individual is more important than the team. If they are upset about their role and playing time, they need to find a way to move past that to continue positively contributing. They need to understand that coaches want what's best for them and for the team. If players put in the work and uphold the mission and goals of the team to the best of their ability, we will find a place for them to be successful in the program. As coaches, we have the responsibility to keep the team moving toward our mission and goals. We do this by holding ourselves, players, and caregivers accountable to the commitments they've made to the team. Finally, as caregivers you must understand that coaches have responsibilities to not only your child but also the rest of the players on the team. There will be times that you do not see eye-to-eye with coaches about your child's playing time or position. In these cases, you must model a positive attitude and encourage your child to do their best in their current position. When they strive to keep getting better and continue to uphold their commitment to the team, we will find them a place on the team where they can contribute and grow."

After fielding questions about the mission and goals of the team as well as related behavioral expectations and consequences, coaches should discuss ways parents can communicate with them throughout the season. Coaches can say something like this,

"We believe it is important for the coaching staff to have frequent communication with parents throughout the season. That being said, you need to understand that we are only able to discuss <u>your child's concerns</u> and not the concerns of other players. Also, coaches will be available for <u>parent meetings upon appointment</u>. Please do not approach the coaching staff immediately before, during, or directly after a game to discuss concerns.

Doing this often causes disruptions for the team and can be distracting for your particular child. One of the most common concerns that parents have about the program relates to their child's role on the team and playing time. This is understandable because we know you care about your kid and want to see them play as much as possible. Over the years, however, we have found that caregivers may have unrealistic expectations for their children because they are not as familiar with their child's athletic ability as coaches are. If you have a concern about your child's role on the team or playing time, trust that we are open to having these conversations with you. Know that when we do talk about this, however, we will share examples from film and practice that support our decisions. As coaches we care deeply for your children and invest tremendous amounts of time and effort to bring the best out of them. We do not want to put kids in positions or roles that they are not ready for because when they fail it has a negative impact on their confidence and the overall performance of the team. Unfortunately, some caregivers may continue to disagree with the coaching staff and this is okay. We just ask that you continue to positively support your child to do the best they can on the team. We have found that it can be really detrimental to players when coaches and parents are in conflict. Let's join together on the goal of promoting the best outcomes for your child this season."

Coaches must be able to set a boundary that protects their own sanity and the interests of the team when parents are unable to communicate in effective ways. If players in these situations are able to continue meeting standards on the team and have a positive attitude, coaches should re-focus efforts on prioritizing their relationship with that player and possibly limit contact with the parent. Inevitably, there will be cases in which parents pull their kids from programs because they are unable to see eye-to-eye with coaches. The best that coaches can do in these situations is feel at ease in the fact that they fulfilled their commitment to the team and attempted to do right by all players who enter their programs.

- The remainder of the parent meeting could cover specific logistics of the season, upcoming events for players and parents, and opportunities for parents to be actively involved in the program.

Booster Clubs. A great way for parents and caring adults to be part of the program would be to join the Booster Club. Having a strong and supportive Booster Club is crucial for many teams at the high school level. Firstly, it is an excellent way for caregivers to be actively invested in the program as well as build and fortify positive relationships with their own child, coaches, players, and other parents. Secondly, many sports teams need outside support from parents because they are unfortunately underfunded. Because of this, most Booster Clubs are involved in fundraising and providing instrumental support throughout the season. Fundraising could support purchasing team equipment and gear that can help players feel more confident and valued in the program. It can also help to cover the cost of travel to camps and other summer activities, which can be great for team cohesion and strengthening bonds between coaches and players. Below are some ideas for Booster Club initiatives and events:

- Booster Clubs commonly play an active role in working the concession stand or gate at games, meets, and matches. They have also been known to help in organizing team dinners throughout the season or the postseason awards banquet.
- In more recent years, boosters have been influential in creating a social media presence for the team that celebrates players' hardwork and progression in the program.
- Booster Clubs could also consider helping to host a youth athletic camp. This would involve coaches, players, and parents working together to organize a single or multi-day camp for youth in the community to participate in fun skills training.
- Boosters could also work with coaches to organize an alumni party and raffle. This can serve as a fundraiser and preseason party in which parents, coaches, and alumni come together for a fun night of dinner and dancing. A similar fundraising event could be organized around a golf tournament.
- Boosters could also attend the preseason team retreat to help with food preparation or other activities.

Celebrating Parents and Caregivers. Apart from the Booster Club, coaches can build positive relationships with players' parents and caregivers by implementing some parent/caregiver initiatives. These would likely involve finding ways to celebrate parents and caregivers and their support of the program.

- Coaches could host a family picnic or potluck for parents, caregivers, and players in the early days of practices. Families can come celebrate the start of the season and get to know each other on a personal level.
- Coaches could also institute a parent/caregiver appreciation night in which parents and caregivers attend practice and take part in fun drills and activities with their kids. This night could culminate in an informal caregiver vs. player scrimmage!
- Toward the end of the season, coaches can encourage seniors on the team to write letters to their parents and caregivers to thank them for their support. It may be meaningful for these players to share their letters at the postseason award banquet. Coaches can help players create/purchase a small token to give to their parents/caregivers at the banquet to also show their gratitude.

2.12 Program Activity: Roles and Responsibilities in the Program

	Physical Needs	**Psychological Needs**	**Team Needs**
Players	Take care of your body and what you put in it. Eat and Sleep well. Don't take unnecessary risks with your health.	Ask for help when you are feeling emotionally upset. Remember people love and care about you.	Uphold your commitment to the mission and goals of the team. Hold teammates accountable to their commitments to the team. Practice humility and openness to feedback.
Coaches	Ensure players are physically prepared for their position. Mitigate the occurrence of injury.	Ensure players feel cared for and valued on the team. Foster positive relationships across every level of the program.	Uphold your commitment to the mission and goals of the team. Hold other coaches, players, and caregivers accountable to their commitments to the team. Practice humility and openness to feedback.
Parents	Ensure children are physically safe and all basic living needs are provided. Consult with coaches if assistance is needed.	Ensure children feel cared for and valued in the home. Be present, positive, and supportive. Consult with coaches if assistance is needed.	Hold children accountable to the commitments they made to the team. Maintain a positive attitude when facing frustration (e.g. playing time or position).

2.13 Coach Activity: Holding Accountability and Operationalizing the Mission Statement

In this activity you will operationalize elements of your mission statement to clarify behaviors associated. You will write a list of what each element looks like and does not look like so that you can communicate this with coaches and players. You may need to further define behaviors and use examples with players and coaches beyond what is listed below. Doing this will ensure that each member of the team fully understands what is expected of them and to what they will be held accountable.

Mission: *We will care about each other on and off the field.*

What does it look like?	What does it *not* look like?
1) *Being patient*	1) *Being impatient*
2) *Being kind*	2) *Being unkind*
3) *Being there*	3) *Not being present*
4) *Being supportive*	4) *Tearing someone down*

Mission: _____

What does it look like?	What does it *not* look like?
1)_____	1)_____
2)_____	2)_____
3)_____	3)_____
4)_____	4)_____

Mission: _____

What does it look like?	What does it *not* look like?
1)_____	1)_____
2)_____	2)_____
3)_____	3)_____
4)_____	4)_____

Mission: _____

What does it look like?	What does it *not* look like?
1)_____	1)_____
2)_____	2)_____
3)_____	3)_____
4)_____	4)_____

Mission: _____

What does it look like?	What does it *not* look like?
1)_____	1)_____
2)_____	2)_____
3)_____	3)_____
4)_____	4)_____

Mission: _____

What does it look like?	What does it *not* look like?
1)_____	1)_____
2)_____	2)_____
3)_____	3)_____
4)_____	4)_____

2.14 Coach Activity: Holding Accountability and Setting Clear Consequences

In this activity you will clarify the ways you will hold yourself, other coaches, and players accountable. You will set clear consequences for success and failure to meet the behavioral standards operationalized from the team mission statement. Upon completion, you can communicate these consequences to the team so that they fully understand what will happen when the standard is unmet, met, or exceeded. Coaches could even use this activity to track individual team members' contributions throughout the season. If players and coaches consistently meet or exceed behavioral standards they should be rewarded. If players and coaches are consistently unable to meet the standards, documentation records such as these can be useful in making decisions about the future of these individuals in the program.

Player: <u>Janice</u>
Standard: "<u>We will care about each other on and off the field</u>": <u>Patient, Kind, Present, Supportive</u>

Unmet:	Met:	Exceeded:
Janice is being impatient with teammates and says hurtful things to them when they make mistakes.	Janice is patient with teammates and encourages them when they make mistakes by saying, "You got this!"	Janice is patient with teammates and encourages them when they make mistakes by saying, "You got this!" Janice also takes time outside of practice to meet with her teammates to discuss how they can better support each other.
1st time: Janice will be reminded of the mission statement, related behaviors, and consequences of their behaviors.	**1st time:** Janice will be recognized for meeting the standard in practice.	**1st time:** Janice will be recognized for exceeding the standard in practice and in team meetings.
2nd time: Janice will sit out from play for a time designated by the coach.	**2nd time:** Janice will be considered for a leadership position on the team.	**2nd time:** Janice will serve as team captain for the week.
3rd time: Janice will be asked to leave practice or the game. They will also have a discussion with the coach about their future on the team.	**3rd time:** Janice will serve as team captain for the week.	**3rd time:** Janice will earn a spot on the player leadership counsel.

Player:_____

Standard: _____

Unmet:	**Met:**	**Exceeded:**
1st time:	1st time:	1st time:
2nd time:	2nd time:	2nd time:
3rd time:	3rd time:	3rd time:

Coach:_____

Standard: _____

Unmet:	**Met:**	**Exceeded:**
1st time:	1st time:	1st time:
2nd time:	2nd time:	2nd time:
3rd time:	3rd time:	3rd time:

2.15 Coach Activity: Being H.U.M.B.L.E.

Hold yourself accountable
Many people automatically become defensive when they hear that they've made a mistake. It is important to recognize this and push past it to take personal responsibility. We can't commit to making ourselves better if we don't take ownership of our mistakes.

Understand where the feedback is coming from
It's easier to accept feedback when we remember that it is given to us by people who care. Members of the team hold each other accountable because we are mutually invested in individual and programmatic success.

Manage your emotions and behaviors
When people face their mistakes they often feel frustrated, worried, and disheartened. These feelings are normal and actually a testament to your investment in the team. You feel this way because you care about doing well. That being said, you have to find ways to recognize and release these emotions so that they do not cloud your ability to own the feedback and implement it. Consider using the acronym O.P.E.N. to help you recognize and release emotions.

Be thankful for the feedback
Expressing gratitude for feedback helps you, the person giving it, and the team as a whole. When we view feedback with gratitude we change the way we see it. Receiving feedback becomes less of a threat and more like a gift that helps us get better.

Learn ways to get better
What went wrong? When and Where did it happen? Why did it happen? Who else was involved? How can I and others improve? Maybe you only make the mistakes in games and not practice or when you are mentally distracted and not calm. Maybe the mistakes happen when you are engaging a specific teammate and not with other members of the team. If you can determine that mistakes happen in a specific context or with specific people, then you can more accurately determine ways to improve. Asking these questions also helps us to quiet negative self-talk that we might slip into when emotionally overwhelmed. If you are feeling upset over some feedback, you might have negative self-talk like, "I'm bad at everything!" or "I'm such a failure." When you take the time to really listen to the feedback and learn specific ways to get better, you can engage in positive self-talk like, "If I could do it the other day, I know it's possible!"

Execute ways to get better
By moving through the above areas you've properly prepared yourself to implement the feedback. Now it's time to do it! When you start to execute strategies to get better, it is important to check-in with teammates and coaches about your progress. Asking them to give you feedback on how you are doing, is crucial to your on-going development as well as the overall success of the team.

2.16 Coach Activity: Being O.P.E.N.

Open yourself to the feeling
You have to open yourself to feelings before you can resolve them. Many times people get caught-up with trying to avoid feelings or fight them off. In doing this, you prevent yourself from doing the things you need to do to make yourself and the team better. Remember that accepting feelings does not mean that you allow yourself to be run by them. It is actually the opposite. Acceptance allows you to understand the emotion more deeply and eventually release it.

Practice patience with yourself
Feelings are not our enemies, rather, they play an important role in our navigation through life. Anger tells us when we have been harmed. Worry keys us into danger and lets us know we need to protect ourselves. Sadness informs us that we have lost something or someone who we care deeply about. It is only our inability to learn from emotions that holds us back, not the emotions themselves. It is important to be patient with ourselves when it comes to emotions because many of us have been taught to fear them or see them as vulnerabilities. In truth, being able to acknowledge our emotions and learn what they have to teach us can be one of our greatest strengths!

Express the feelings
By expressing our emotions, we release them. Some people express their emotions by talking to others about them, writing about them, letting themself cry, or engaging in some other activity to express them. When we avoid our emotions, they have a tendency to build-up to the point where we can't ignore them anymore. Unexpressed emotions can render us unable to physically and mentally function and can also get in the way of our relationships and goals.

Never give up
We need to understand that emotions will always be with us because they serve a purpose and it is up to us to improve our relationship with them. Continually letting ourselves feel and listen to our emotions may be challenging at first, but it gets easier overtime. With practice, the next time anger, worry, and sadness tells us that something is wrong we will be less overwhelmed by their message.

2.17 Coach Activity: Filters and How We Communicate

Everytime we communicate the actual words we say and how we say them go through a filter. Our filters are made-up of our histories, experiences in past relationships, and values. All these things sometimes get in the way of us communicating effectively. In this activity you will be given an opportunity to reflect on your personal filter and how this can obstruct communication. It would be useful for coaches to share their reflections within the coaching staff.

What in your <u>history</u> impacts the way you communicate?

Example: *When I was younger, I had a stutter that made me really self-conscious about being understood. I would choose not to communicate what I was thinking or feeling because it was easier to stay quiet. I think sometimes this still impacts me today. I worry that I will come across as unclear so I only speak when I have to.*

_____
_____
_____
_____

What in your <u>past relationships</u> impacts the way you communicate?

Example: *When I was younger, my parents were pretty strict and seemed to not listen to me or want my opinion. I really resented that and so when I got older, I always try to speak my mind. Sometimes this impacts my communication because people tell me that I can come across angry or stubborn when I'm not trying to be.*

_____
_____
_____
_____

What in your <u>values</u> impacts the way you communicate?

Example: *In my culture, we have a strong value of respecting elders. People have told me that this helps me be humble and listen to people in authority, like coaches. I like this about myself, but a part of me feels like it can get in the way of speaking my mind when I need to.*

_____
_____
_____
_____

2.17a Coach Activity: Clearing the Filter…

Now that you know more about yourself and your communication filter, you can practice clearing your filter and communicating differently. Review the below examples and write about how you can better communicate in each scenario. It would be useful for coaches completing the exercise to share their reflections within the coaching staff.

You are concerned about an assistant coach on staff because you see them missing practices and being more short with the kids. You really want to talk to them about it but hesitate because you are new to the program and worry that you haven't built a strong enough relationship with them yet. They may take the feedback negatively and quit the team which could be detrimental to the program. Knowing how your filter can be clouded, what are you going to do to clear it and communicate more effectively in this situation?

I can use the acronym O.P.E.N. to understand that my fear is normal and just shows how much I care. I've got to challenge myself to speak-up so that things don't get worse. Maybe I can try talking with the coach one-on-one after a coaches' meeting. I could use the feedback sandwich to say something I appreciate about their coaching, share my concerns about the situation, then end on my hope that things will improve. They may have personal stuff going on that they are afraid to share with me and feel relieved that they get a chance to talk about it.

You are frustrated with a player's parent who continually posts on social media their distaste for you and your coaching. You've tried to talk with them individually, but they have not changed their behavior. You hesitate to engage them more in communication because you fear they might pull their kid from the program. If this particular player were to leave, that would be hard on you and the team because they are so hard-working and athletically talented. Knowing how your filter can be clouded, what are you going to do to clear it and communicate more effectively in this situation?

_____
_____
_____
_____
_____

You are highly irritated with a player who just doesn't seem to buy into the team culture and is continually disrespectful to their teammates and you as their position coach. You've tried to correct the player several times, but nothing seems to change their attitude. You've even talked with your head coach about it, but they don't see the same things you do on the daily. It doesn't help that this player is highly talented and knows that the team needs them to win games. Knowing how your filter can be clouded, what are you going to do to clear it and communicate more effectively in this situation?

_____
_____
_____
_____
_____

2.18 Coach Activity: Filters and How We Receive Communication

Everytime we receive communication, the actual words people say and how they say them go through a filter. Our filters are made-up of our histories, experiences in past relationships, and values. All these things sometimes get in the way of us hearing messages clearly. In this activity you will be given an opportunity to reflect on your personal filter and how this can obstruct your ability to receive communication. It would be useful for coaches to share their reflections within the coaching staff.

What in your <u>history</u> impacts the way you receive communication?

Example: *My family immigrated to the U.S. before I was born. I remember having to translate for my parents all the time. People would be frustrated with my parents and disrespectful because they didn't know the language. I think this impacts how sensitive I am to the ways people talk with me. I've been told that I worry too much about what people say to me.*

_____
_____
_____
_____

What in your <u>past relationships</u> impacts the way you receive communication?

Example: *When I was younger my parents got divorced. I had to go back and forth between my parents' houses and always felt the pressure to make them happy. I think I'm like that with other people, too. When people talk to me about a problem, I get so invested in solving it and making them happy. Sometimes, I think this gets in the way of me being happy.*

_____
_____
_____
_____

What in your <u>values</u> impacts the way you receive communication?

Example: *As a man in my culture, I've been taught to be tough and strong. I think this has helped me get through some hard times in my life, but it may be something that holds me back today. It's difficult for me to acknowledge when I've made a mistake and this prevents me from getting better. I also think people see this and it makes them less likely to give me feedback.*

_____
_____
_____
_____

2.18a Coach Activity: Clearing the Filter…

Now that you know more about yourself and your communication filter, you can practice clearing your filter and receiving communication differently. Review the below examples and write about how you can better receive communication in each scenario. It would be useful for coaches completing the exercise to share their reflections within the coaching staff.

One of your assistant coaches has approached you with a concern they have about the line-up for this week's game. They appeared frustrated with your decision to play one athlete over another saying, "I know you're the boss, but I've seen some good things coming out of this kid and I think we ought to give them a shot." Knowing how your filter can be clouded, what are you going to do to clear it and receive communication more effectively in this situation?

I can use the acronym H.U.M.B.L.E. to remind myself about how to better receive feedback. I can also tune into my initial emotions and reactions in the situation. Knowing me, I may be irritated that this coach is questioning my judgment. I need to understand that this communication is less about me and more about this coach's concern and care for her players. I will try to push past defensiveness to really listen to this coach's ideas about the line-up. Maybe she has a different order that we could try this week that might be better than what I came up with.

A player's parent approaches you after practice to let you know that their kid might be missing a couple games due to family concerns that she does not specify. She also says she can't take him to all his practices anymore saying, "I don't have the time and his dad won't do it!" You feel frustrated because this is a good kid and one of your starters. You hate to see him miss out because of parental issues. Knowing how your filter can be clouded, what are you going to do to clear it and receive communication more effectively in this situation?

_____
_____
_____
_____
_____

A player yelled at you during practice after you tried to correct a mistake she was making shouting, "I don't have to fucking listen to you!" She ran off the field before you had a chance to respond, and you could tell that she was starting to cry. You know that she lost her grandmother recently who was pretty much the only person who would attend her games and show her support to the program. You want to be patient with the player, but she cannot go unpunished. Knowing how your filter can be clouded, what are you going to do to clear it and receive communication more effectively in this situation?

_____
_____
_____
_____
_____

2.19 Coach Activity: Communication B.A.S.I.C.S.

*B*e H.U.M.B.L.E. and O.P.E.N.
It's important to be **H.U.M.B.L.E.** and **O.P.E.N.** when you approach communication. These are especially helpful when you are receiving feedback and want to better understand and manage your emotions surrounding the communication.

*A*ttend to context
One must attend to the context of communication in order to respond effectively. Helpful context questions: *Who are you and who are you talking to? What are both of your roles and responsibilities in this situation? What is the communication about? How are your communication filters impacting the ways you both express yourselves and receive messages?*

*S*et goals and make a plan
You should organize your thoughts, how you want to communicate them, and in what context. Sometimes we might have the goal of just expressing our feelings and concerns and it would best be done outside of practice time. Other times we might need to approach the other person during practice so we can give them feedback about their sport related performance.

I-statements
I-statements are phrases that people use to more effectively communicate. They start with owning how you feel. Then they let the other person know how you see them in the situation. Finally, they end in a request for change. Example: *"I feel frustrated when I give you feedback and it doesn't seem to be implemented. Can we talk more about what is happening in this situation so we can get on the same page?"*

*C*ommunicate clearly and concisely
Many times people get caught-up in their emotions or non-relevant details and their message gets lost. It is important to stick to your goals in the situation and use emotions and details that help you to achieve those goals.

*S*how respect
You show respect to yourself by staying true to your values and goals in the communication. You show respect to others by being patient, calm, caring, and understanding.

Chapter 3: Recognizing Risks and Building on Resilience

Definitions:

After identifying one's purpose and promoting the shared destiny of the team, coaches can look to the third dimension of The Warrior Mentality to help them recognize risks and build on resilience within their programs. Coaches understand that they, the coaching staff, players, players' families, and the communities in which they live have risks that threaten individual and programmatic success. Risks can exist at the individual level, within each person, including: physical make-up and functioning, intellectual ability, neurodiversity, and psychological or emotional challenges.

People can also be negatively impacted by marginalization of the groups in which they belong, according to their: race, ethnicity, immigration status, gender, sexual orientation, socio-economic status, language, stage of development, and religion/spirituality. Even life experiences can also pose challenges at the individual level including: neglect or abuse, parental separation or divorce, death of a loved one, having a loved one use substances or experience a psychological disorder, traumatic events, illness or injury, self/familial immigration experiences, living within a neighborhood with high rates of community violence, attending a low-resource and underperforming school, and self/familial involvement in the justice system.

In addition to the above, programs are also impacted by the systems in which they exist. This would involve negative influences at the school, organizational, community, state, and country levels. The most striking example of this would be the chronic underfunding of high school sports teams in low-resource schools. These programs and schools exist in economically struggling communities that are shaped by underinvestment in education at the state and federal levels.

In the midst of risk, coaches also build upon resources and strengths within themselves, fellow coaches, players, and communities to promote the success of their programs. At the individual level coaches can reinforce the incredible resilience of people who shoulder daily physiological, cognitive, or emotional challenges and keep going. They can also recognize their own and players' persistence through the barriers caused by societal, institutional, interpersonal, and internalized oppression of the identities and cultural groups in which they belong. Further, coaches champion the courage it takes for them and their players to move through loss and other painful life experiences. Finally, coaches can draw from the vitality of families, schools, and communities toward fostering the wellness of individuals and the overall team.

Because of the shared destiny of the team, what happens to one individual has ripple effects for all other members of the program. When a head coach battles a life-threatening illness, he relies on his assistants to pick up the slack and reassure the players. When an assistant coach is alone in a new town, he looks to his coaching staff to become the family he is missing. When a player has no food at home or access to running water, he can count on his coach to have a sandwich and shower ready for him before school starts in the morning.

Similarly, when a physically challenged player makes athletic gains, she inspires her teammates to try harder. When a coach becomes the first African American female hired for her position at her school, she blazes a trail for other women of color with similar hopes. When a player and their parents earn U.S. citizenship and no longer live in fear of deportation, the team celebrates it as a collective victory. When a coach is there to award an Eagle Scout pin to a player who recently lost his father, the whole team brims with pride.

Key Concepts:

1) <u>Physiological Risks:</u> Injury, physical violence, death, and poverty are risks that threaten an individual's physical safety and wellness. While coaches mitigate the risk of injury for all players, they especially attend to the needs of athletes with certain experiences, identities, and cultural backgrounds. The first player group that has an increased risk of injury would be those with physical or intellectual challenges. For these players, the risk of injury depends upon: their specific physical and intellectual abilities, their previous training and conditioning, sport type, accessibility of the sport, inclusivity of coaches and teams, level of competition, and relative abilities of teammates and opponents.

   Along with injury, physical violence and death are other risks that threaten players' physical safety and wellness. While coaches attend to these risks for all athletes, they must pay special attention to the needs of ethnic and racial minority players, athletes living in poverty, and LGBTQ+ players. Coaches must recognize that their ethnic and racial minority players are statistically more likely to live in low-income neighborhoods with low-resource schools that contribute to their risk of being victims to crime, community violence, and murder. Similarly, coaches must also acknowledge that their LGBTQ+ players are statistically much more at risk of being homeless, using substances, engaging in self-harm, and considering suicide due to their experiences of bullying, assault, and abuse in homes, schools, and communities.

   In addition to these, poverty also poses a risk to physiological safety and wellness. Coaches must understand that players who are homeless and/or lacking basic living needs are much more likely to suffer the ill effects of poor nutrition and limited health care. Because of this, players living in poverty may experience detriments to their physical and cognitive ability to perform in sport and in the classroom. In the worst of cases, these players also risk serious, long-term illness and disability if they are unable to access preventative and/or ongoing health care.

2) <u>Physiological Resilience:</u> Individual players, coaches, teams, families, schools, and communities are responsible for supporting team members' physiological resilience. Initially, players must ensure their own safety (as much as they are able) by avoiding instances in which they put themselves in danger of injury, violence, or death and reaching out for help to get their basic needs met. When athletes need more assistance, coaches must step-in to assess the situation and provide as much immediate support as they are able. In the area of injury, coaches ensure that players are matched with

teammates and opponents that are at their relative physical level. They also take the time to physically prepare players for their positions and avoid putting players in roles that are outside of their current range of ability. In the area of violence and death, coaches assess players' neighborhoods and current living conditions and do their best to advocate for athletes' safety when they are not on the field. In the area of poverty, coaches secure immediate housing, food, clothing, and emergency health care for players and look to connecting players and their families with on-going support. Ongoing support can be found in the team, players' families, schools, and communities.

In this chapter, we will present ideas, strategies, and activities that coaches can use to identify physiological risk and promote resilience within players who: have physical or intellectual differences, live in high violence communities, have LGBTQ+ identities, and struggle with poverty.

3) Psychological Risks: Low self-esteem, self-worth, confidence, and competence as well as depression, anxiety, and negative coping behaviors are just a few of the psychological and socio-emotional risks that players and coaches face in programs. While coaches seek to identify and address all these risks within themselves, other coaches, and players, they especially attend to the needs of individuals with certain experiences, identities, and cultural backgrounds.

The first group of players with increased risk of psychological and socio-emotional concerns would be physically or cognitively diverse players. Depending on their level of functioning and the coach's ability to provide accessible and inclusive spaces for participation, athletically challenged players can struggle to feel successful and accepted within a team. In similar ways, athletically talented players have their own psychological risks related to depression and anxiety when their strong athletic identities are threatened.

Players with intellectual challenges, neurodiversity (e.g. Autism, ADHD), or academic struggles are also at an increased risk of psychological concerns. Depending on their level of functioning and coach's ability to provide accessible and inclusive spaces for participation, intellectually challenged players and players with neurodiversity may feel frustrated, confused, or ostracized on teams. Similarly, athletes with academic struggles may face concerns related to confidence, stress, helplessness, and hopelessness when they experience obstacles in the classroom that threaten their ability to continue playing.

The next group of players with increased risk of psychological and socio-emotional concerns would be players living in high poverty and community violence areas. Players who live in poverty must contend with the propensity to confuse *not having enough with not being enough*. These players may also carry the burden of caring for younger siblings and holding an outside job to help support their families. In addition, players living in high community violence areas feel the burden of stress and hypervigilance necessary to keep themselves, younger siblings, and friends safe.

Further, players with specific identities and cultural backgrounds are at increased risk of psychological and socio-emotional issues. Players from ethnic and racial minority backgrounds as well as those from families who have recently immigrated shoulder the burden of daily racism and xenophobia in the U.S. today. Additionally, women and players holding LGBTQ+ identities navigate daily sexism, homophobia, and transphobia. Because of this, these players are at risk of stress and the internalization of negative self-beliefs that limit their abilities to be successful within and beyond the team.

Coaches should also consider the psychological and socio-emotional risks of themselves and their players in the context of grief and loss as well as other mental health concerns. When death hits individual athletes or coaches, it is felt by the entire program. Players and coaches who have challenges grieving are at a higher risk of experiencing symptoms of depression and anxiety. Teams who are unable to support each other may also feel helpless and without direction. In the same way, coaches and players who have pre-existing struggles with psychological symptoms or familial concerns may be at higher risk of developing stress, frustration, social issues, and behavioral concerns on teams. These, in turn, may lead them to have conflictual relationships with other coaches or teammates, increased disciplinary actions, and higher chances of discontinuing in sport.

Finally, coaches face psychological risk associated with being part of the profession. Coaches of high school athletes often struggle with finding a work-life balance because of their tendency to be overtasked in schools. This becomes even more apparent for coaches in low-resource and high need communities. Coaches care so much for their players that they also run the risk of emotional burn-out. Many coaches are so concerned for players' well-being and caring for their families that they fail to meet their own needs. This becomes even more distressing for coaches of players who need sport to survive and thrive. Coaches in high competition districts are also more at risk of burn-out related to high expectations to win and fear of losing their job if they don't. In the end, coaches with marginalized backgrounds and identities face all of the above risks in the context of increased strain and psychological burden (e.g. coaches of color and LGBTQ+ coaches).

4) <u>Psychological Resilience</u>: Individual players, coaches, teams, families, schools, and communities are responsible for supporting team members' psychological and socio-emotional resilience. Initially, players must ensure their own socio-emotional needs are met (in as much as they are able) by tuning into how they feel on and off the team and reaching out to others when they need assistance. When players are unable to meet their own psychological needs, coaches must be able to assess the situation and support coping. When coaches identify that players' concerns are beyond their ability to address, they must engage experts and resources within and beyond the program. The same can be said for coaches assessing and addressing their own psychological and socio-emotional needs. Teammates, families, schools, and communities must be able to provide safe and caring spaces for athletes and coaches to take advantage of the growth-fostering possibilities within sport.

Sport and teams, in and of themselves, promote psychological wellness in young people. Teens who engage in sport, especially those from the at-risk groups described above, can build self-confidence and competence in setting athletic goals and progressing toward them. Further, they can build relationships with coaches and teammates that increase their sense of self-esteem and personal worth. These psychological benefits can, in turn, positively shape the academic and occupational trajectory of players well into adulthood. Many times at-risk players persist in school and go on to higher education and successful careers because sport kept them hopeful about their future. In truth, many coaches are in this profession because they were those same kids that benefited from transformational coaching and teams.

In this chapter, considerations, strategies, assessments, and activities will be presented to assist coaches in their abilities to meet the psychological and socio-emotional needs of themselves and their players. Ways to build upon resilience with specific player groups will be discussed as well as avenues toward mitigating stress and burn-out in coaching.

Activities:

3.1 Coach Activity: Identifying Risks and Resources is the first activity in this chapter. In this activity (3.1, 3.1a, and 3.1b), coaches will be given the opportunity to reflect upon their strengths and challenges across the individual, familial, team, school, and community levels. Then they will brainstorm ways to use these strengths to address challenges across each level. This would be a great activity for coaches to use in preseason meetings to get to know themselves and each other a little better. It would also be useful to revisit when issues and concerns arise related to the burdens of coaching (e.g. work-life balance, dual relationships, contextual concerns, etc.).

3.2 Coach Activity: Supporting the Physical and Mental Health of Differently Abled Players is the second activity in this chapter. In this activity (3.2 and 3.2a), coaches will be given a list of considerations and questions to guide their assessment of risk and resilience in work with differently abled players. Coaches will then practice utilizing athletes' strengths to address growing areas and promote physiological and psychological safety and development in these players.

3.3 Coach Activity: Supporting the Physical and Mental Health of High Talent Athletes is the third activity in this chapter. In this activity (3.3 and 3.3a), coaches will be given a list of considerations and questions to guide their assessment of risk and resilience in work with high talent players. Coaches will then practice utilizing athletes' strengths to address growing areas and promote the psychological and physiological wellness of these players.

3.4 Coach Activity: Supporting the Physical and Mental Health of LGBTQ+ Players is the fourth activity in this chapter. In this activity (3.4 and 3.4a), coaches will be given a list of considerations and questions to guide their assessment of risk and resilience in work with LGBTQ+ players. Coaches will then practice utilizing athletes' strengths and resources to mitigate risks for these players.

3.5 Coach Activity: Supporting the Physical and Mental Health of Players Living in Poverty is the fifth activity in this chapter. In this activity (3.5 and 3.5a), coaches will be given a list of considerations and questions to guide their assessment of risk and resilience in work with players living in poverty. Coaches will then practice utilizing athletes' strengths and resources to mitigate risks for these players.

3.6 Coach Activity: Supporting the Physical and Mental Health of Players Living in High Violence Areas is the sixth activity in this chapter. In this activity (3.6 and 3.6a), coaches will be given a list of considerations and questions to guide their assessment of risk and resilience in work with players living in high violence communities. Coaches will then practice utilizing athletes' strengths and resources to mitigate risks for these players.

3.7 Coach Activity: Supporting Immigrant, Ethnic, and Racial Minority Athletes is the seventh activity in this chapter. In this activity (3.7 and 3.7a), coaches will be given a list of considerations and questions to guide their assessment of risk and resilience in work with immigrant athletes and those from ethnic and racial minority backgrounds. Coaches will then practice utilizing athletes' strengths and resources to mitigate risks for these players.

3.8 Coach Activity: Helping a Team Cope with Grief and Loss is the eighth activity in this chapter. In this activity (3.8 and 3.8a), coaches will be given a list of considerations and questions to guide their assessment of risk and resilience in the context of weathering grief and loss on teams. Coaches will then practice utilizing strengths and resources to mitigate risks for themselves and players on the team.

3.9 Coach Activity: Supporting Your Own Mental Health in Coaching is the ninth activity in this chapter. In this activity (3.9 and 3.9a), coaches will be given a list of considerations and questions to guide their assessment of personal risk and resilience in the context of coaching. Coaches will then practice utilizing strengths and resources to mitigate risks across coaching case examples.

3.1 Coach Activity: Identifying Risks and Resources

In this activity, you will brainstorm specific strengths and resources you have across the individual, family, team, school, and community levels. Examples for **Individual** could be things like "strong" and "motivated." Examples for **Family** could be things like "caring" and "supportive." Examples for **Team** could be things like "patient" and "pushes me." Examples for **School & Community** could be things like "safe" and "cares about athletics."

Identifying Strengths

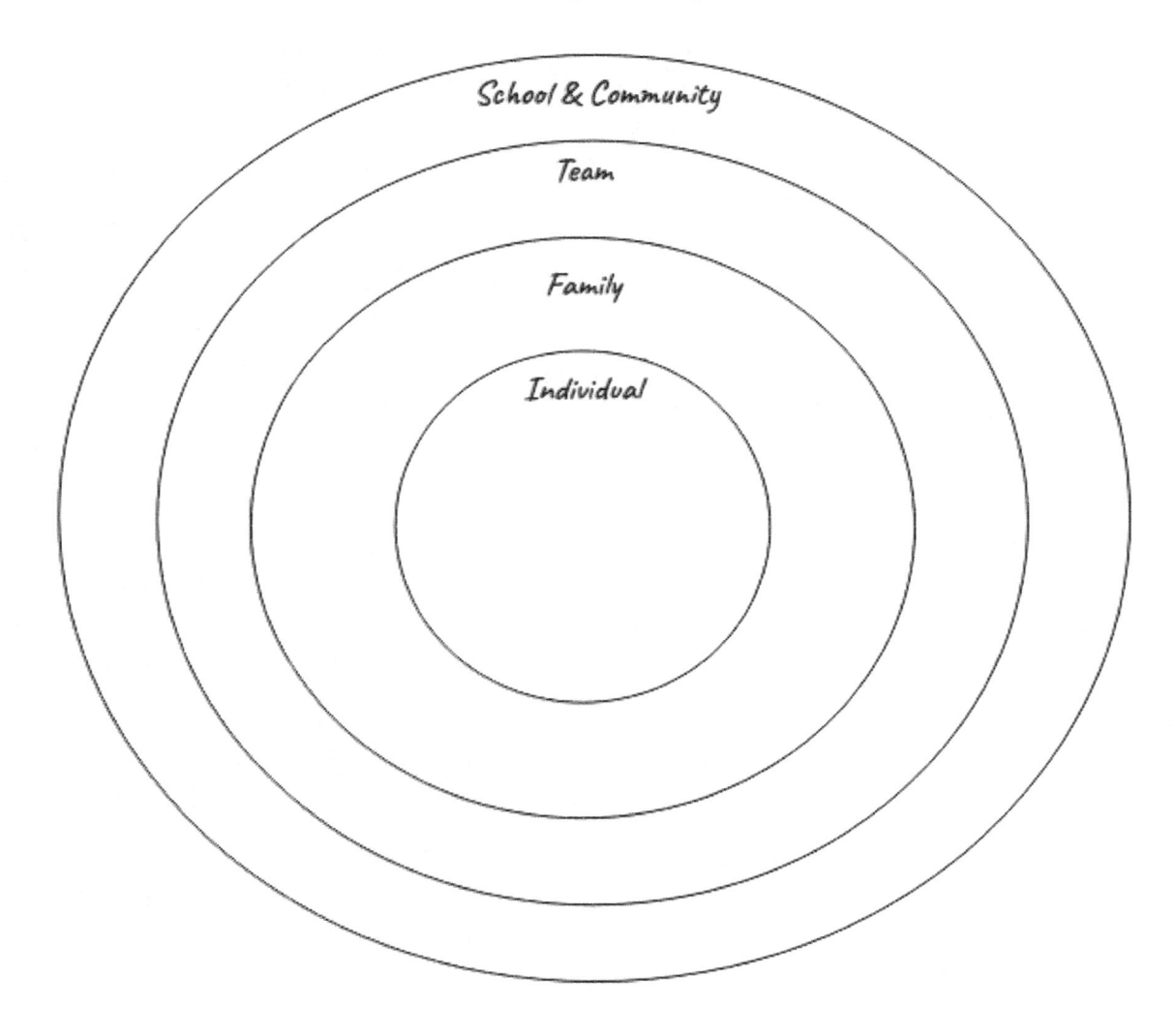

- School & Community
- Team
- Family
- Individual

3.1a Coach Activity: Identifying Risks and Resources

In this activity, you will brainstorm specific challenges you have across the individual, family, team, school, and community levels. Examples for **Individual** could be things like "get down on myself" and "get frustrated." Examples for **Family** could be things like "busy" and "stressed." Examples for **Team** could be things like "demanding" and "some conflicts." Examples for **School & Community** could be things like "unsafe" and "doesn't care about athletics."

Identifying Challenges

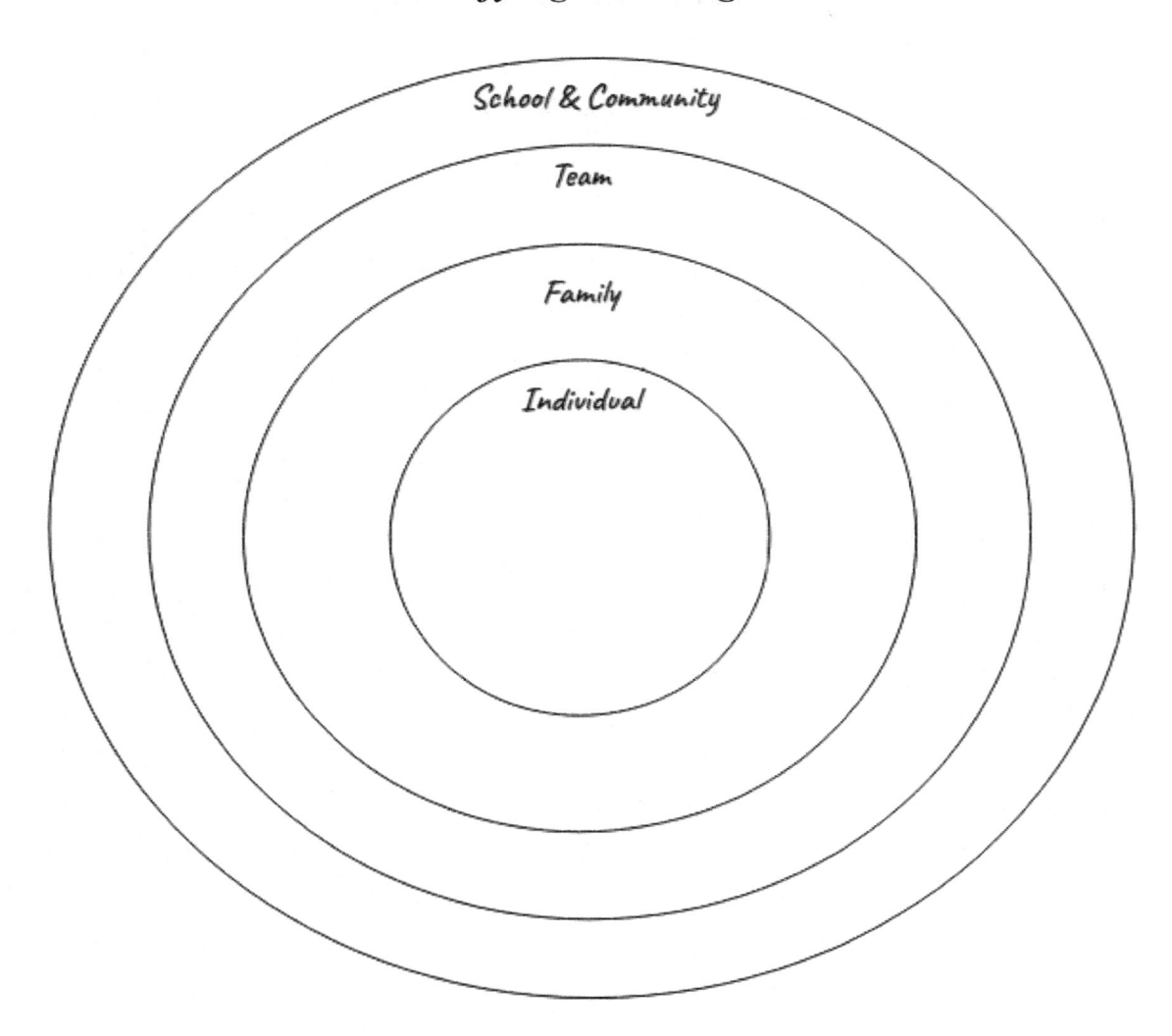

3.1b Coach Activity: Using Strengths to Help Challenges

In this activity you will use your strengths to address and overcome your challenges. See the example to help you complete the exercise.

Challenges	Strengths
Individual Level: • I get down on myself easily.	**Individual Level:** • I am motivated to keep going even when I'm upset.
Family Level: • Sometimes my wife isn't as supportive as I would like.	**Family Level:** • My wife works hard to help provide for the family.
Team Level: • Sometimes the players don't seem motivated.	**Team Level:** • My fellow coaches see this as well and we can develop a plan to address it.
School & Community Level: • My principal is too busy to answer my calls or emails.	**School & Community Level:** • My athletic director is a great resource and is highly supportive.

3.2 Coach Activity: Supporting the Physical and Mental Health of Differently Abled Players

Risk and Resilience

In order to effectively include and support differently abled players on teams, coaches must understand some research trends related to risks and resilience for these young people. As far as socio-emotional experiences of young people with learning challenges, there has been multiple studies showing higher levels of negative self-views (Kaukiainen et al., 2002), loneliness, and secrecy regarding disability because of feared stigmatization (Corsano, et al., 2017). Despite this, studies have found that psychosocial educational programs for youth with learning disabilities can help promote self-esteem and decrease loneliness (Musetti, 2019).

Similarly, research has found that adolescents with neurodiversity have an increased likelihood to suffer socio-emotional distress and decreased hope (Moody et al., 2022). These findings, however, evidenced that social skills and having maternal support can contribute to higher levels of hope (Moody et al., 2022). While hope is an important resiliencey factor for all people, it is especially crucial for children with neurodivergence. For them, hope holds protective relationships with depression, anxiety, life satisfaction, optimism, self-esteem, and academic achievement (Yarcheski & Mahon, 2016).

Research supports the notion that sports can offer important pathways toward health promotion, enhanced functional abilities, increased optimism, relationship development, and engagement of meaningful life activities for persons with physical and intellectual disabilities (Wilhite & Shank, 2009). Sports can also provide opportunities for these players to build a sense of confidence around an athlete identity that enables connection with others (Svanelov et al., 2020). While Title IX has ushered in more equitable access to sports for young women, there is yet to be legislation supporting students with disabilities who would like to participate in school sanctioned sports (Wilson & Clayton, 2010). This has put the onus on coaches to find ways to include athletes of all ability levels.

Ideas for Assessing Risks:

In order to more effectively engage players with physical and intellectual challenges, neurodiversity, and academic struggles, coaches must first understand and assess risks. Areas of risk for these young people typically relate to their ability to access and engage in sport in the context of environments that may discount or fail to accommodate their needs. Many times experiences of ableism can cause young people to internalize negative feelings about themselves, their relationships, and their future. It is important for coaches to understand the impact of contextual obstacles on differently abled young people so that they can better support them. Below are some questions to assess accessibility and inclusivity of programs for differently abled players:

- Gauge players' familiarity with athletics and exercise in general.
    - Have they played any sports before or engaged in physical activity?
    - If so, for how long and in what context?
    - What was successful or unsuccessful about their previous participation that could be useful for coaches to know in assessing their fit for the team?

- Gauge players' familiarity with this particular sport.
    - Have they played the sport before?
    - If so, for how long and in what context?
    - What was successful or unsuccessful about their previous participation that could be useful for coaches to know in assessing their fit for the team?

- Gauge players' understanding of the rules of this sport and what is expected of them as a player on the team.
    - Do they understand the different positions and goals of a game?
    - Are they familiar with the responsibilities of each position?
    - Do they understand how teammates work together to achieve a goal?
    - Do they understand how coaches will make decisions about playing time and in what circumstances they will play?

- Gauge players' understanding of what is involved in becoming a player on your team.
    - Do they understand training, practice, and game commitments within and beyond the season?
    - To what extent can they understand and live-out the mission and goals of the team?
    - Do they understand what happens when they are unable to uphold their commitments to the team?

- Gauge all the above considerations with players' caregivers and their overall interest, investment, and expectations related to their child being part of the program.
    - Do caregivers understand all that would be involved in their teen playing on the team?
    - Do they personally support their teens' desires to be part of the team?
    - To what extent can they invest in supporting their teens' ability to be successful in the program?
    - What are their expectations for their teens' involvement in the program and do they match with coaches' expectations?
    - What other questions do they have about their teens' involvement in the program?

- Gauge players' experiences of ableism and how it impacts the ways they see and feel about themselves.
    - In what contexts are you reminded of your ability?
    - When have you felt treated differently because of your ability on the team, in school, or in the community (e.g. being made fun of by teammates, being called bad names by others, having assumptions made about your physical ability, being singled out by teachers, having threats of violence made toward you)?

- Do you ever question yourself for having these experiences and wonder if you are just reading into things?
- Do people discount your ability (e.g. don't talk about ability when it does matter to you)?
- Do people make decisions about accommodations for you without asking you first?
- Have you ever felt bad about or less of a person because of your ability?
- Have you ever wished that you had a different ability?
- Have you tried to not affiliate yourself with others who share your ability?
- What have your caregivers, family members, and other adults taught you about your ability?
- When and in what contexts have you ever felt unsafe because of your ability?
- Do you ever feel worried, stressed, hopeless, frustrated, guilty, or embarrassed related to your ability?
- Do these feelings ever impact what you feel in your body (e.g. trouble sleeping, digestive concerns, unexplainable pain within the body, loss of appetite or overeating, heart racing, sweating, breathing fast, feeling shaky, dizzy or lightheaded, feeling like something terrible will happen, having a hard time concentrating, or having racing thoughts)?
- Do these feelings ever cause you to be mean or hurt someone else when you don't really want to?
- Do these feelings ever cause you to be mean or hurt yourself when you don't really want to?
- Do these feelings ever cause you to want to drink or engage in other substance use or behaviors to feel better?
- Have you considered not being alive anymore or ending your own life because of challenging experiences or emotions?

If a player answers yes to a fair number of these questions it would be useful to connect them with a school counselor or social worker as soon as possible. They may be experiencing clinical levels of anxiety, depression, panic, or traumatic stress that would benefit from immediate intervention. In emergency situations, you can also call 911 or take your player to their local emergency room. You can also call or text 988, the mental health crisis line created by the Substance Abuse and Mental Health Services Administration (SAMHSA). SAMHSA is the national government agency tasked with promoting the mental health and wellness of persons residing in the U.S. They created 988 and 988lifeline.org (to chat) for emergency mental health support. Here is SAMHSA's website for more details about this national service,
https://www.samhsa.gov/find-help/988/

Ideas for Building on Resilience:

A great way for coaches to address risks is to identify and build upon the strengths and resources of players with physical challenges, intellectual challenges, neurodiversity, and academic struggles within and beyond the team. Below are a list of considerations to achieve this:

- If a player has had past experience in this sport or any athletic pursuits, build upon it.
    - What did they learn about being an athlete?
    - In what ways did they learn to move their body that works for them and helps them to achieve a goal?
    - What positive feelings did they have related to previous sport participation?
    - What feelings do they want to have again when joining this team?

- After allowing them time to try out different positions, help them find a role that they can feel confident and successful in. Ensure that it is a role that allows them the most playing time.
    - What position on the team do they feel most comfortable and confident?
    - What position(s) currently needs to be filled?
    - If there are no starting positions across roles that the player could fill, what position(s) do they most enjoy, and wouldn't mind being 2nd or 3rd string?
    - Which position(s) would give them the most playing time?

- Find ways to highlight these players' programmatic contributions apart from their physical achievements on the field.
    - In what ways has this player embodied the mission, values, and goals of the team?
    - How can you recognize their commitment to the team as well as their commitment to personal growth?
    - What physical (e.g. increasing weight lifting maxes) and non-physical accomplishments (e.g. attended every preseason practice or meeting) has this player achieved that you and the team can celebrate?

- Explore ways to psychologically support this player when they become frustrated or disheartened at their personal progress or playing time in games.
    - In what ways can you remind the player of their motivations for joining the team?
    - In what ways can you remind the player of their commitment to the mission and goals of the team?
    - In what ways can you remind the player of their commitment to personal progress?
    - What are some individual strengths that the player can tap into to push through frustration or fear?
    - What are some familial/community resources that the player can tap into to push through disheartenment?

- If their caregivers are highly invested in their involvement on the team and available to support that goal, use them as a resource.

    - How and to what extent can caregivers be involved in training, practices, and/or games?
    - What other information and tips can they offer to promote this player's success on the team?
    - Are their other caregivers or adults at school or in the community that can also be helpful toward promoting this player's success on the team?

- If more assistance is needed, identify ways that teammates and other coaches can help support this player in the program.
    - Are their coaches available to keep a close eye on this player to promote safety at practice and in games?
    - Are there players on the team that can commit to checking-in with this player and assisting them in practice and games when the need arises?

- If after all these strategies have been implemented and the athlete is not able or interested in continuing in the program as a player, other opportunities for continued involvement should be explored.
    - Would they be interested in opportunities for supporting the team as a manager, film person, coach's assistant, etc.?
    - Would they be interested in other opportunities to partner with the sports program through initiatives within the school and/or community?

Other considerations to support these players' psychological health:

- What are some strengths that this player has that could mitigate psychological risk?
    - Level of self-esteem and affiliation toward their ability
    - Ability to assess personal functioning
    - Desire to grow and progress
    - Short and long-term goals for their future within and beyond athletics

- What are some strengths this player can access from within their family and home?
    - Caregivers and other adults who are able and motivated to support a player's psychological health
    - Caregivers and other adults who accept the player and encourage them to have a pride in their ability
    - Caregivers and other adults who teach the player about the history and successes of people with their ability
    - Caregivers and other adults who help a player identify coping skills and strategies to protect themselves in the context of navigating life with their ability (e.g. finding friendships with others who share their same abilities)
    - Caregivers and other adults who serve as models of success who share their same ability

- What are some strengths this player can access from within their team?
    - Coaches, teammates, and booster club families who are able and motivated to support a player's psychological health
    - Coaches who are culturally representative of these players on the team
    - Coaches and teammates who are sensitive to the experiences of a player with this ability (e.g. do not make jokes related to ability)
    - Coaches who discipline team members for their negative treatment or insensitivity toward others based on their ability

    - Coaches and teammates who are accommodating to the experiences of a player with this ability (e.g. creating a different technique to achieve a goal)
    - Coaches and teammates who recognize the impact of historical and systemic oppression of differently abled people (e.g. academic, occupational, economic, and health disparities)
    - Coaches and teammates who recognize the impact of interpersonal oppression on the experiences of differently abled people (e.g. unconscious biases impacting how people see, interact with, or avoid differently abled people)
    - Coaches and teammates who recognize the impact of internalized oppression on the experiences of differently abled people (e.g. a player starting to see themselves as less deserving, less intelligent, or less capable compared to others from majority abilities)

- What are some strengths this player can access from within their schools and communities?
    - Peers, teachers, staff, and mentors who are able and motivated to support a students' psychological health
    - Peers, teachers, staff, and mentors who value students of different abilities and help them feel comfortable and confident in them
    - Schools that teach accurate and complete histories of differently abled persons in the U.S.
    - Schools that emphasize the achievements, contributions, and resiliency of differently abled persons in the U.S.
    - Schools that are composed of teachers, staff, and administrators that are culturally representative of the student population
    - Peers, teachers, and staff who are sensitive to the experiences of differently abled students (e.g. do not make jokes related to ability)
    - Teachers and staff who discipline school members for their negative treatment or insensitivity toward differently abled people
    - Teachers and staff who are accommodating to the experiences of differently abled students and involve them in discussions about accommodations
    - Peers, teachers, and staff who recognize the impact of historical and systemic oppression on the experiences of differently abled students (e.g. academic, occupational, economic, and health disparities)

- Peers, teachers, and staff who recognize the impact of interpersonal oppression on the experiences of differently abled students (e.g. unconscious biases impacting how people see, interact with, or avoid people of different abilities)
- Peers, teachers, and staff who recognize the impact of internalized oppression on the experiences of differently abled people (e.g. a student starting to see themselves as less deserving, less intelligent, or less capable compared to others from majority abilities)

3.2a Coach Activity: Utilizing Strengths to Mitigate Risks with Differently Abled Players

In this activity coaches will brainstorm ways to utilize the strengths of differently abled players to mitigate psychological risks. Review the below cases and write your reflections on the space provided. This would be a great activity to conduct within a staff meeting at the start of a season to help coaches better understand inclusivity and accessibility on teams.

You were just emailed by a parent indicating that their child has an interest in joining the basketball team next year as an incoming freshman. This parent indicated that their child has a limb difference in which they wear a right foot prosthetic. The parent noted that their child has played basketball for the past two years in middle school and really enjoyed being part of the team. The parent indicated that their child does have a tendency to get down on themselves, though, when they fall behind other players. How can you assess this player's needs and strengths to support their overall participation in the program?

First off, this player has a caring and supportive parent who wants them to be successful in a game they really enjoy. That is a big strength. Since they have played basketball in middle school for two years, that is also really good. They should not have that many issues with joining the freshman team as competition at this level is not as high compared to the JV or Varsity. Now, since the kid has a pattern of getting down on himself, I would want to spend time with him talking about team expectations and our goals. I could also help him to identify strengths and set specific goals preseason that are attainable. This would help him to focus on his own progress and not compare himself to other players.

You are a head varsity football coach in a small town who has a couple players on the team who struggle with intellectual challenges. You are having a hard time figuring out the best place for them on the team because they work hard, the team loves them, and you want to see them play. They really struggle with knowing and remembering what to do in most positions but are physically able to run and hold onto the ball without falling. Their teammates go easy on them in practice, but you worry what might happen if you put them in a game. How can you assess these players' needs and strengths to support their overall participation in the program?

_____
_____
_____
_____
_____
_____

You are an assistant coach on the girls' and boys' swim team in a suburban school in a moderately competitive school district. You usually work with the athletes who are struggling on the team and give them extra guidance and coaching. This season a freshman with very little experience in athletics joined the team. You have been working with her on finding a race that she can excel in, but she seems to get frustrated with herself easily. Last week she said, "I should just give up, because I'll never win a race." Her parents are very supportive of her participation and have become active in the booster club. How can you assess this player's needs and strengths to support their overall participation in the program?

___

You were approached by a parent at the incoming freshman meeting who indicated that their child has a strong desire to join the freshman football team next season. The parent noted that their child has high functioning autism and has played flag football for city leagues in the past. The parent indicated that autism impacts their child's ability to understand social cues and know when they are overstepping boundaries. Despite this, their child is cognitively capable of understanding the game and meeting expectations. He has not engaged in tackle football before, however, and she is not sure how he will do with this level of physicality. How can you assess this player's needs and strengths to support their overall participation in the program?

You are a head varsity baseball coach in a rural area and competitive district. You have a player who is one of your star athletes on the team, but who continually struggles to maintain eligibility due to his grades being so low. You've talked with the kid and it doesn't seem to be an effort issue. You talk with his teachers and they think he may have attention problems, but he hasn't been assessed for special education eligibility. His parents are good people, but haven't been too concerned with his grades. They say, "He's always been a little slow." How can you assess this player's needs and strengths to support their overall participation in the program?

You are an assistant coach on the girls' and boys' track and field team in an urban school and moderately competitive school district. This season an athletically gifted sophomore sprinter has been having behavioral issues in his math class. He has almost been sent to the office on several occasions and his teacher has complained to you about his behavior. You speak with him and find out that he "hates the class and the teacher" and "doesn't know what's going on half the time." You do a little more digging and see that he has struggled in math since he was young, but no one really took the time to assess him. How can you assess this player's needs and strengths to support their overall participation in the program?

3.3 Coach Activity: Supporting the Physical and Mental Health of High Talent Athletes

High Talent Athletes and CTE

Much has been researched and written about Chronic Traumatic Encephalopathy, CTE, and its impact on athletes in high contact sports like football. CTE can occur when one's head is met with collision that causes brain impairment and neuropathologic damage (Van Itallie, 2019). CTE development risk increases alongside a number of factors, including: years playing the sport, number of blows to the head, and the position one plays in their sport. For football, increased risks have been found for offensive lineman, running and defensive backs, and wide receivers (Baugh et al., 2015). High talent athletes may be more likely to develop CTE due to their longer careers on the field.

CTE entered the conversation less than a decade ago with a study that examined the brains of deceased football players. 99% of the NFL players and 87% of the participants at all levels of play could be diagnosed with CTE neuropathologically (Mez et al., 2017). At the mild and severe levels of pathology, researchers found behavioral and/or mood symptoms, cognitive concerns, as well as signs of dementia through interviews with those who were familiar with these players' symptoms and behaviors prior to death (Mez et al., 2017). Research related to CTE onset and severity has found that earlier exposure to tackle football was associated with developing CTE and its subsequent severity (Mez et al., 2020).

Although CTE can only be diagnosed through brain imaging after death, many have discussed the possible behavioral impact of brain injury on current players, particularly those that engage in aggression and violence off the field (Washington-Childs, 2017; Ventresca et al., 2022, Simonetto et al., 2022). Scholars interested in the area cite mood and behavioral implications of CTE as well as the culture of toxic masculinity within high contact sports as contributing to the ways some players victimize others off the field. While it is important to analyze these possible spill-over effects and address them, it is also essential to recognize the work of coaches who are actively attempting to challenge toxic masculinity and champion more prosocial values.

Coaches often discuss fears related to high contact sports falling away due to societal concerns associated with CTE. Without these sports, coaches anticipate many more young men (high talent and otherwise) engaging in violence, using substances, dropping-out of school, and ending up in jail. These coaches' worries are consistent with the incredible risks and obstacles many young people, particularly youth of color, face in America. Homicide is the leading cause of death for African American youth today (CDC, 2023), largely due to the fact that they are more likely to live in high community violence areas with greater economic, educational, medical, and mental health disparities (Butcher et al., 2015; Deutsch et al., 2012).

Fears of Being Injured

Risk of injury is often at the top of high talent athletes' minds and the cause of significant stress and worry. Research has found that athletes can have several emotional responses to being injured such as anger, sadness, anxiety, irritation, identity confusion, and hopelessness (Tracey, 2003; Ruddock-Hudson et al., 2012). Depressive symptoms, in particular, seem to be more frequent in injured athletes who have strong athlete identification (Park et al., 2023). That is, players who view themselves as an athlete above all else are more likely to feel sad and hopeless when they are no longer able to engage in their sport. In addition to depressive symptoms, athletes may live in fear of becoming re-injured, which often puts a hamper on their recovery and future performance (Hsu et al., 2017). If depression and anxiety weren't bad enough, many high talent athletes also struggle with deep feelings of regret after injury because they can't contribute to the team in the ways they are accustomed.

In Warrior Mentality research (Ocampo, 2024), coaches discussed providing and reinforcing opportunities for high talent players to invest in the betterment of the team beyond their athletic contributions (e.g. leadership roles and consulting with coaches on schemes and team preparation). This was useful for these players because they were able to diversify the ways they and others see them. In the unfortunate event, high talent athletes become hurt, they can have a consistent source of esteem and still feel valued for their contributions. Further, when high talent athletes feel more autonomous in leadership roles and invested in team outcomes, they are more likely to commit to the program and act in ways that support its culture.

Ideas for Assessing Risks:

In order to more effectively engage high talent athletes, coaches must first understand and assess factors that could contribute to injury and challenges adapting to injury. Below are some considerations for assessing players' risks in these areas:

- Gauge players' attitudes toward sport and their participation in it.
    - How do they feel about playing sports?
    - Have they chosen to play this sport or has someone else encouraged/forced them to do it?
    - Are there other sports they enjoy or would prefer to play?
    - What prevents them from playing these sports?
    - What do they like and not like about playing sports?
    - What makes them worried about playing on the team this season?

- Gauge players' understanding of the physical expectations of the sport and what is expected of them as a player on the team.
    - What positions do they want to pursue this season and why?
    - Do they understand how coaches will make decisions about playing time and in what circumstances they will play and not play?

- Gauge players' understandings of their physical potential and ability/desire to set goals for improvement.
    - Do you and they have a good understanding of their potential in this sport?
    - Are they willing to make short and long-term goals to achieve/surpass their potential?
    - Do they have an understanding of what it will take to achieve/surpass their goals?
    - Do they have a desire to do what it takes to achieve/surpass their goals?

- Gauge individual, familial, school, and community risk factors that could detract from players' abilities to achieve/surpass their goals.
    - Do any individual level challenges exist for <u>you</u> that would impact this player?
        - Past physical or psychological stressors and concerns
        - Past experiences in coaching
        - Current physical or psychological stressors and concerns
        - Current experiences in coaching
        - Biased or invalidating attitudes or beliefs
    - Do any familial level challenges exist for this player?
        - Struggles with poverty
        - Parental separation, absence, or strain
        - Death and loss in the family
    - Do any school level challenges exist for this player?
        - Struggles with low resources
        - Overburdened coaches
        - Overburdened teachers
        - Overburdened administrators
        - Faculty and staff that are ill equipped to support the needs of marginalized students of different identities and cultural backgrounds.
    - Do any community level challenges exist for this player?
        - Living in a high poverty areas
        - Living in a high crime and violence area
        - Living in a community that actively invalidates, oppresses, and perpetuates the struggles of young people from marginalized identities and cultural backgrounds.

- Gauge all the above considerations with players' caregivers and their overall interest, investment, and expectations related to their child being part of the program.
    - Do caregivers understand all that would be involved in their child playing on the team?
    - Do they personally support their child's desires to be part of the team?
    - To what extent can they invest in supporting their child's ability to be successful in the program?
    - What are their expectations for their child's' involvement in the program and do they match with coaches' expectations?
    - What other questions do they have about their child's involvement in the program?

- Gauge players' experiences of psychological distress.
    - Do you ever feel worried, stressed, hopeless, frustrated, guilty, or embarrassed related to your sport, your school, your family, your neighborhood, or other things going on in your life?
    - Do these feelings ever impact what you feel in your body (e.g. trouble sleeping, digestive concerns, unexplainable pain within the body, loss of appetite or overeating, heart racing, sweating, breathing fast, feeling shaky, dizzy or lightheaded, feeling like something terrible will happen, having a hard time concentrating, or having racing thoughts)?
    - Do these feelings ever cause you to be mean or hurt someone else when you don't really want to?
    - Do these feelings ever cause you to be mean or hurt yourself when you don't really want to?
    - Do these feelings ever cause you to want to drink or engage in other substance use or behaviors to feel better?
    - Have you considered not being alive anymore or ending your own life due to challenging experiences or emotions?

If a player answers yes to a fair number of these questions it would be useful to connect them with a school counselor or social worker as soon as possible. They may be experiencing clinical levels of anxiety, depression, panic, or traumatic stress that would benefit from immediate intervention. In emergency situations, you can also call 911 or take your player to their local emergency room. You can also call or text 988, the mental health crisis line created by the Substance Abuse and Mental Health Services Administration (SAMHSA). SAMHSA is the national government agency tasked with promoting the mental health and wellness of persons residing in the U.S. They created 988 and 988lifeline.org (to chat) for emergency mental health support. Here is SAMHSA's website for more details about this national service, https://www.samhsa.gov/find-help/988/.

Ideas for Building on Resilience:

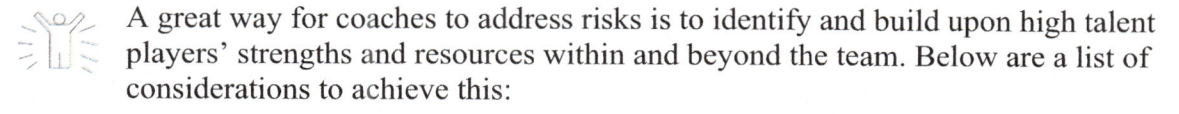

A great way for coaches to address risks is to identify and build upon high talent players' strengths and resources within and beyond the team. Below are a list of considerations to achieve this:

- If a player has had both positive and negative experiences in sport, determine how you can build upon the positive to mitigate the negative this season.
    - What do they look forward to this season?
    - What excites them about their athletic potential?
    - What do they look forward to that does not involve their athletic contributions (e.g. preseason retreat, making new friends, or strengthening relationships with old friends)?

- After allowing them time to try out different positions, help them find a role that they can feel confident in but that also allows them to grow. Ensure that their position/training holds their interest to prevent boredom and distraction.
    - What position on the team do they feel most comfortable and confident?
    - What position(s) currently needs to be filled?
    - What position can they grow in?

- Find ways to highlight these players' programmatic contributions apart from their physical achievements on the field. *Even though they may be able to exceed physical standards or expectations, they must continue to give their best efforts.*

    - In what ways has this player embodied the mission, values, and goals of the team?
    - How can you recognize their commitment to the team as well as their commitment to personal growth?
    - What physical (e.g. pass completions or yards rushing) and non-physical accomplishments (e.g. attended every preseason practice or meeting) has this player achieved that you and the team can celebrate?

- Explore ways to psychologically support this player when they become frustrated or disheartened by injury or negative feedback.
    - In what ways can you remind the player of their motivations for joining the team?
    - In what ways can you remind the player of their commitment to the mission and goals of the team?
    - In what ways can you remind the player of their short and long-term goals as well as commitments to personal progress?
    - In what ways can you help this player adjust short and long-term goals after an injury to help them re-focus on more attainable outcomes?
    - What are some individual strengths that the player can tap into to push through frustration or fear?
    - What are some familial/community resources that the player can tap into to push through disheartenment?

- If their caregivers are highly invested in their involvement on the team and available to support that goal, use them as a resource.
    - How and to what extent can caregivers be involved in training, practices, and/or games?
    - What other information and tips can they offer to promote this player's success on the team?
    - Are their other caregivers or adults at school or in the community that can also be helpful toward promoting this player's success on the team?

- If more assistance is needed, identify ways that teammates and other coaches can help support this player in the program.
    - Are their coaches or players available to check-in with this player and encourage them through challenging emotions or circumstances?

- If after all these strategies have been implemented and the athlete is not able or interested in continuing in the program as a player, other opportunities for continued involvement and support should be explored.
    - Would they be interested in opportunities for supporting the team as a manager, film person, coach's assistant, etc.?
    - Would they be interested in other opportunities to partner with the sports program through initiatives within the school and/or community?
    - Would they be interested in focusing more effort in another sport or pursuit?
    - If so, how can you support them toward that goal?

3.3a Coach Activity: Utilizing Strengths to Mitigate Risks with High Talent Players

In this activity coaches will brainstorm ways to utilize the strengths of athletically gifted players to support physiological and psychological health. Review the below cases and write your reflections on the space provided. This would be a great activity to conduct within a staff meeting at the start of a season to help coaches better support high talent players.

You are the offensive lineman coach in a very successful football program in a highly competitive district. You have a sophomore who is 6'6, 350 lbs who is an absolute force and can push a sled for a mile. The only challenge, however, is that he really has a hard time remembering the blocking schemes. When he gets in a real play situation, he kind of freezes. Luckily he's big enough to get in the way of somebody, but you want to help him reach his full potential. You can also see how this gets to him because he doesn't like making mistakes and letting his teammates down. How can you assess this player's needs and strengths to support their overall participation in the program?

One way I would leverage his strengths to address his needs would be to give him visual and auditory reminders from the sidelines as well as having other lineman and offensive players remind him before every down. Overtime, he may need less reminders and will become more confident in his ability to execute his job successfully. He's still young so that is really good. He also seems invested in the program and wants to do right by his teammates which is great. If he only freezes during scrimmage or games, maybe the issue is more psychological and less that he can't actually remember. If this were the case, I would also find ways to coach him up and remind him that he can do it. We believe in him.

You are a head varsity cross country coach in a rural school close to a reservation. You have two Native American sibling girls (sophomore and junior) who decided to join the team to improve their conditioning for basketball. At their first practice, they consistently led the pack and ran low 5's for the last mile interval! You are not getting too excited, though, because they said they may not be able to make all the practices and races because of basketball responsibilities. You don't want to step on the toes of the basketball program, but these kids could really do something for your team. Maybe with some training, they could even use running to take them to the next level. How can you assess these players' needs and strengths to support their overall participation in the program?

_____
_____
_____
_____
_____

You are the head varsity football coach at a moderately successful program in a suburban school. You have a highly talented junior who plays wide receiver for you who just got hit really hard in the 3rd quarter of the game in the last game before playoffs. He was down for a bit and you assessed if he was concussed, but weren't sure if he should go back in and play the rest of the game. This would be his second or third concussion this season. You know that he wants to play and is currently building up his highlights to be more competitive for recruiting. How can you assess this player's needs and strengths to support their overall participation in this game, their future in the program, and career in college?

You were just emailed by a parent indicating that their child will be joining the wrestling team next year as an incoming sophomore. This parent indicated that their child was a state champion last year in another district. The parent noted that their child has grown-up wrestling and is following in his father's footsteps. His father wrestled at a Division I school back in the day. The parent mentioned that their child also has an interest in football, but his father wants him to start specializing to increase his chance at earning a scholarship. How can you assess this player's needs and strengths to support their overall participation in the program?

You are a head varsity dance coach in a suburban town whose program has won multiple championships. Your girls are hard workers and highly talented. You pride yourself on your high standards for the program and each girl. You've noticed one of your top girls has been distracted in practice lately and honestly seems lower energy than usual. You approach her after practice and she admits to not eating as much lately because she is concerned about gaining weight. You are worried about her and have also struggled with eating issues. How can you assess this player's needs and strengths to support their overall participation in the program?

___

You are an assistant coach on the boys' varsity basketball team in an urban school with a strong winning record. Your head coach relies on you to work with the kids who have a hard time showing-up or putting in full effort. You have a junior this season that has the potential to be one of the best athletes this school has ever seen, however he just does not seem motivated to get there. You've talked with him and tried to discipline him, but those didn't work. You recently reached out to his mother and she thinks you're wasting your time because, "He's a lost cause." She compared him to his father who has been incarcerated due to drugs and other charges for the past 4 years. How can you assess this player's needs and strengths to support their overall participation in the program?

3.4 Coach Activity: Supporting the Physical and Mental Health of LGBTQ+ Players

Mental Health and LGBTQ+ Youth

In order to more effectively engage gender and sexual minority youth on teams, coaches must understand these players' specific physical and psychological risks. There is a plethora of research surrounding mental health risks for LGBTQ+ youth. According to the Trevor Project's 2023 U.S. National Survey on the Mental Health of LGBTQ Young People, 67% of LGBTQ youth reported anxiety symptoms, 54% indicated depressive symptoms, 41% considered ending their own lives, and 14% actually attempted suicide this past year. This number grows exponentially when looking at transgender and nonbinary youth experiences.

Transgender and nonbinary young people reported consistently higher percentages of both depression and anxiety symptoms, while 1 out of 5 of them have attempted suicide this past year (Trevor Project, 2023). Similarly, high percentages of gender and sexual minority youth become homeless and detached from familial relationships (Deal & Gonzales, 2023) which increases their risk of victimization, health concerns and engaging in risky behaviors to survive (Alessi et al., 2021; Deal et al., 2023; Cochran et al., 2002). It is important to note that intersectionality for LGBTQ+ people can increase their risk of negative physical and psychological outcomes. Trans and non-binary youth of color are much more likely to experience intersectional discrimination and violence that impact increased rates of self-harm, foregone health care, suicide ideation, and attempting suicide (Chan et al., 2022).

Apart from mental and physical health risks, LGBTQ+ athletes could also experience negative academic and athletic performance outcomes due to the discrimination they receive on the teams in which they play. The discomfort associated with discrimination, in turn, can contribute to LGBTQ+ young people leaving sports altogether (Griffin, 1994). When LGBTQ+ youth have people in their lives, like coaches, that love and accept them they are protected from many of the risk factors discussed above. Other protective factors against LGBTQ+ suicide include: family support, LGBTQ+ affirming curriculums and school policies, mental health care, and peer support (Gorse, 2022).

Ideas for Assessing Needs:

In order to more effectively engage gender and sexual minority athletes, coaches must fully understand and assess these players' specific physical and psychological needs. Below are some questions that coaches can ask themselves and players to better achieve this goal.

- Gauge these players' sense of safety on the team.
    - Do you feel comfortable on the team?
    - Do you feel cared for, accepted, and supported by coaches on the team?
    - Do you feel cared for, accepted, and supported by your teammates?
    - Are there times you feel unsafe on the team?
    - If so, say more about how and in what context and times you feel unsafe.

- Gauge these players' sense of safety in their schools.
    - Do you feel comfortable in your school?
    - Do you feel cared for, accepted, and supported by your teachers?
    - Do you feel cared for, accepted, and supported by your classmates?
    - Are there times you feel unsafe in your school?
    - If so, say more about how and in what context and times you feel unsafe.

- Gauge these players' sense of safety in their homes.
    - When you are at home, do you feel comfortable there?
    - Do you feel loved, accepted, and supported by your parents and caregivers?
    - Do you feel loved, accepted, and supported by other family members?
    - Are there times you feel unsafe in your home?
    - If so, say more about how and in what context and times you feel unsafe.

- Gauge these players' sense of safety in their communities.
    - When you are in your community, do you feel comfortable there?
    - Do you feel cared for, accepted, and supported by members of your community?
    - Are there times you feel unsafe in your community?
    - If so, say more about how and in what context and times you feel unsafe.

- Gauge psychological risks associated with sexism, homophobia, and transphobia for gender and sexual minority athletes.
    - In what contexts are you reminded of your gender and sexual orientation?
    - When have you felt treated differently because of your gender or sexual minority identity on the team, in school, or in the community (e.g. being made fun of by teammates, being called bad names by others, having assumptions made about your physical ability, being singled out by teachers, having threats of violence made toward you)?
    - Do you ever question yourself for having these experiences and wonder if you are just reading into things?
    - Do people discount your experience as a gender or sexual minority person (e.g. don't talk about this when it does matter to you)?
    - Have you ever felt bad about or less of a person because of your gender or sexual minority identity?
    - Have you ever wished that you had a majority gender or sexual orientation?
    - Have you ever tried to suppress your identities or been asked to do so by others?

    This is a really important risk factor. In the last couple decades research has determined that engaging gender and sexual minority young people in treatment to change or suppress their gender identity or sexual orientation, can cause serious and long-lasting psychological damage. Because this treatment (conversion therapy) actually increases risk of psychological issues, substance use, self-injury and suicide in gender and sexual minority young people, it has been outlawed in several states.

- Have you tried to not affiliate yourself with others who share your gender or sexual minority identity?
- What have your caregivers, family members, and other adults taught you about your gender and sexual identity?
- Were you taught about things that happened to other people sharing your gender and sexual identity in the U.S. and/or other countries historically and today?
- If so, was this accurate to what you have learned in other places?
- When and in what contexts have you ever felt unsafe to be a gender or sexual minority person?
- When and in what contexts have you ever felt your friends or family were unsafe to be gender or sexual minority people?
- To what extent is your relationship with parents impacted by your gender or sexual identity (e.g. parents' religious beliefs in conflict with your identity)?
- Does living with your gender and sexual identity (and all of the above experiences) cause you to feel stressed, worried, exhausted, lonely, hopeless, guilty, frustrated, or embarrassed?
- Do these emotions and experiences cause you to feel physically unwell (e.g. trouble sleeping, digestive concerns, unexplainable pain within the body, loss of appetite or overeating, heart racing, sweating, breathing fast, feeling shaky, dizzy or lightheaded, feeling like something terrible will happen, having a hard time concentrating, or having racing thoughts)?
- Do any of these feelings get in the way of your ability to hang out with friends, focus in school, complete homework, focus in practice, or compete to the best of your ability?
- Do these feelings ever cause you to be mean or hurt someone else when you don't really want to?
- Do these feelings ever cause you to be mean or hurt yourself when you don't really want to?
- Do these feelings ever cause you to want to drink or engage in other substance use or behaviors to feel better?
- Have you considered not being alive anymore or ending your own life because of challenging experiences or emotions?

If a player answers yes to a fair number of these questions it would be useful to connect them with a school counselor or social worker as soon as possible. They may be experiencing clinical levels of anxiety, depression, panic, or traumatic stress that would benefit from immediate intervention. In emergency situations, you can also call 911 or take your player to their local emergency room. You can also call or text 988, the mental health crisis line created by the Substance Abuse and Mental Health Services Administration (SAMHSA). SAMHSA is the national government agency tasked with promoting the mental health and wellness of persons residing in the U.S. They created 988 and 988lifeline.org (to chat) for emergency mental health support. Here is SAMHSA's website for more details about this national service, https://www.samhsa.gov/find-help/988/.

Ideas for Assessing Resources:

In order to more effectively engage gender and sexual minority athletes, coaches must fully understand and assess these players' specific strengths and resources. Below are some questions that coaches can ask themselves and players to better achieve this goal:

- Gauge these players' individual resources.
    - What are some strengths that this player has that could mitigate risk?
        - Level of self-esteem and pride in their gender and sexual identity
        - Ability to assess and advocate for their personal safety needs
        - Short and long-term goals for their future within and beyond athletics

- Gauge these players' familial or home based resources.
    - What are some strengths this player can access from within their family and home?
        - Caregivers and other adults who are able and motivated to support a player's psychological health
        - Caregivers and other adults who accept the player and encourage them to have a pride in their gender and sexual identity
        - Caregivers and other adults who teach the player about the history of people within their gender and sexual identity
        - Caregivers and other adults who help a player identify coping skills and strategies to protect themselves in the context of navigating life with their gender and sexual identity (e.g. finding friendships within the LGBTQ+ community)
        - Caregivers and other adults who serve as models of success who share their same gender and sexual identity

- Gauge these players' team based resources.
    - What are some strengths this player can access from within their team?
        - Coaches, teammates, and booster club families who are able and motivated to support a player's psychological health
        - Coaches who are culturally representative of these players on the team
        - Coaches and teammates who are sensitive to the experiences of a player from a gender and sexual minority background (e.g. do not make jokes related to gender and sexual identities)
        - Coaches who discipline team members for their negative treatment or insensitivity toward others based on gender and sexual identity
        - Coaches and teammates who are accommodating to the experiences of a player from a gender and sexual minority background (e.g. creating separate dressing space for female athletes on the football team)
        - Coaches and teammates who recognize the impact of historical and systemic oppression on the experiences of gender and sexual minority persons (e.g. academic, occupational, economic, and health disparities)

- Coaches and teammates who recognize the impact of interpersonal oppression on the experiences of gender and sexual minority persons (e.g. unconscious biases impacting how people see, interact with, or avoid gender and sexual minority people)
- Coaches and teammates who recognize the impact of internalized oppression on the experiences of gender and sexual minority persons (e.g. a player starting to see themselves as less deserving or less capable compared to others from majority identities)

- Gauge these players' school and community resources.
  - What are some strengths this player can access from within their schools and communities?
    - Peers, teachers, staff, and mentors who are able and motivated to support students' psychological health
    - Peers, teachers, staff, and mentors who value students' gender and sexual minority experiences and help them feel comfortable and confident in them
    - Schools that teach accurate and complete histories of gender and sexual minority persons in the U.S.
    - Schools that emphasize the achievements, contributions, and resiliency of gender and sexual minority persons in the U.S.
    - Schools that are composed of teachers, staff, and administrators that are culturally representative of the student population
    - Peers, teachers, and staff who are sensitive to the experiences of gender and sexual minority students (e.g. do not make jokes related to gender and sexual identity)
    - Teachers and staff who discipline school members for their negative treatment or insensitivity toward others based on their gender or sexual minority identities
    - Teachers and staff who are accommodating to the experiences of students with gender and sexual minority identities (e.g. adjust records to acknowledge students' names and gender markers)
    - Peers, teachers, and staff who recognize the impact of historical and systemic oppression on the experiences of gender and sexual minority students (e.g. academic, occupational, economic, and health disparities)
    - Peers, teachers, and staff who recognize the impact of interpersonal oppression on the experiences of gender and sexual minority students (e.g. unconscious biases impacting how people see, interact with, or avoid people from these identities)
    - Peers, teachers, and staff who recognize the impact of internalized oppression on the experiences of gender and sexual minority students (e.g. a student starting to see themselves as less deserving, less intelligent, or less capable compared to others from majority identities)

- *To learn more about the mental and physical health risks of gender and sexual minority youth as well as ways to better support them, please visit: https://www.thetrevorproject.org/*

- *To learn more about supporting the needs of LGBTQ+ athletes visit:* [GLSEN Changing the Game](#).

3.4a Coach Activity: Utilizing Strengths to Mitigate Risks for LGBTQ+ Players

In this activity coaches will brainstorm ways to utilize players' strengths and resources to mitigate risks faced by LGBTQ+ young people. Review the below cases and write your reflections on the space provided. This would be a great activity to conduct within a staff meeting at the start of a season so that coaches can better appreciate the risks and resilience of these players.

You are a head varsity wrestling coach in your 15th year of coaching. You currently work at a rural school in a moderately competitive district. Your assistant coach talked with you recently about a player having a scuffle with another player at practice because one called the other "gay." The assistant coach thought there was something more to what they were saying, but he didn't catch it all. You haven't really run into this type of thing before, but things have been changing over the past few years related to players coming out. How can you assess these players' risks and resources to support their overall safety and participation in the program?

Well, I would first figure out if the players had resolved the issue amongst themselves since the incident had passed. If they still have big problems with each other I would resolve those first. All players need to know that if they work hard and maintain their commitment to the team, they belong here. Also, there is absolutely no room for bullying on this team. The player who was calling names will be addressed and punished. The player who was called the name will be talked to separately. I will probably meet with him and the assistant coach to talk about how he feels on the team and let him know he can come to us with any concerns he has.

You are a JV girls' lacrosse coach at a suburban school in a high competition school district. One of your best players recently came out as lesbian to the team during the preseason retreat. She became very emotional about it and mentioned sometimes feeling unsafe in her home because her family is very religious. You followed-up with her individually to get more information about her safety risk at home and she did not seem willing to share more. You continue to be concerned and remember your friend in college who was part of the LGBTQ+ community and who ended her own life due to feeling unsafe and unaccepted. How can you assess this player's risks and resources to support her overall safety and participation in the program?

⚾ You are the freshman baseball coach at a rural school in a small town in the South. You have a player who's been a little distracted in practice over the past few days and decide to follow-up with him individually. After several conversations over a two week period, the player finally confides in you that his father found out that he had been sending romantic messages to another boy in school. The player said that he has been spending the night at his aunt's house for the past week because his father said that he was going to "kick the shit out of him" if he sees him again. How can you assess this player's risks and resources to support his overall safety and participation in the program?

_____
_____
_____
_____
_____
_____
_____

🥎 You are the new head varsity softball coach at a rural high school in a moderately competitive district who is a woman and who is married to a woman. You have a couple players on the team who have come out as lesbian within the team but have not done so in their families or in school. One player's parent learned about this and was upset that "this type of thing" is happening in the team. She threatened to call the principal and school board about you "indoctrinating" players. How can you assess these players' risks and resources to support their overall health and participation in the program?

_____
_____
_____
_____
_____
_____
_____

🏈 You are the JV football coach at a suburban high school in a competitive district. This season a female athlete came out for the team and completed all the summer workouts. She's struggled with some of the physicality, but she's really positive and motivated to earn a spot on the team. You've put her in on special teams a couple of times but you can tell that she's a little disappointed that she hasn't played more. In truth, you are worried about her getting hurt. Male athletes on the team and on opposing teams are starting to get bigger and stronger in comparison to her. You don't want to discourage her from playing, but you do have responsibilities for her safety. How can you assess risks and resources to support this player's overall health and participation in the program?

_____

_____

_____

_____

_____

_____

_____

_____

🌐 You are the head varsity girls' basketball coach at a suburban high school. You have a player on the team that recently came out as transgender. You have been coaching for almost 20 years and have not really run into this before. This player has asked the team to refer to them as a different name and use different pronouns. Since the team has started to do this, the player has started to be more positive, perform better, and become more confident. You want to keep encouraging this player, but still feel uncomfortable with referring to them in this way. How can you assess your discomfort as well as other risks and resources to support this player's overall health and participation in the program?

_____

_____

_____

_____

_____

_____

_____

_____

3.5 Coach Activity: Supporting the Physical and Mental Health of Players Living in Poverty

Poverty in the U.S.

According to the U.S. Census Bureau (2023), nearly 38 million people live in poverty in the U.S. today. For a family of four, that's a household income less than $29,950 per year. As discussed in a previous section, poverty is more concentrated in communities of color. The Board of Governors of the Federal Reserve System (2023), for example, found that for every $100 of wealth held by a typical White family the typical Hispanic and African American family has held around $10-$15 since the Great Recession in 2008. Scholars have theorized that contextual barriers in the short and long run have kept people of color in the position of being unable to accumulate and pass on generational wealth within their families and communities. Research supports this notion and has identified a number of factors that contribute to wealth inequality. The most influential to the gap was differences in income (despite commensurate levels of education) and less stock and business ownership (Herring & Henderson, 2016).

Among all children in the U.S. the rates of poverty have more than doubled between 2021 and 2022 (U.S. Census Bureau, 2023). This change has been attributed to the expiration of the Child Tax Credit within the American Rescue Plan that brought child poverty rates to an all-time low in 2021 (Koutavas, et al., 2023). Many children living in poverty in the U.S. attend Title I schools in which they receive free and reduced breakfast and lunch as well as other benefits to support their and their families' basic needs.

Living in poverty puts physical and psychological stress on young people and their families. According to Santiago and colleagues (2011), poverty can contribute to symptoms of anxiety, depression, and social problems as well as worsen delinquency, somatic issues, attention problems, and other mental health symptoms. Many young athletes' participation in sports offers them a glimmer of hope, a respite from everyday stress, belongingness that heightens self-worth, important instrumental supports, as well as avenues toward feeling confident and competent when battling the stressors of poverty.

Ideas for Assessing Needs:

In order to more effectively engage athletes living in poverty, coaches must fully understand and assess these players' specific physiological and psychological needs. Below are some questions that coaches can ask themselves and players to better achieve this goal:

- Gauge these players' access to basic living needs.
    - Do you currently have a home or stable housing?
    - If not, where are you currently staying?
    - Are your parents or caregivers working?
    - Do you hold a job outside of school and sports to support your family?
    - Are you responsible for caring for someone other than yourself in the home (e.g. younger siblings, ill parents, elderly grandparents)?
    - Do you ever have to skip a meal because there is no food in the home?

- - Does your home have electricity, heating/cooling, running water?
  - Do you have access to personal hygiene supplies?
  - Do you have access to clothes and shoes as well as laundering facilities?
  - Do you have physical space and time to sleep, relax, and complete homework in the place you are living?
  - Do you have access to medical and mental health care for check-ups or immediate issues?
  - Do you have access to transportation to get to school and back home after practice and games?
  - Do you have funds to purchase necessary school supplies or sport fees and equipment?
  - Do you have funds to pay for food that the school or program does not provide for you during the school year and season?

- Once an athlete has been identified as having concerns related to poverty, coaches should ask the player the following questions:
  - Do you worry about where you will sleep at night?
  - Do you worry that your caregivers are out of work or will lose their job?
  - If you hold a job, do you ever feel stressed, exhausted, hopeless, worried, guilty, frustrated, or embarrassed in relation to balancing this and your schoolwork and sport?
  - If you are responsible for caring for someone other than yourself in the home (e.g. younger siblings, ill parents, elderly grandparents), do you ever feel stressed, hopeless, exhausted, worried, guilty, frustrated, or embarrassed?
  - Do you ever have these same feelings when you have to skip a meal because there is no food in your home or you do not have money to purchase food?
  - Do you ever feel stressed, hopeless, worried, guilty, frustrated, or embarrassed to invite people to your home because of its condition?
  - Do you feel these same ways about your appearance because you do not have access to personal hygiene supplies, laundry, new clothes, or shoes?
  - Do you feel unable to sleep, relax, and complete homework in the place you are living?
  - Do you worry about having access to medical and mental health care for check-ups or immediate issues?
  - Do you feel stressed, hopeless, worried, guilty, frustrated, or embarrassed related to your access to transportation?
  - Do you ever have these same feelings related to your ability to purchase necessary school supplies or sport fees and equipment?
  - Do all these feelings get in the way of your ability to hang out with friends, concentrate in school, complete homework, focus in practice, or compete to the best of your ability?
  - Do these feelings ever cause you to be mean or hurt someone else when you don't really want to?
  - Do these feelings ever cause you to be mean or hurt yourself when you don't really want to?

- Do these feelings ever cause you to want to drink or engage in other substance use or behaviors to feel better?
- Have you considered not being alive anymore or ending your own life because of challenging experiences or emotions?

If a player answers yes to a fair number of these questions it would be useful to connect them with a school counselor or social worker as soon as possible. They may be experiencing clinical levels of anxiety, depression, panic, or traumatic stress that would benefit from immediate intervention. In emergency situations, you can also call 911 or take your player to their local emergency room. You can also call or text 988, the mental health crisis line created by the Substance Abuse and Mental Health Services Administration (SAMHSA). SAMHSA is the national government agency tasked with promoting the mental health and wellness of persons residing in the U.S. They created 988 and 988lifeline.org (to chat) for emergency mental health support. Here is SAMHSA's website for more details about this national service, https://www.samhsa.gov/find-help/988/.

Ideas for Assessing Resources:

In order to more effectively engage athletes living in poverty, coaches must fully understand and assess these players' specific strengths and resources. Below are some questions that coaches can ask themselves and players to better achieve this goal:

- Gauge these players' individual resources.
    - What are some strengths that this player has that could mitigate risk?
        - Level of personal responsibility and conscientiousness
        - Ability to assess personal and familial needs
        - Desire to provide for personal and familial needs
        - Short and long-term goals for their future within and beyond athletics

- Gauge these players' familial or home based resources.
    - What are some strengths this player can access from within their family and home?
        - Caregivers and other adults who are able and motivated to support a player's physiological health (e.g. a parent working two jobs to keep the family afloat)
        - Caregivers and other adults who are encouraging of a player's short and long-term goals within and beyond athletics (e.g. a grandfather encouraging the player to use athletics as a means of accessing education and escaping poverty)

- Gauge these players' team based resources.
  - What are some strengths this player can access from within their team?
    - Coaches, teammates, and booster club families who are able and motivated to support a player's physiological health (e.g. a booster club raising funds for players to access school supplies and sport equipment)
    - Coaches and teammates who are encouraging of a player's short and long-term goals within and beyond athletics (e.g. coaches having discussions with the player about their goals for after graduation and helping them make a plan toward achieving them)

- Gauge these players' school and community resources.
  - What are some strengths this player can access from within their schools and communities?
    - Friends, teachers, staff, and mentors who are able and motivated to support a player's safety (e.g. instituting community programs that teach transferable occupational skills for unemployed persons)
    - Teachers, staff, and mentors who are encouraging of a player's short and long-term goals within and beyond athletics (e.g. instituting mentorship programs to support academic and occupational success).
    - School or community case managers that can connect the player and their family with free or low-cost access to: medical and mental health treatment, emergency and long-term housing, and sustainable sources of food and basic living essentials.
    - *If you would like to explore resources available in your community like food, housing, financial assistance, healthcare, and other services visit this website:* FindHelp.org

Advocating for Local Communities. Teams and coaches often engage in service work and activities that promote the individual interests of players and the overall community. Service work has been shown to positively shape young people who engage in it. Further, teams who work together toward service initiatives increase cohesion across all levels of a program. Below is a list of service activities that sport teams could consider instituting:

- Having a drive to collect clothing, shoes, basic hygiene supplies, toys, school supplies and other items for local shelters.
- Having a fundraiser for local charitable organizations as part of a game raffle.
- Having the team assist in moving furniture or other items for non-profits or charitable organizations.
- Assisting in and/or hosting English language learning classes for adults in the community.
- Assisting in and/or hosting computer literacy classes for adults in the community.
- Having a food drive for the local food pantry.
- Having the team assist in cleaning-up a local park or roadway.
- Having the team assist in painting homes or landscaping for elderly members of their communities.

- Having the team visit with elderly folks at a local senior citizen center to share a meal, play games, and listen to stories.
- Volunteering at or hosting a free/low cost festival for families in the community with games, face painting, food, and fun!
- Pairing players up with students in the local elementary school to read together and/or have lunch together.
- Pairing players up with students in the local elementary school to do homework and play games together in an afterschool program.
- Pairing players up with elementary or middle school students as part of an on-going mentorship program. Players would spend time with these students in fun and educational activities across the school year.
- Pairing players up with other high school students who have special needs as part of an on-going buddy program. Players would spend time with these students in fun activities across the school year (e.g. having lunch together, reading books, playing games, etc.).

3.5a Coach Activity: Utilizing Strengths to Mitigate Risks for Players Living in Poverty

In this activity coaches will brainstorm ways to utilize players' strengths and resources to mitigate risks associated with players living in poverty. Review the below cases and write your reflections on the space provided. This would be a great activity to conduct within a staff meeting at the start of a season so that coaches can better appreciate the risks and resilience of these players.

You are the new head varsity girls' basketball coach at an urban high school in a competitive district. Your school is in one of the poorest neighborhoods in your city. You live in a nicer suburb 35 minutes away from the school, but grew-up here and attended this school yourself. Most of your players have never been outside the city. You are concerned about a couple players who say they won't be able to pay the cost of attending the team's preseason retreat. How can you assess these players' risks and resources to support their overall health and participation in the program?

Well, it's good that she grew up there and knows what it's like for these kids. It depends on how many kids can't attend and the possibility for fundraising. If it is only 2 that need help, we might be able to get money together for them to go. If it is more, then I would have to think about where the retreat is, what is the cost, and whether it might be better to change it up. It actually might be better to change it anyway because it sounds like it is a poor area and exorbitant fees for a retreat would put stress on all the families even if they don't say anything.

You are the softball coach in a small school in a rural town. One of your player's has been consistently going home with another player after practice, then coming to school together the next morning. You joke that they are "joined at the hip" but learn later that one of these player's families recently got evicted. This player is currently living with the other player, while her mother and younger sister stay in emergency housing. You feel terrible because she is a great student and athlete and know that this experience may threaten her progress. How can you assess this player's risks and resources to support their overall health and participation in the program?

_____
_____
_____
_____
_____
_____
_____

You are the head freshman football coach in a small school and rural farming community. Most of your players' families work in the fields and some players help them before or after school. You notice that your players are more tired than usual because they have been helping their families pick. They have also been late to practice or had to leave early some days. You want to hold these players to the practice standard and their commitment to the team, but you don't want to punish them for something out of their control. How can you assess these players' risks and resources to support their overall safety and participation in the program?

_____

_____

_____

_____

_____

_____

_____

You are the boys' varsity baseball coach in a medium sized school in a rural community. Many of your player's families work in the oil fields and some make decent money doing it. You have one high talent junior who's a good kid and pretty coachable. You are worried about him, though, because he said he would probably not play next season. He said that his family needs him to take a job in the oil fields. His father has been out of work due to an injury and his mother has to stay home to watch the new baby. How can you assess this player's risks and resources to support their overall health and participation in the program?

_____

_____

_____

_____

_____

_____

_____

You are the new head varsity girls' lacrosse coach at a suburban high school in a competitive district. Your school is fairly affluent, but you do have players who bus in to play from poorer areas. You enjoy the mix of players because it's hard to work with some athletes (and their parents) from privileged and entitled backgrounds. You've noticed issues on the team, however, with some affluent players having negative attitudes toward the players who bus in. Honestly, they may be a little jealous of these players' athletic abilities and starting positions. How can you assess these players' risks and resources to support their overall health and participation in the program?

___

You are the varsity football coach in a small school in a rural community near the U.S./Mexico border. Many of your players have family on either side of the border. You understand that it is challenging for these players to make ends meet because their caregivers are often limited in the jobs that they can get without documentation. One of your juniors is the oldest of his siblings and the first child born in the U.S. You've had conversations with him about attending college because he is pretty bright and could get a scholarship to a smaller school. He says that he would want to, but feels that he ought to get a decent paying job to support his family after graduation. How can you assess this player's risks and resources to support their overall health and participation in the program?

3.6 Coach Activity: Supporting the Physical and Mental Health of Players Living in High Violence Areas

Ideas for Assessing Needs:

In order to more effectively engage athletes living in high violence communities, coaches must fully understand and assess these players' specific physiological and psychological needs. Below are some questions that coaches can ask themselves and players to better achieve this goal:

- Gauge these players' sense of safety in their homes.
    - Where do you spend most of your time outside of school and practice?
    - If you spend it at home, what are you usually doing?
    - If you are at a friends or family member's house, what are you usually doing?
    - Where do you sleep most nights?
    - If you sleep most nights in your home, who also lives there?
    - How long have you and your family members lived in that home?
    - Are there times you feel unsafe in your home?
    - If so, say more about how and in what context and times you feel unsafe.

- Gauge these players' sense of safety in their neighborhoods.
    - Who are your neighbors?
    - Do you or your family members feel comfortable going to your neighbors if there is a concern about safety?
    - Do you or your family members feel comfortable walking outside during the day and night in your neighborhood?
    - Has violence occurred in your neighborhood?
    - If so, say more about how and in what context this violence happened?
    - Are there any safety precautions that you or your family members take in your neighborhood?

- Once an athlete has been identified as having concerns related to living in a high violence community, coaches should ask the player the following questions:
    - How much do you worry about your safety in your community?
    - How much do you worry about the safety of your family and friends in your community?
    - Does this worry cause you to feel physically unwell (e.g. trouble sleeping, digestive concerns, unexplainable pain within the body, loss of appetite or overeating, heart racing, sweating, breathing fast, feeling shaky, dizzy or lightheaded, feeling like something terrible will happen, having a hard time concentrating, or having racing thoughts)?
    - Do you ever feel stressed, hopeless, worried, guilty, frustrated, or embarrassed to invite people to your home or neighborhood because it is not safe?

- Do all these feelings get in the way of your ability to hang out with friends, focus in school, complete homework, focus in practice, or compete to the best of your ability?
- Do these feelings ever cause you to be mean or hurt someone else when you don't really want to?
- Do these feelings ever cause you to be mean or hurt yourself when you don't really want to?
- Do these feelings ever cause you to want to drink or engage in other substance use or behaviors to feel better?
- Have you considered not being alive anymore or ending your own life because of challenging experiences or emotions?

If a player answers yes to a fair number of these questions it would be useful to connect them with a school counselor or social worker as soon as possible. They may be experiencing clinical levels of anxiety, depression, panic, or traumatic stress that would benefit from immediate intervention. In emergency situations, you can also call 911 or take your player to their local emergency room. You can also call or text 988, the mental health crisis line created by the Substance Abuse and Mental Health Services Administration (SAMHSA). SAMHSA is the national government agency tasked with promoting the mental health and wellness of persons residing in the U.S. They created 988 and 988lifeline.org (to chat) for emergency mental health support. Here is SAMHSA's website for more details about this national service, https://www.samhsa.gov/find-help/988/.

Ideas for Assessing Resources:

In order to more effectively engage athletes living in high violence communities, coaches must fully understand and assess these players' strengths and resources. Below are some questions that coaches can ask themselves and players to better achieve this goal:

- Gauge these players' individual resources.
  - What are some strengths that this player has that could contribute to their safety?
    - Level of personal responsibility and conscientiousness
    - Ability to assess risks and avoid harm
    - Desire to keep themselves and others safe
    - Short and long-term goals for their future within and beyond athletics

- Gauge these players' familial or home based resources.
  - What are some strengths this player can access from within their family and home?
    - Caregivers and other adults who are able and motivated to support a player's safety (e.g. a parent ensuring that another trusted adult will be at home with the player when they are working the night shift)

- ■ Caregivers and other adults who are encouraging of a player's short and long-term goals within and beyond athletics (e.g. a grandmother checking her son's homework every night and regularly attending conferences with teachers)

- Gauge these players' team based resources.
    - What are some strengths this player can access from within their team?
        - ■ Coaches and teammates who are able and motivated to support a player's safety (e.g. a teammate giving the player a ride home or allowing them to stay the night during risky times)
        - ■ Coaches and teammates who are encouraging of a player's short and long-term goals within and beyond athletics (e.g. coaches having discussions with the player about their goals and helping them make a plan toward achieving them)

- Gauge these players' school and community resources.
    - What are some strengths this player can access from within their schools and communities?
        - ■ Friends, teachers, staff, and mentors who are able and motivated to support a player's safety (e.g. instituting programs to decrease community violence)
        - ■ Teachers, staff, and mentors who are encouraging of a player's short and long-term goals within and beyond athletics (e.g. instituting mentorship programs to support academic and occupational success).

3.6a Coach Activity: Utilizing Strengths to Mitigate Risks for Players Living in High Violence Areas

In this activity coaches will brainstorm ways to utilize players' strengths and resources to mitigate risks associated with life in high violence communities. Review the below cases and write your reflections on the space provided. This would be a great activity to conduct within a staff meeting at the start of a season so that coaches can better appreciate the risks and resilience of these players.

You are the new head varsity boys' basketball coach at an urban high school in a competitive district. Your school is in a somewhat decent neighborhood compared to where most of the players live. You live in a nicer suburb 35 minutes away from the school. These players bus into your school because they like the team and have taken to your coaching. You heard some of them talking about a recent shooting in their neighborhood two nights ago. No one they knew got hurt, but they could hear the gunshots through their windows. The guys joked about it, but you are worried about their safety. How can you assess these players' risks and resources to support their overall safety and participation in the program?

Well, that is tough. My guess is that these players probably know more about their safety than I do because I don't live in that neighborhood. They probably have lived there most their life, too, and know how to stay safe. That being said, they shouldn't be in charge of taking care of themselves on their own. Especially when they are not at school or at practice and games. They need adults at home that can watch them and make sure they are good. I would probably check-in with the players and talk to them about their homes and neighborhoods. I would also talk with caregivers to let them know I am concerned and there to help. If caregivers are concerned and want to get out of the neighborhood, I might try to get them connected with people who could help guide them through it.

You are the freshman head girls' volleyball coach at an urban school. You have a player who's been a little distracted in practice over the past few days because her older sister was recently arrested for selling drugs. You learn from other players that her sister is afraid that the people she works for may be coming after her. This player's older sister currently lives in the home with the player, their mother, and their younger brother. How can you assess this player's risks and resources to support their overall safety and participation in the program?

You are the girls' and boys' head track and field coach at an urban school in a city with one of the highest crime rates in the country. Two girls on the team approached you last week with a concern about another athlete. They were worried because their teammate started "talking to" an older guy who is known for being gang affiliated and who's been arrested in the past for assault. They want you to talk with her because she isn't listening to them. They also said that no one is really at home to keep an eye on her because her mom works two jobs and the dad's out of the picture. You have a pretty good relationship with this athlete and also feel concerned for her. How can you assess this player's risks and resources to support their overall safety and participation in the program?

_____
_____
_____
_____
_____
_____
_____
_____

You are the boys' and girls' cross country coach in a rural school on a Native American reservation. One of your athletes has been looking stressed and a bit distracted in practice this week. You learn that her cousin went missing recently. There have been other women missing from the reservation over the past few years with very few being found. You want to encourage this athlete to take some time off to deal with her concerns, but also appreciate that the team is keeping her emotionally and physically safe. How can you assess this player's risks and resources to support their overall health and participation in the program?

_____
_____
_____
_____
_____
_____
_____
_____

⚾ You are the head varsity baseball coach in a small school and rural community that recently experienced a tragedy that resulted in two young people losing their lives. One of the teens was a relief pitcher on the team and well-liked by other players and coaches. Even though he didn't play that much, he had a great attitude and was a good kid. The other players on the team (and parents) are incredibly upset and worried. They are grieving and don't want this to happen again. How can you assess players' risks and resources to support their overall safety and participation in the program?

_____
_____
_____
_____
_____
_____
_____
_____

🏃🏃 You are the new head varsity track and field coach at an urban school in a community that has seen increases in crime and violence over the past few months. When you relocated, you moved to the less well-off part of town because it was more affordable. Recently, your home got broken into when you were out of town for the weekend and they took your electronics and some jewelry. The players who live in that part of town reassured you saying that it's happened to them, too. They gave you some ideas on how to prevent it from happening in the future. You are pretty shaken-up and worry that they are used to feeling this way. How can you assess these players' risks and resources to support their overall health and participation in the program?

_____
_____
_____
_____
_____
_____
_____
_____

3.7 Coach Activity: Supporting Immigrant, Ethnic, and Racial Minority Athletes

Oppression and Disparity

Youth of color experience exposure to higher numbers of adverse childhood experiences and have a higher likelihood of suffering challenges related to poor physical health, substance use, and mental distress across the lifespan (Sheats et al., 2018). When African American youth, in particular, are not being victimized they find themselves more likely to fall into the juvenile justice system (Crosby, 2016) which, in and of itself, sets the stage for adult involvement (Gatti et al., 2009). Consequently, involvement within these systems often results in continued generational cycles of poverty, familial upheaval, and negative overall health outcomes (Dragomir & Tadros, 2020).

The majority of people living in poverty in the U.S. today are people of color (U.S. Census Bureau, 2023). Nearly half of African American youth attend high-poverty schools (National School Board Association, 2020), in which there are struggles to purchase and maintain sufficient learning materials and resources as well as recruit and maintain high quality teachers. According to the National Assessment of Educational Progress (NAEP, 2023a), only 9 out of 100 African American students performed at or above proficient levels in mathematics and only 16 out of 100 performed at or above proficient levels in reading in 2022 (NAEP, 2023b). Latinx and Native American youth proficiency levels in these same academic areas were also alarming.

Further, when African American students move into secondary and post-secondary education, they continue to show disproportionately high rates of drop-out and low enrollment in college (National Center for Educational Statistics, 2023a; 2023b). For those African Americans that do complete post-secondary education, there remain barriers to obtaining gainful employment. Research consistently shows higher unemployment rates among African American men (Bureau of Labor Statistics, 2021), as well as lower wages for the same jobs, independent of education and qualification levels (Payscale, 2019). Lower college graduation rates and disproportionately higher rates of unemployment and poverty are also seen in Latinx and Native American communities in comparison to non-Hispanic, White populations. Racism across communities of color has been associated with poor physical and mental health outcomes like: anxiety (Soto et al., 2011), depression (English et al, 2020), PTSD (Sibrava et al., 2019), diabetes (Bacon et al., 2017), obesity (Sewell, 2017), and high blood pressure (Forde et al., 2020).

Immigration and acculturation have been and continue to be salient battles for many Latinx people and other immigrant communities within the U.S. Many times, challenges associated with immigration further exacerbate educational, occupational, and health disparities already faced by people of color in America. Trauma in home countries that influences migration (Kaltman et al., 2011), as well as traumatic events happening during people's journeys, negatively influences those crossing the border (de Arellano et al., 2018; Fulginiti, 2008). Family separation and deportation of family members has been linked to various harmful outcomes for children as well as poorer relationship quality between parents and kids (Conway et al., 2020). Living with discrimination and acculturative stress as well as fear of deportation and shame surrounding documentation status all negatively impact many Latinx families today (Golash-Boza & Hondagneu-Sotelo, 2013; Hurwich-Reiss & Gudino, 2016; Ayon, 2018; Abrego, 2011).

Ideas for Assessing Needs:

In order to more effectively engage athletes from immigrant, ethnic, and racial minority backgrounds, coaches must fully understand and assess these players' specific needs. Below are some questions that coaches can ask themselves and players to better achieve this goal.

- Gauge psychological risks associated with racism and xenophobia for immigrant, ethnic, and racial minority players.
    - In what contexts are you reminded of your immigrant, ethnic, and racial minority background?
    - When have you felt treated differently because of your immigrant, ethnic, and racial minority background on the team, in school, or in the community (e.g. being made fun of by teammates, being called bad names by others, being singled out by teachers, being asked if you speak English or if you are a immigrant, having assumptions made about your intelligence, having assumptions made about your religion, or being followed by store workers or police)?
    - Do you ever question yourself for having these experiences and wonder if you are just reading into things?
    - Do people discount your experience as an immigrant, ethnic, or racial minority person (e.g. don't talk about these when it does matter to you)?
    - Have you ever felt bad about or less of a person because of your immigrant, ethnic, or racial background?
    - Have you ever wished that you had a different cultural background?
    - Have you tried to not affiliate yourself with others who share your immigrant, ethnic, or racial background?
    - What have your caregivers, family members, and other adults taught you about your immigrant, ethnic, or racial background?
    - Were you taught about things that happened within the history of your culture, race, or ethnicity in the U.S. and/or other countries?
    - If so, was this accurate to what you have learned in other places?
    - What have your caregivers, family members, and other adults taught you to look out for or protect yourself from due to your immigrant, ethnic, or racial background?
    - When and in what contexts have you ever felt unsafe to be an immigrant or have your ethnicity or race?
    - When and in what contexts have you ever felt your friends or family were unsafe to be an immigrant or have your ethnicity or race?
    - If you are a child of immigrant parents, to what extent do cultural differences impact your relationship with parents (e.g. parents having different goals or expectations for you than other non-immigrant parents)?

- If you are a child of immigrant parents, to what extent have you had to translate for your parents outside of the home (e.g. school, doctor's office, grocery store)?
- Does living with your immigrant status, race, or ethnicity (and all of the above experiences) cause you to feel stressed, worried, exhausted, lonely, hopeless, guilty, frustrated, or embarrassed?
- Do these emotions and experiences cause you to feel physically unwell (e.g. trouble sleeping, digestive concerns, unexplainable pain within the body, loss of appetite or overeating, heart racing, sweating, breathing fast, feeling shaky, dizzy or lightheaded, feeling like something terrible will happen, having a hard time concentrating, or having racing thoughts)?
- Do any of these feelings get in the way of your ability to hang out with friends, focus in school, complete homework, focus in practice, or compete to the best of your ability?
- Do these feelings ever cause you to be mean or hurt someone else when you don't really want to?
- Do these feelings ever cause you to be mean or hurt yourself when you don't really want to?
- Do these feelings ever cause you to want to drink or engage in other substance use or behaviors to feel better?
- Have you considered not being alive anymore or ending your own life because of challenging experiences or emotions?

If a player answers yes to a fair number of these questions it would be useful to connect them with a school counselor or social worker as soon as possible. They may be experiencing clinical levels of anxiety, depression, panic, or traumatic stress that would benefit from immediate intervention. In emergency situations, you can also call 911 or take your player to their local emergency room. You can also call or text 988, the mental health crisis line created by the Substance Abuse and Mental Health Services Administration (SAMHSA). SAMHSA is the national government agency tasked with promoting the mental health and wellness of persons residing in the U.S. They created 988 and 988lifeline.org (to chat) for emergency mental health support. Here is SAMHSA's website for more details about this national service, https://www.samhsa.gov/find-help/988/.

Ideas for Assessing Resources:

In order to more effectively engage athletes from immigrant, ethnic, and racial minority backgrounds, coaches must fully understand and assess these players' specific psychological resources. Below are some questions that coaches can ask themselves and players to better achieve this goal:

- Gauge these players' individual resources.
    - What are some strengths that this player has to mitigate psychological risk?

- Level of self-esteem and affiliation toward their cultural background
- Ability to assess personal and familial needs and safety
- Desire to provide for personal and familial needs and safety
- Short and long-term goals for their future within and beyond athletics

- Gauge these players' familial or home based resources.
  - What are some strengths this player can access from within their family and home?
    - Caregivers and other adults who are able and motivated to support a player's psychological health
    - Caregivers and other adults who teach the player about their cultural background and history
    - Caregivers and other adults who stronging identify with their cultural background and feel proud of it
    - Caregivers and other adults who encourage the player to have an affinity for their cultural background
    - Caregivers and other adults who help a player identify coping skills and strategies to protect themselves in the context of navigating life with their cultural background (e.g. working hard, prayer).
    - Caregivers and other adults who serve as models of success within their same cultural background

- Gauge these players' team based resources.
  - What are some strengths this player can access from within their team?
    - Coaches, teammates, and booster club families who are able and motivated to support a player's psychological health
    - Coaches who are culturally representative of the players on the team
    - Coaches and teammates who are sensitive to the experiences of a player from an immigrant, ethnic, or racial minority background (e.g. do not make jokes related to cultural background)
    - Coaches who discipline team members for their negative treatment or insensitivity toward others based on their immigrant status, language, ethnicity, or race.
    - Coaches and teammates who are accommodating to the experiences of a player from an immigrant, ethnic, or racial minority background (e.g. adjust practices to accommodate religious holidays or cultural gatherings/celebrations)
    - Coaches and teammates who recognize the impact of historical and systemic oppression on the experiences of a player from an immigrant, ethnic, or racial minority background (e.g. academic, occupational, economic, and health disparities)

- Coaches and teammates who recognize the impact of interpersonal oppression on the experiences of a player from an immigrant, ethnic, or racial minority background (e.g. unconscious biases impacting how people see, interact with, or avoid people from these cultural backgrounds)
- Coaches and teammates who recognize the impact of internalized oppression on the experiences of a player from an immigrant, ethnic, or racial minority background (e.g. a player starting to see themselves as less deserving, less intelligent, or less capable compared to others from majority cultural backgrounds)

- Gauge these players' school and community resources.
  - What are some strengths this player can access from within their schools and communities?
    - Peers, teachers, staff, and mentors who are able and motivated to support a students' psychological health
    - Peers, teachers, staff, and mentors who value students' cultural backgrounds and experiences and help them feel comfortable and confident in their cultural background
    - Schools that teach accurate and complete histories of immigrants and other ethnic and racial minority persons in the U.S. prior to, during, and after colonization
    - Schools that emphasize the achievements, contributions, and resiliency of immigrants and other ethnic and racial minority persons in the U.S.
    - Schools that are composed of teachers, staff, and administrators that are culturally representative of the student population
    - Peers, teachers, and staff who are sensitive to the experiences of students from an immigrant, ethnic, or racial minority background (e.g. do not make jokes related to cultural background)
    - Teachers and staff who discipline school members for their negative treatment or insensitivity toward others based on their immigrant status, language, religion, ethnicity, or race.
    - Teachers and staff who are accommodating to the experiences of students from an immigrant, ethnic, or racial minority background (e.g. adjust school days to accommodate religious holidays or cultural gatherings/celebrations)
    - Peers, teachers, and staff who recognize the impact of historical and systemic oppression on the experiences of students from an immigrant, ethnic, or racial minority background
    - Peers, teachers, and staff who recognize the impact of interpersonal oppression on the experiences students from an immigrant, ethnic, or racial minority background
    - Peers, teachers, and staff who recognize the impact of internalized oppression on the experiences of students from an immigrant, ethnic, or racial minority background

3.7a Coach Activity: Utilizing Strengths to Mitigate Risks for Immigrant, Racial, or Ethnic Minority Athletes

In this activity coaches will brainstorm ways to utilize players' strengths and resources to mitigate risks associated with their experiences as immigrants and/or racial or ethnic minority persons. Review the below cases and write your reflections on the space provided. This would be a great activity to conduct within a staff meeting at the start of a season so that coaches can better appreciate the risks and resilience of these players.

You are the new head varsity football coach at a suburban high school in a moderately competitive district. Your school has a relatively high number of players from Pacific Islander backgrounds. You feel excited about your chances to win district this year because of these players' athletic abilities, coachability, and familial support of football. You know alot about this culture because you are also Polynesian. After two games, you start to hear some mumblings of frustration from White parents on the booster club about you, "playing favorites." How can you assess these players' risks and resources to support their overall health and participation in the program?

Well, it would be hard for me because I would probably get upset about those comments. It's like a perfect example of racism to you and to those players. I would probably have to consult with my staff to cool off and come up with a plan to address the situation. If you ignore it, resentment would probably grow making it a much harder year (or couple years) for you as a new coach. I would probably remind the team and parents about the mission statement and team goals as well as how we decide playing time and positions.

You are the JV boys' basketball coach in an urban school in a highly competitive district. You and most of the players at the school are African American. During a recent game with a private parochial school in the city, one of your players got into a fight with an opposing team's player. It was hard to make-out what happened but your player had to ride the bench for the remainder of the game and the other player did not. You talk with the player later and he tells you that the White kid on the other team called him the n-word. You are sensitive to the kid but know you have to teach him to better manage his emotions. He's lucky that he only had to ride the bench, if he got in a fight on the street things would be much worse for him. How can you assess this player's risks and resources to support their overall health and participation in the program?

_____
_____
_____
_____
_____
_____

⚽ You are the head varsity girls' soccer coach in a medium sized school and rural community near the U.S./Mexico border. Your team is pretty competitive for your district and has won a handful of state championships over the past few years. You like to take the girls to tournaments in and around the state to increase their level of competition. On one preseason trip, you forgot to check with new players about their documentation. You have to do this for the kids whose families come from Mexico so that you don't run into issues at border check-points. Because you forgot, there was an issue at a check-point in which a player was almost detained. Although she seemed okay, you felt terrible and want to find ways to check-in with her about it later. How can you assess this player's risks and resources to support their overall safety and participation in the program?

_____
_____
_____
_____
_____
_____
_____
_____

🥍 You are the girls' varsity lacrosse coach at a suburban school in a moderately competitive district. You were approached by a student in your P.E. class who wants to join the team. This student is Muslim and recently immigrated from a Middle Eastern country with her family. She really enjoys P.E. and seems to be pretty athletic in class. She asked if you could talk to her parents about joining the team. They want her to focus on school and fear that she will become "like those American girls who just think about boys and make bad decisions." You want to support this young person, but are unsure as to what you can do in this situation. How can you assess this player's risks and resources to support their overall health and participation in the program?

_____
_____
_____
_____
_____
_____
_____
_____

You are the head varsity girls' volleyball coach in a suburban school within a highly competitive district. You have players on the team that bus into your school from the city to play on your team because of the legacy you built over your 10 years coaching here. Most of these players are African American from low-income homes in dangerous neighborhoods. One White player on the team recently got into an argument with one African American player on the team and called her a "ghetto bitch." This resulted in a near physical altercation between several teammates and a couple African American players saying they were going to transfer to other programs. How can you assess these players' risks and resources to support their overall safety and participation in the program?

___

You are the head varsity baseball coach at a rural school in a moderately competitive district. Since your school is in a college town, you have a large number of players that are the children of students and university professors from all over the world. At times it is difficult when these kids come out for the team, especially if there are language barriers or misunderstandings related to what being on the team entails. Also, some issues have come up between local kids and players from different countries. You think these may be due to their vastly different lived experiences. How can you assess these players' risks and resources to support their overall health and participation in the program?

3.8 Coach Activity: Helping a Team Cope with Grief and Loss

Death on the Field

All coaches dread the idea of a player losing their life to a sport related injury. Football, as one of the highest contact sports in high school, has come under fire in recent decades surrounding risk of brain injury and death. According to relatively recent research, examining 243 football related deaths (happening between 1990 and 2010 at the high school and college levels), approximately 12 deaths occurred each year (1 death out of 100,000 players). Fatalities were due to indirect causes during practice and conditioning as well as brain injury due to blunt force trauma during play (cardiac failure 41.2%, brain injury 25.5%, heat illness 15.6%, and sickle cell traits 4.5%). Deaths at the college level were more common than those seen at the high school level, but there was less of a difference between the two when considering fatalities due to brain injury (Boden et al., 2013). Due to this, the rules around physical engagement in football and other high contact sports have changed to promote player safety. For more information on CTE and traumatic brain injury please visit the National Institute of Neurological Disorders and Stroke website:
https://www.ninds.nih.gov/health-information/disorders/traumatic-brain-injury-tbi

Additionally, more awareness has been brought to the sudden death of athletes due to cardiac concerns across sports. Seeing fairly healthy looking young people lose their lives suddenly due to overexertion on the news has caused fear in many caregivers and coaches. Ghani and colleagues (2023) discuss their findings related to this phenomenon indicating that younger athletes tended to have hereditary/genetic causes to sudden cardiac death, while older athletes were more likely to have coronary artery disease. Because of this, the majority of professional cardiology organizations recommend that athletes undergo physical examinations and screenings to determine their levels of risk (Ghani et al., 2023). Being able to screen for concerns that would heighten risks of death as well as changing rules of the game toward safer play, are excellent ways to decrease the incidences of players losing their lives on the field. The most common heart condition attributed to sudden cardiac arrest is called hypertrophic cardiomyopathy (HCM). HCM causes thickening and stiffening in the walls of the heart that limits blood flow. 1 in 500 people are estimated to have HCM, but many go undiagnosed. More information on HCM in young athletes can be found at The American Heart Association's website:
https://www.heart.org/en/health-topics/cardiomyopathy/what-is-cardiomyopathy-in-adults/hcm-in-young-adults-and-student-athletes

Death Due to Gun Violence

In the U.S. the leading cause of death for children and teens between the ages of 1 and 19 years old is death by firearm (including injuries, homicides, and suicides) (CDC, 2023b). African American youth are at a much higher risk of death by homicide in comparison to other groups (CDC, 2022) largely due to many living in low resource and high violence neighborhoods. Death by firearm (due to suicide or unintentional injury) is much higher for teens that live in home with firearms compared to those without (Grossman et al., 2005; Anglemyer et al., 2014). Despite this, caregivers can decrease the risk of firearm injury or death by storing guns unloaded and locked (Grossman et al., 2005) away from ammunition.

Most parents who are gun owners believe that they take these safety precautions and, thus, don't anticipate that their children are able to access guns. This, however, does not appear to be consistent with what their teenagers say. In a recent study, nearly 40% of teens whose parents owned guns noted that they could access a gun in their home in less than 5 minutes or less than an hour (Salhi et al., 2021). Further, younger children may be at increased risk of firearm injury and death because of recent gun safe failures and recalls (Shering, 2024). For more information about gun safety and recommendations, please visit the American Academy for Pediatrics website: https://www.aap.org/. To learn more about gun laws related to young people and the flow of guns from legal to criminal usage, please visit The Bureau of Alcohol, Tobacco, Firearms, and Explosives (ATF) website: https://www.atf.gov/

Death Due to Suicide

According to the CDC (2023c) the suicide rate between 2007 to 2021 has risen by 62% in young people between the ages of 10 and 24 years old. In 2021 it sat at approximately 11 deaths per 100,000. As mentioned in a previous section of the workbook, the risk of LGBTQ+ youth taking their own lives is astronomical, with 1 out of 5 trans and nonbinary young people attempting suicide in the past year (Trevor Project, 2023). Similarly, the Covid-19 pandemic was found to have increased the overall observed number of youth suicides by over 200 people (Bridge et al., 2023).

Adolescent girls are more likely to engage in self-harm and attempt suicide (CDC, 2023d), while adolescent boys are more likely to die from it, largely due to the lethality of means they use. Along with gender and sexual minorities, indigenous youth are also at a higher risk of death by suicide compared to other racial and ethnic groups (CDC, 2023d). Research into this health disparity in indigenous populations points to contextual factors like substance use and limited access to mental health services as well as emergency services like 24-hour hotlines that can help stop these teens from attempting to harm themselves in pivotal moments (Qiao & Bell, 2017).

According to the CDC (2022), a suicide cluster happens when there are multiple suicides taking place in close time and geographic proximity (e.g. schools). Students do not necessarily need to know one another, but just hearing about a peer's suicide via social media can contribute to clustering (CDC, 2022). Studies have found that media surrounding suicide that uses graphic details and pictures as well as romanticizes or idealizes it can actually contribute to greater incidences through imitation (Gould et al., 2003; Romer et al., 2006). To decrease the incidences of suicide caregivers and communities should: address contextual factors that intersect with the problem, increase access to suicide and mental health care, promote connectedness between people and their families and communities, teach problem solving and coping skills to increase people's ability to manage distress, identify and supporting people at risk, and lessen the harm of suicide to prevent future risk (Stone et al., 2017). For more information on suicide and it's prevention visit this SAMHSA webpage: https://www.samhsa.gov/mental-health/suicidal-behavior

Losing Loved Ones

While losing a player is hard, supporting a player who has lost loved ones presents its own challenges. Several factors contribute to young people's increased risk of developing psychological challenges after the death of a parent or sibling in childhood. These include: the age of the child at the time of the loss, their gender and the gender of their parent who passed, pre-existing psychological problems, the quality of the relationship the child had with the deceased person before their death, having a surviving parent who is excessively vulnerable and dependent on the child, lack of community and/or family supports, unstable or inconsistent routine and environment, lack of prior understanding or knowledge about death, death that is unanticipated, and a death caused by homicide or suicide (Osterweis et al., 1984).

Farella Guzzo and Gobbi's (2023) review of literature surrounding adolescents' adjustment to the death of a parent found that teens who lose parents are at a higher risk of depression, anxiety, insomnia, suicidal ideations, addiction, and impaired functioning at home and in school. Similarly, Farella Guzzo and Gobbi (2023) note a number of factors that influence adjustment to and coping with the loss of a parent for adolescents, including: peers, family, school life, and the wider social environment. Losing a loved one is considered a traumatic event in people's lives and can cause mental health symptoms associated with trauma. If you would like to learn more about helping children and adolescents cope with a loss of a loved one or another traumatic event please visit the National Institute of Mental Health (NIH) website: https://www.nimh.nih.gov/health/publications/helping-children-and-adolescents-cope-with-disasters-and-other-traumatic-events

Wisdom from The Warrior Mentality

Coaches can utilize dimensions of The Warrior Mentality (Ocampo, 2024) to inform their approach to weathering grief and loss in their programs. Firstly, coaches reflect upon their underlying purpose in work with individual players as well as the team when someone passes away. As discussed above, coaches understand that they are tasked with supporting the physical and psychological needs of players and must also consider their own wellness within the context of the team. Players and coaches facing the death of loved ones (on and off the team) need special attention and care in the form of time, proximity, and emotional processing. In this, coaches give players time to adjust, are physically present for them in multiple capacities, sit in the sadness with players, and encourage engagement of professional support when more help is needed.

Coaches do these things because they acknowledge a shared destiny within the team. Grief and loss hits differently *because* of the reciprocal relationships and emotional investments coaches and players have within their teams and one another. When a player or coach passes away, part of the team is gone. When a player's friend or family member dies, their teammates can feel the loss as if it were their own. Players and coaches do not want to see each other suffering and will go to great lengths to help each other shoulder that pain.

Coaches can lighten players' emotional loads by finding ways to build upon resilience and mitigate possible challenges in the grieving process. Often this is done by coaches modeling humility and an openness to asking for help. This may look like proactively inviting mental health providers or religious clergy to consult with the team after a loss. Additionally, this might also include opening time outside of practice for players to meet with each other and coaches to discuss concerns and gain support. Just in the act of helping players commemorate loved ones in ceremonies on and off the field, coaches offer opportunities for the team to show solidarity and express care to players (and families) when they need it the most.

With all that being said, situations of grief and loss are complicated when coaches fear that ruminating on death or commemorating lost players puts other players at risk or causes detriment to moving the team forward. This is most often seen in relation to suicide. The fear of suicide clusters happening in schools and communities is very real. While some coaches view over-discussing suicide as dangerous, other coaches believe that talking about suicide (and other mental health issues) is preventative.

Although it may be scary to ask young people about suicide because we fear that this will put the idea in their heads, research supports having these difficult conversations. Encouraging kids to disclose their thoughts about suicide within families can be helpful toward decreasing risk and increasing positive outcomes as long as caregivers are able to have healthy conversations and move toward getting kids the help they need (Frey & Fulginiti, 2017). Giving words to what we fear, provides us with some semblance of control. Talking about suicide and training parents and coaches to identify warning signs and concrete steps toward seeking help is essential. If you feel unable to assess the risk of suicide in your players, you should seek out mental health providers and other resources for assistance. For more information on suicide and it's prevention in young people visit The American Academy of Child and Adolescent Psychiatry (AACAP) at: https://www.aacap.org/AACAP/Families_and_Youth/Resource_Centers/Suicide_Resource_Center/Home.aspx.

Ideas for Assessing Psychological Needs:

In order to more effectively engage athletes struggling with grief, coaches must fully understand and assess these players' specific psychological needs. Below are some questions that coaches can ask themselves and players to better achieve this goal.

- Gauge psychological risks related to grief.
    - Have you lost someone in your life before?
    - If so, what was that like for you and for your family, team, school, and community?
    - What has your family members, culture, and/or religion taught you about death and dying?
    - What do you believe about death and dying?
    - What do you know about this recent death and what do you still wonder?
    - How does the way the person died impact your feelings now?
    - What are your feelings about this recent death?
    - What are other people's feelings and responses to this death (e.g. your family, friend group, team, school, or community)?
    - In what contexts are you reminded about this recent death?
    - Do you currently feel physically and emotionally safe?
    - Have you tried to avoid feelings you have had to the death or become numb?
    - If so, what feelings have you become numb to or tried to avoid?

- Do these emotions and experiences cause you to feel physically unwell (e.g. trouble sleeping, digestive concerns, unexplainable pain within the body, loss of appetite or overeating, heart racing, sweating, breathing fast, feeling shaky, dizzy or lightheaded, feeling like something terrible will happen, having a hard time concentrating, or having racing thoughts)?
  - Do any of these feelings get in the way of your ability to hang out with friends, focus in school, complete homework, focus in practice, or compete to the best of your ability?
  - Do these feelings ever cause you to be mean or hurt someone else when you don't really want to?
  - Do these feelings ever cause you to be mean or hurt yourself when you don't really want to?
  - Do these feelings ever cause you to want to drink or engage in other substance use or behaviors to feel better?
  - Have you considered not being alive anymore or ending your own life because of this recent death?
  - What do you wish you had right now to feel better?

If a player answers yes to a fair number of these questions it would be useful to connect them with a school counselor or social worker as soon as possible. They may be experiencing clinical levels of anxiety, depression, panic, or traumatic stress that would benefit from immediate intervention. In emergency situations, you can also call 911 or take your player to their local emergency room. You can also call or text 988, the mental health crisis line created by the Substance Abuse and Mental Health Services Administration (SAMHSA). SAMHSA is the national government agency tasked with promoting the mental health and wellness of persons residing in the U.S. They created 988 and 988lifeline.org (to chat) for emergency mental health support. Here is SAMHSA's website for more details about this national service, https://www.samhsa.gov/find-help/988/.

Ideas for Assessing Psychological Resources:

In order to more effectively engage athletes experiencing grief, coaches must fully understand and assess these players' specific psychological resources. Below are some questions that coaches can ask themselves and players to better achieve this goal:

- Gauge these players' individual resources.
  - What are some strengths that this player has that could mitigate psychological risk?
    - Level of psychological resilience
    - Ability to assess their personal and familial coping with death
    - Desire to provide for personal and familial psychological wellness
    - Short and long-term goals for their future to pursue through grieving

- Gauge these players' familial or home based resources.
    - What are some strengths this player can access from within their family and home?
        - Caregivers and other adults who are able and motivated to support a player's psychological health
        - Caregivers and other adults who accept that the player is grieving and give them space and time to do so in ways that feel right to them
        - Caregivers and other adults who are able to manage their own grief
        - Caregivers and other adults who can teach and engage the player in individual and collective, cultural or religious, beliefs and practices that promote coping with grief

- Gauge these players' team based resources.
    - What are some strengths this player can access from within their team?
        - Coaches, teammates, and booster club families who are able and motivated to support a player's psychological health
        - Coaches and teammates who understand that the psychological impact of death and grieving may not show-up in the same way and in the same time for every person
        - Coaches and teammates who accept that the player is grieving and give them space and time to do so in ways that feel right to them
        - Coaches and teammates who are able to manage their own grief and reach out for support when needed
        - Coaches who can invite mental health professionals into team meetings who can normalize grief, assess when more services are needed, and provide basic coping strategies to feel better
        - Coaches who can invite spiritual/religious/cultural leaders and elders into team meetings to normalize grief and how it is viewed and navigated within their traditions
        - Coaches and teammates who are willing and able to sit in the sadness or any other challenging emotions with a player so that they do not feel alone
        - Coaches, teammates, and booster clubs who are willing and able to help commemorate the person who died and support the player by: implementing programmatic tributes or symbols, attending events and ceremonies in the community, helping to set-up or take down chairs at events, helping to fundraise or provide food and other items for events, helping as pallbearers, giving eulogies or remembrances, etc.

- Gauge these players' school and community resources.
    - What are some strengths this player can access from within their schools and communities?
        - Peers, teachers, staff, and mentors who are able and motivated to support a students' psychological health

- Peers, teachers, staff, and mentors who understand that the psychological impact of death and grieving may not show-up in the same way and in the same time for every person
- Peers, teachers, staff, and mentors who accept that the student is grieving and give them space and time to do so in ways that feel right to them
- Peers, teachers, staff, and mentors who are able to manage their own grief and reach out for support when needed
- Teachers and staff who can invite mental health professionals (from within the school and beyond) into meetings who can normalize grief, assess when more services are needed, and provide basic coping strategies to feel better
- Teachers and staff who can invite spiritual/religious/cultural leaders and elders to normalize grief and how it is viewed and navigated within their traditions
- Peers, teachers, staff, and mentors who are willing and able to sit in the sadness or any other challenging emotions with a player so that they do not feel alone
- Peers, teachers, staff, and mentors who are willing and able to help commemorate the person who died and support the student by implementing school or community-wide tributes as well as attending, helping to organize, and fundraising for events in the community

3.8a Coach Activity: Utilizing Strengths to Mitigate Risks for Grieving Players

In this activity coaches will brainstorm ways to utilize strengths and resources to mitigate risks associated with grief. Review the below cases and write your reflections on the space provided. This would be a great activity to conduct within a staff meeting at the start of a season so that coaches can better appreciate ways to support themselves and players through grief..

You've coached the girls' varsity lacrosse team for the past 5 years in a suburban city in a moderately competitive district. This week you got a call from one of your player's mothers saying that her husband passed away over the weekend. She had a hard time talking through tears, but let you know that it was sudden and unexpected. She said the player will likely be out for some time to cope. You learn from another player that the father actually killed himself while the mother and daughter were out of town. They both found him when they walked in the house. How can you assess this player's risks and resources to support their overall health and participation in the program?

Goodness, this is really tough. The player is probably traumatized by the whole thing and should take as much time as she needs to get through this. I would probably send the mother and the player some nice flowers and a card from me and see if the team and boosters want to do more. I would have to be respectful of their wishes because suicide is different from other types of death. Some people don't want to draw attention to it, but I need the player to know that me and the team will be here for her.

You are the wrestling coach at an urban school in a competitive district. This season one of your players' grandmothers has been really sick. This has been tough on the player because his grandmother is his caregiver and closest thing to any loving adult he has had apart from you. You got news yesterday that she passed away, but the player still attended practice. You let them know they could go home, but they got angry saying, "I don't have anywhere else to go!" It breaks your heart to hear this and really worry about what happens next for this player. How can you assess this player's risks and resources to support their overall health and participation in the program?

You are the head varsity swimming coach at a suburban school in which you've taught and coached for 7 years. You had a player last season who took their own life causing incredible grief within the community. You talked with the parents and have done your best to be available to the family. You also talked with players and came up with ways to commemorate their teammate. You haven't allowed yourself to grieve, though, because it brings up past experiences in your own life you've tried to overcome. If you stop to feel what you need to, you may not come back from it. How can you assess and address your own psychological needs and resilience to promote more adaptive coping and fulfill your commitments to the team?

You are the varsity football coach in a small rural school known for producing several high talent athletes. This season one of the coaches on staff lost his life due to a sudden heart attack he had in his home. This coach was well liked by players and could always be relied on to lighten up a staff meeting with his jokes. He was a close personal friend of yours and your families traveled on vacation together. He even confirmed your oldest son. You know that you need to be there for the team and the other coaches, but you are also feeling the loss in yourself and your family. How can you assess and address your own psychological needs and resilience to promote more adaptive coping for yourself and your team?

🏀 You are the head varsity boys' basketball coach at a urban school in which you've taught and coached for 2 years. You just received a call from your principal saying that one of your players was found dead this morning due to what looks like a drug overdose. You are feeling overwhelmed with the news and are unsure of what to do next. You are new to teaching and coaching and have not experienced anything like this as a coach or a player. How can you determine the right course of action in this situation to support your own mental health and the overall health and adjustment of the team?

_____
_____
_____
_____
_____
_____
_____
_____

⚾ You are the varsity softball coach in a rural school in a moderately competitive district. One former player on the team recently passed away after battling leukemia for the past several years. She was loved by you, other coaches, teammates, friends, teachers, and pretty much the whole community. Everyone knew that her health was suffering in the final months, but you had held out hope for a miracle. Her parents are planning the funeral and would like you and the team to be involved. How can you determine the right course of action in this situation to support your own mental health and the overall health and adjustment of the team?

_____
_____
_____
_____
_____
_____
_____
_____

3.9 Coach Activity: Supporting Your Own Mental Health in Coaching

Changing Times

Coaches have experienced a multitude of challenges and stressors related to the Covid-19 pandemic. Researchers have noted that the pandemic has forced today's young people to carry fears, navigate change, weather isolation, and manage stress unlike any other generation before them (Imran, et al., 2020). The pandemic has caused some children to endorse symptoms of anxiety, post-traumatic stress, and depression (Marques de Miranda et al., 2020) which has been exacerbated by increased exposure to media and children's already existent mental health issues and special needs (Panchal et al., 2023). While adjusting standards to give kids time to catch-up after the pandemic is reasonable, many coaches cite this as a frustration because they are the ones who are often alone in motivating kids and helping them persist in school.

Along with the psychological impact of the pandemic, coaches also express concerns related to navigating social media and its influence on young people. In recent years social science research has sought to better understand the impact of social media on individuals' socio-emotional adjustment and mental health. Vogel and colleagues (2014) found that social media usage was related to lower self-esteem through upward social comparisons. When people compare themselves to others on social media whom they view as better than themselves, they have a tendency to feel bad. More recent research has sought to understand the impact of social media use on athletes in particular. David and colleagues (2018) found that Division I athletes saw advantages and disadvantages of Twitter. Social media as a means to advocate for causes, obtain moral support, and build team cohesion were seen as advantages; while managing critical tweets and detrimental performance outcomes were seen as disadvantages (David et al., 2018).

Coaches also experience stresses related to social media and generational shifts in players' attitudes and values. Prioritization of personal needs over the needs of the group is something that has been discussed in recent years related to Gen Z's focus on self-direction, individual achievement, and personal security (Sakdiyakorn et al., 2021). Coaches from older generations like Baby Boomers and Gen X often attribute this shift to social media access, easy living, and over indulgent parenting, while Millennial coaches may see things differently. Millennials may be more apt to acknowledge the psychological and socio-emotional challenges that Gen Z'ers endure and see the strength they bring in drawing attention to important causes and the struggles of marginalized groups.

Finally, coaches experience challenges associated with developing positive relationships with players' caregivers. Coaches often have strong feelings about parental over-involvement and under-involvement in athletics. Parents who are absent and invest little in their children's teams leave kids and coaches disheartened, while overcontrolled parents leave kids embarrassed and coaches upset. Overcontrolled parenting prevents children from developing crucial behavioral and emotional regulation skills necessary to be successful throughout their lives (Perry et al., 2018), and absent parents prevent children from developing protective sense of worth, trust, and esteem.

Challenges of Being a Minority Coach

Coaches from ethnic and racial minority backgrounds discuss challenges related to finding a coaching job and keeping it within the context of racism. When they are able to obtain a coaching position, they often face stereotypes related to being untrustworthy or deficient. These become obstacles to gaining trust from players and their parents to perform their job effectively. High school coaches' stories in Warrior Mentality research (Ocampo, 2024) are consistent with research surrounding the lack of leadership diversity in collegiate and professional athletics (TIDES, 2022; Washington Post, 2022). TIDES (2022) found that among the 131 FBS collegiate teams, only 16.8% of them had head coaches of color.

This is a troubling number due to the fact that 65.7% of all players in FBS schools were athletes of color (49.1% of these players were African American). The Washington Post (2022) article series on racial disparities in NFL coaching found similar trends in professional football. The majority of players in the NFL are African American, nearly 60%, whereas the number of African American head or coordinator coaches is 11%. According to the Washington Post (2022) when NFL teams won at least nine games in a season, Black head coaches were fired 8% of the time compared to White coaches being fired 2% of the time. Connectedly, a good portion of the African American coaches that are fired in the NFL were hired for interim positions in clubs facing tumult, which lowered their chances of being successful from the start (Washington Post, 2022).

Coaches also express concerns surrounding advocating for their racial and ethnic minority players when experiencing racial strain on their coaching staffs. One coach interviewed in Warrior Mentality research (Ocampo, 2024) compared himself to a "house negro" trying to align himself with a White head coach to advocate for his Black players on the team. He said this caused conflict between himself and his Black players, who viewed him as "a sucker." Oppression causes within group conflict, which leads people of color to distrust each other and perpetuates cycles of familial strain and disconnection. Despite these obstacles and challenges, African Americans and other ethnic and racial minority coaches have found ways to cope with racism, support one another, and promote the best interests of their players.

In order to promote the best interests of their athletes, coaches often mentor them on and off the field which brought about positive outcomes that are also noted in past research including: benefits in socio-emotional wellbeing, academics, mental health, interpersonal relationships, prevention of risky behaviors, and positive racial identity (Sanchez et al., 2018). Connectedly, coaches also share how they act as father figures who offer guidance, support, social access, and encouragement (Richardson, 2012) as well as offering protection, correction, coping skills, and affection to their players in contexts where racism threatens self-esteem and self-concepts (Coard, 2022). Similarly, coaches give players advice related to doing well academically and planning for the future (Hicks et al., 2016), which is incredibly important when considering the propensity for African American student-athletes to experience racism (Beamon, 2014) as well as feel used and exploited for their athletic ability by universities (Beamon, 2008).

Underfunding of Schools

Coaches experience stressors associated with working in low-resource and high need schools. According to the Center on Budget and Policy Priorities (Leachman et al., 2017) since the 2007-2009 recession, school districts across the country have had to find ways to recover and re-invest in students. Districts faced obstacles related to property values plummeting and political challenges to raising taxes (both of which directly contribute to public school funding). Further, CBPP (Leachman et al., 2017) noted that school districts had cut over 350,000 teaching and other employee jobs between 2008 and 2012, a number that is slowly being remedied over the years.

Through the American Rescue Plan the federal government invested $130 billion dollars into supporting K-12 schools' reopening and recovery from the COVID-19 pandemic (U.S. Department of Education, 2022). While this is a substantial amount, schools across the country are facing a "funding cliff" as this money is set to run out in late 2024. Schools with the highest needs were given more money and, thus, face even more drastic consequences when this money is gone (Barnum, 2023). Some school superintendents noted that they will likely have to cut jobs (e.g. tutors, classroom assistants, and teachers) as well as summer programming due to expiration of these federal dollars (Marketplace, 2023).

Overtasking of Coaches

Coaches indicate being spread too thin and fear they are the last of a dying breed. One of the foremost factors contributing to the shortage of coaches today is schools' pervasive overtasking and undervaluing of coaches (Saffici, 2015; Gould et al., 2009). Coaches that are teachers typically get paid a stipend for coaching that is in addition to their salary as a teacher. Most coaches around the country are earning abysmal stipends in comparison to the years of work they put into their programs. According to a stipend schedule for an Arizona school district, the range of pay for coaches and organizers is between $537 and $7,243 for one school year of service (Phoenix Union High School District, 2021). Similarly, a school district in New Mexico increased its yearly stipend for varsity coaches to between $5,000 and $7,000 (Rio Grande Sun, 2022). Other states and school districts list very similar stipend ranges for their coaches depending on years of service and wealth of the school district.

Although coaching stipends have increased in some school districts to adjust for the amount of time and effort coaches expend, there continues to be a pattern of underpayment even for the most experienced coaches. Let's use the example of a head varsity football coach with 20 years of experience who earns $7,000 a year at the top of the stipend schedule. This hypothetical coach is spending an average of 20 hours per week (during the academic year and summer) completing all tasks related to leading a coaching staff and preparing his team for the season. That would be $6.73 per hour, which is well below the federal minimum wage (National Conference of State Legislatures, 2023). While this calculation is shocking, it is important to acknowledge that head varsity football coaches tend to be at the top of the stipend schedule. They typically earn more than assistant coaches, coaches of other sports, and other extracurricular activity organizers.

Work -Life Balance

The strain of work responsibilities in coaching and the ability to meet familial obligations has been researched within female coaches (Dixon & Bruening, 2007) and male coaches (Graham & Dixon, 2014). Ryan and Sagas (2011) explored the experiences of coaches in small colleges and their ability to strike a work-family balance. They found that spousal support, supervisory support, and feelings of autonomy were related to lower conflict and an increased sense of enrichment. Further, past research has indicated that a healthy work-family balance can increase organizational and career commitment as well as job and life satisfaction (Schenewark & Dixon, 2012). Coaches discuss how crucial it is to work in a program that allows them the time and flexibility to be with their family. Similarly, coaches share that having patient and loving partners and children also make coaching less stressful and more enjoyable. Many coaches describe their wives as the "quarterbacks" at home that made sure everything runs smoothly (Ocampo, 2024).

Dual Relationships

Not only do coaches navigate a work-life balance, so too, do they navigate dual roles as coaches to their team and fathers to their biological children who may play for them. In developing The Warrior Mentality framework (Ocampo, 2024), coaches discussed guilt and fear related to coaching their children. Many coaches in this position transfer the high standards they have for themselves to their own children. They tend to be harder on their own kids than they are on other players because they expect more.

This may be due to parents' tendencies to view their children as reflections of themselves. These high expectations may cause resentment and conflict in the coach-parent/ player-child relationship. To prevent this strain, it is crucial to have coaches on staff and a partner at home who can let coaches know when they are being too hard on their children in either context. Once a conflict has already occurred, parent-coaches should acknowledge that their actions or words were wrong, apologize for causing hurt, and commit to implementing changes to prevent conflict from happening again.

Pressure to Win

Even when coaches champion the personal development of their athletes, winning is often associated with their credibility and job security (Banwell & Kerr, 2016). This fixation on winning causes psychological risks for coaches as well as their players. Coaches who get caught-up in an obsessive pursuit of the 'W' can leave their players behind. Research surrounding the downfalls of obsessive passion has found that it causes detriment to athlete autonomy and decreases players' satisfaction in the athlete-coach relationship (Lafreniere et al., 2011). Even worse, research has outlined a number of other harms players have experienced due to coaches' behavior, including: neglect, discrimination, hazing, psychological abuse, physical injury, and sexual assault (Kerr et al., 2019).

Coaches must find ways to escape or manage the pressure to win so that they do not cause harm to themselves or their players. This often involves expanding the ways they see winning and re-focusing on players' character development. Coaches also come to a place of acceptance and appreciating competition and all its outcomes. Coaches must learn to accept that winning and losing are part of the game and energy expended in loss prevention is wasted. According to veteran coaches, energies are better invested in caring for players and making sure they win at life.

Blaming Yourself When Players Walk Away

Coaches who invest so much physical and psychological energy into their players have a hard time not blaming themselves when players walk away from programs. Research tells us that kids quit sports for a number of reasons, including: not having fun, not feeling athletically competent, feeling negative about coaches or teammates, parental pressures, losing time with friends, injuries, and not having enough money or resources to play (Witt & Dangi, 2018). While many of these reasons are related to coaches' efforts or approaches to a team, there are other things that pull players away. For many caring coaches, players walking away triggers unconscious processes that activate fear, guilt, frustration, and sadness. Coaches see themselves and loved ones in their players, and internalize losing players as a personal loss.

Coaches need to find ways to focus on what is in their control. Veteran coaches find ways to de-personalize players walking away and think about what they have achieved. They understand that spending too much time on regret or worry makes them less available to other players, themselves, and their families. Coaches plant seeds and find hope in players who come back to their programs years after they leave the team. They feel immense joy and pride in hearing that they made a positive impact on players, especially those that struggled the most.

Ideas for Assessing Psychological Needs:

In order to more effectively address stress related to coaching, coaches must fully understand and assess their specific psychological needs. Below are some questions that coaches can ask themselves to better achieve this goal.

- Gauge psychological risks related to Covid-19.
  - In what ways has the Covid-19 pandemic impacted you and your family, team, school, and community?
  - In what ways does the Covid-19 pandemic still impact you and your family, team, school, and community?

- Gauge psychological risks related to social media.
  - How competent are you in social media?
  - In what ways can you understand and use social media to support the mission and goals of the team?
  - In what ways can you teach responsible social media usage to players?
  - In what ways can you communicate expectations and boundaries of social media to players and their caregivers?

- Gauge psychological risks related to generational differences.
  - What generational values and worldviews do you ascribe to?
  - What generational values and worldviews do your coaches ascribe to?
  - What generational values and worldviews do your players ascribe to?

- What generational values and worldviews do your players' caregivers ascribe to?
- In what ways do these generational worldviews collide?

- Gauge psychological risks related to working with caregivers.
    - What have been your own experiences with caregivers growing-up?
    - How do these personal experiences shape the way you work with players' caregivers?
    - What makes you frustrated, worried, and disheartened in your work with caregivers?
    - Why do these things cause you to feel this way?
    - How many players on the team have absent or uninvolved caregivers?
        - In what ways do these caregivers impede your ability to coach?
    - How many players on the team have past or current relational strain with caregivers?
        - In what ways does this strain impede your ability to coach?
    - How many players on the team have controlling or overbearing caregivers?
        - In what ways do these caregivers impede your ability to coach?

- Gauge psychological risks related to being a minority coach.
    - What cultural identities do you hold that impact your ability to obtain a coaching job and be successful in it (e.g. race, gender, sexual orientation, etc.)?
    - In what ways does oppression of your individual or cultural identities limit your ability to coach (e.g. racism, sexism, homophobia, etc.)?
    - What at the systemic level limits your ability to coach (e.g. lack of mentors available to guide you)?
    - What at the interpersonal level limits your ability to coach (e.g. parents distrusting of your ability to lead and question you)?
    - What at the intrapersonal level limits your ability to coach (e.g. unconsciously adopting the belief that you will never be able to be hired in a head coaching position)?

- Gauge psychological risks related to underfunding in schools.
    - Do you work in a school that is low-resource and high need?
    - If so, how does this impact your ability to coach (e.g. high stress, limited ability to provide players with assistant coaches, equipment, and opportunities that will make them better)?

- Gauge psychological risks related to overtasking in schools.
    - Are you often called upon to do things that are outside of your job description (e.g. work games of other sports, open the school early, close the school late)?
    - Do you complete unpaid tasks for your school because no one else will do it?
    - Do you make yourself available to players outside of school and sport?
    - In your relationships with players, do you often engage in conversations or exchanges that feel emotionally tasking?
    - Do you often worry about your players and their well-being?
    - How much time do you spend thinking about coaching and your sport?

- o How much of your own money do you invest in the development of the program?
- o Do you feel that your coaching stipend alone is commensurate with the amount of time and energy you expend in coaching and/or completing tasks asked of you by the school, other coaches, players, and players' caregivers?

- Gauge psychological risks related to work-life balance.
    - o If you have a partner and children, what do they think about your coaching?
    - o To what extent are they willing and able to complete tasks and responsibilities in the home when you are unable to do so because of coaching?
    - o To what extent are they interested and supportive of your career as a coach?
    - o To what extent do they engage in tasks that help the program (e.g. cooking dinners for the team)?
    - o To what extent do they engage in relationships with other coaches, their families, players, and players' families?

- Gauge psychological risks related to dual relationships.
    - o Do you currently coach your child or children?
    - o What are your feelings toward this?
    - o What are their feelings toward this?
    - o How has being a parent impacted the ways you coach your child?
    - o Are the expectations you hold for your child consistent with the expectations you hold for other players?
    - o Do you find yourself becoming more irritated or embarrassed when your child makes a mistake?
    - o Do you find yourself yelling or correcting your child more often or more stringently than other players?
    - o Do you find yourself being less hard on your child as their coach?
    - o Do you give your child more leeway or opportunities than you might give other players?
    - o What is your emotional reaction when another coach corrects your child or gives them feedback?
    - o Do you talk to your child about how you will handle setting a boundary between athletics and family time?
    - o Do you have a plan that will help you maintain these boundaries (e.g. limit the time you talk about sport in the home)?
    - o Are you able to assess when you have overstepped a boundary or do you have people who can point this out to you when it happens (e.g. other coaches, partner, the child themself)?
    - o To what extent are you able to apologize for overstepping?
    - o To what extent are you able to commit to not overstepping again?

- Gauge psychological risks related to the pressure to win.
    - o To what extent are you worried about losing your job if you have a losing season?
    - o To what extent do you feel the program, school, and community support you as a coach and your trajectory in the position?

- To what extent do you feel the program, school, and community value your mission and goals apart from winning games?
- To what extent does the pressure to win impact your coaching identity?
- To what extent does the pressure to win impact your thoughts and feelings about yourself?
- To what extent does the pressure to win impact your feelings toward your staff as well as the ways you treat them?
- To what extent does the pressure to win impact your feelings toward your players as well as the ways you treat them?

• Gauge psychological risks related to athletes or coaches walking away.
- To what extent do you view a coach's resignation or leaving as a personal failure?
- What within yourself and your history contributes to you feeling this way?
- To what extent are you able to see other factors contributing to this coach leaving?
- To what extent do you view players leaving a program as a personal failure?
- What within yourself and your history contributes to you feeling this way?
- To what extent are you able to see other factors contributing to this player leaving?

• Gauge overall levels of psychological risk.
- Do any of the emotions and experiences listed above cause you to feel physically unwell (e.g. trouble sleeping, digestive concerns, unexplainable pain within the body, loss of appetite or overeating, heart racing, sweating, breathing fast, feeling shaky, dizzy or lightheaded, feeling like something terrible will happen, having a hard time concentrating, or having racing thoughts)?
- Do any of these feelings get in the way of your ability to maintain relationships with friends and family, focus on your job outside of coaching, focus on coaching, or complete other tasks?
- Do these feelings ever cause you to be mean or hurt someone else when you don't really want to?
- Do these feelings ever cause you to be mean or hurt yourself when you don't really want to?
- Do these feelings ever cause you to want to drink or engage in other substance use or behaviors to feel better?
- Have you considered not being alive anymore or ending your own life because of these feelings?

If you answer yes to a fair number of these questions it would be useful to connect with a counselor or mental health provider as soon as possible. You may be experiencing clinical levels of anxiety, depression, panic, or traumatic stress that would benefit from immediate intervention. In emergency situations, you can also call 911 or go to a local emergency room. You can also call or text 988, the mental health crisis line created by the Substance Abuse and Mental Health Services Administration (SAMHSA). SAMHSA is the national government agency tasked with promoting the mental health and wellness of persons residing in the U.S. They created 988 and 988lifeline.org (to chat) for emergency mental health support. Here is SAMHSA's website for more details about this national service, https://www.samhsa.gov/find-help/988/.

Ideas for Assessing Psychological Resources:

In order to promote their own psychological wellness, coaches must fully understand and assess specific resources. Below are some questions that coaches can ask themselves to better achieve this goal:

- Gauge individual resources.
    - What are some strengths that you have that could mitigate psychological risk?
        - Level of psychological resilience
        - Ability to assess your personal ability to cope
        - Desire to provide for your own psychological wellness
        - Short and long-term goals for your future to pursue through stress

- Gauge familial or home based resources.
    - What are some strengths you can access from within your family and home?
        - Partners and children who able and willing to support your coaching career
        - Partners and children who are able and willing to take responsibility for tasks at home that you may not be able to do because of coaching
        - Partners and children who are interested in building relationships within the team and contribute to the betterment of the team
        - Partners who are able to encourage you when you become emotionally overburdened with contextual and relational issues that impact coaching (e.g. the pandemic, generational differences, stress in working with players' caregivers, racism and other types of oppression, underfunding of schools, and overtasking of coaches)
        - Partners who can help you maintain healthy boundaries between coaching and family
        - Partners and children who are able to give you feedback about your management of dual relationships and ensure you are promoting your child's growth and development as a parent and coach
        - Partners and children who are able to ground you when you get caught up in the pressure to win
        - Partners and children who can remind you of your worth apart from winning
        - Partners who can encourage you to depersonalize coaches or players leaving the program
        - Partners who are able to assess and provide you feedback regarding your overall emotional state and help you connect with outside resources and support as needed

- Gauge team based resources.
  - What are some strengths you can access from within the team and program?
    - Coaches on staff who able and willing to support your coaching career
    - Coaches on staff who are able and willing to take responsibility for tasks in the program that you may not be able to do
    - Coaches on staff and players who are invested in the mission statement and goals of the team
    - Coaches on staff and players who are able to encourage you when you become emotionally overburdened with contextual and relational issues that impact coaching (e.g. the pandemic, generational differences, stress in working with players' caregivers, racism and other types of oppression, underfunding of schools, and overtasking of coaches)
    - Coaches on staff who can help you maintain healthy boundaries between coaching and family
    - Coaches on staff who are able to give you feedback about your management of dual relationships and ensure you are meeting your commitments to the team and promoting your child's growth and development
    - Coaches on staff and players who are able to ground you when you get caught up in the pressure to win
    - Coaches on staff and players who can remind you of your worth apart from winning
    - Coaches on staff who can encourage you to depersonalize when other coaches or players leave the program
    - Coaches on staff and players who are able to assess and provide you feedback regarding your overall emotional state and help you connect with outside resources and support as needed

- Gauge school and community resources.
  - What are some strengths you can access from within your school and community?
    - School administrators, teachers, staff, coaching mentors, and community members who able and willing to support your coaching career
    - School administrators, teachers, staff, coaching mentors, and community members who are able and willing to take responsibility for tasks in the program that you may not be able to do
    - School administrators, teachers, staff, coaching mentors, and community members who are invested in the mission statement and goals of the team
    - School administrators, teachers, staff, coaching mentors, and community members who advocate for, institute, and maintain policies that help you better navigate contextual and relational issues that impact coaching (e.g. the pandemic, generational differences, stress in working with players' caregivers, racism and other types of oppression, underfunding of schools, and overtasking of coaches)
    - Coaching mentors who are able to encourage you and give you strategies to prevent and/or manage burn-out

- School administrators who can advocate for, institute, and maintain policies that help you maintain healthy boundaries between coaching and family
- Coaching mentors who are able to give you feedback about your management of dual relationships and ensure you are meeting your commitments to the team and promoting your child's growth and development
- Coaching mentors who are able to ground you when you get caught up in the pressure to win
- School administrators, teachers, staff, coaching mentors, and community members who can remind you of your worth apart from winning
- Coaching mentors who can encourage you to depersonalize when coaches or players leave the program
- School administrators and coaching mentors who are able to assess and provide you feedback regarding your overall emotional state and help you connect with outside resources and support as needed

3.9a Coach Activity: Utilizing Strengths to Mitigate Risks for Coaches

In this activity coaches will brainstorm ways to utilize their own strengths and resources to mitigate risks associated with coaching. Review the below cases and write your reflections on the space provided. This would be a great activity to conduct within a staff meeting at the start of a season so that coaches can better appreciate each others' risks and resilience.

You've coached the girls' and boys' wrestling team in a small rural school for the past 4 years. You grew-up in this town and came back to it after college because you want to be closer to family and really care about building up the community. This past year, you and your wife suffered two miscarriages and the emotional pain related has caused her to be out of work for a while. Your teaching and coaching salary has barely been enough to keep you afloat and you are unsure how long you can make it. You want to take on more responsibilities at the school to make some extra cash, but that means less time at home with your wife who is already in bad shape. How can you assess your risks and resources in this situation to support you and your family's overall health and the betterment of the program?

This is so common, and it really sucks. He's got to find a way to balance time supporting his wife emotionally while also supporting the family. He is probably very emotionally drained, himself, and that has detriment for his ability to lead the team. The good news is he seems to really care about his community and gives back. He also said he has family there. I wonder if he could tap into those resources to help him out. Maybe the family could spend more time with his wife to help her cope or maybe there's some community programs that could help her get into counseling. School administrators should also see this coach's commitment and find ways to reward that with higher pay and a more flexible schedule.

You are the varsity baseball coach at a rural school in a relatively competitive district. You have some great players coming in that you think could help you win district and go far in state. You've coached for the program for the past 10 years and have built pretty good relationships with the community. This year the school got a new principal who is pretty unsupportive of athletics. She really cut your already small budget and now you aren't able to get the guys new gear. The families in town can't afford to do it, so the kids will do without. You find yourself getting really angry with this new principal and hope she doesn't hurt your chances at doing well this season. How can you assess your risks and resources in this situation to support your emotional health and the betterment of the program?

___
___
___
___
___

You are the head varsity football coach at a rural school in a competitive district. You've coached for the program for the past 12 years and currently have one son who plays quarterback for the team. He is a junior and has the talent to pursue playing at the next level. You played in Junior College before an injury prevented you from going further. Your wife says that you need to be careful about pressuring him too much and assistant coaches have said you need to go a bit easier on him in practices and games. How can you assess your ability to manage dual roles in this situation and what can you do differently to promote the health and wellness of your child?

___

You are currently the head varsity girls' volleyball coach at a rural school in which you've taught and coached different sports for the past 30 years. Your kids have graduated and left the nest and it is just you and your husband at home. The pandemic hit your husband pretty hard because of some physical issues he's had and left him out of work for the past couple years. Being the sole breadwinner in the family is somewhat okay because the kids are now able to support themselves. But you feel like it takes a toll on you and your relationship with your husband. He's kind of old school about that stuff and you can tell his self-esteem suffers not being able to contribute like he used to. How can you assess your risks and resources in this situation to support you and your family's overall health and the betterment of the program?

You are currently the head boys' and girls' track and field coach at a rural school in a low resource, high need community. Many of the athletes on the team live in poverty and use public assistance, while some are even considered homeless by the district. Over your 15 years coaching here you have bought food, clothing, shoes, hygiene essentials, and other items for kids at school and on the team. You have even driven kids to school and doctor's appointments, provided childcare for younger siblings of athletes, and helped many parents get connected with jobs and other resources. You are getting closer to retirement and want to be able to spend more time with your grandchildren, but you worry about who will take care of your kids at school if you are not there to do it. How can you assess your risks and resources in this situation to support your overall health and the needs of young people at your school?

___

You are the athletic director and have served as the varsity football, basketball, baseball, and track coach across your 40 years working at a small, rural school. You miss teaching and coaching and would help out if the school needed it, but you had to take the administrator position a few years back because it was better for your family. You really understand the struggles that your coaches face and wish you could do more for them. Being an administrator, however, shows you the other side of things and how much money is really available for sports. You worry about seeing fewer and fewer coaches coming down the pipeline who are willing to dedicate their lives to a position that asks so much and provides so little. How can you assess your risks and resources in this situation to support your coaches and the future of high school athletics?

Appendices

Appendices: Player Leadership Council Lesson Plans

A. Forming Leadership Platoons……………………………………………………………………..157
B. Instagram, SnapChat, Tiktok, Twitter, etc……………………………………………..………….160
C. Approaches to Leadership……………………………………………………………………..….163
D. Troubleshooting Leadership Issues with Teammates…………………………………………......167
E. Goal Setting ………………………………………………………………………………………172
F. Mental Health Issues and Getting Support……………………………………………………….176
G. Communication Filters……………………………………………………………………………180
H. Being H.U.M.B.L.E……………………………………………………………………………....187
I. Communication B.A.S.I.C.S…………………………………………………………………......192
J. Diversity and Inclusion in Teams………………………………………………………………...195
K. Sport Psychology and Mental Performance……………………………………………………...197
L. Navigating Injury………………………………………………………………..………………202
M. Looking toward the Future……………………………………………………………...………..205

Forming Leadership Platoons

Background:

Most people are not born leaders. Although some may have in-born personality characteristics or communication styles that can help them to lead, even they must find ways to utilize these talents most effectively as leaders. The best way to practice honing leadership skills is by taking on roles that require them within a team. Below is an overview of one such opportunity that can be implemented to build leadership skills within a team.

Objectives:

1. Identify elements of Leadership Platoons in sport programs
2. Describe ways platoons provide opportunities to practice leadership skills and increase team cohesion
3. Plan and create Leadership Platoons on the team

Materials:

- List of team members
- Spiral notebooks
- Writing utensils
- White board or chalkboard

Leadership Council Check-ins (optional):

- Address any team issues that have come-up since last meeting
- Discuss any mentee issues that have come-up since last meeting

Activities:

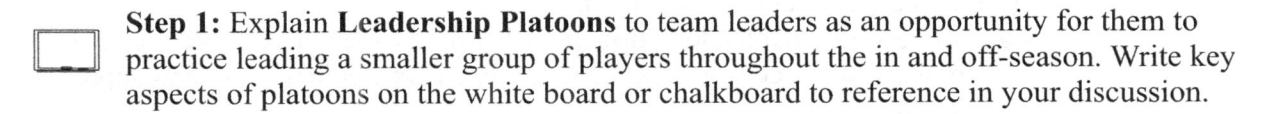

Step 1: Explain **Leadership Platoons** to team leaders as an opportunity for them to practice leading a smaller group of players throughout the in and off-season. Write key aspects of platoons on the white board or chalkboard to reference in your discussion.

- **Leadership Platoons** are 'teams' within the team. Depending on the size of the team, each platoon could contain 5 to 10 players. Platoons should be co-lead by two leaders so that they can support one another and their teammates throughout the year.

Step 2: Explain how **Leadership Platoons** earn points across the year by completing different activities. The platoon with the most points should be **rewarded** with a dinner out with coaches, gift-cards, recognition at games or matches, a symbol for their uniforms, recognition at the end of year banquet, etc.

- Point earning **activities** could include:

    - Attendance to meetings and practices
      (1 point for each teammate attending)
    - Promptness to meetings and practices
      (1 point for each teammate being on-time)
    - Conditioning or weight training gains
      (1 point for each teammate meeting goals)
    - Winning practice competitions
      (1 point for each teammate win/success)
    - Earning a certain GPA each semester
      (1 point for each teammate earning a B average or better per quarter)
    - Taking part in community service projects
      (1 point for each teammate that participates in a community clean-up or other service activity)
    - Supporting other sports or activities on campus
      (1 point for each teammate that attends another sport's games or program's extracurricular events)

Step 3: Have leaders engage in a draft to determine the teammates they would like to have on their platoons. Ask them to reflect upon the following considerations as they decide who they would want to lead on their platoons. *Leaders must understand that their ability to foster cohesion and motivate their teammates is much more important than their platoon composition.*

- As leaders, choose players that you feel you can most effectively guide (e.g. consider personality and communication styles).
    - Understand that leaders must be flexible in their approach and engagement of whoever joins your platoon.
- As leaders, choose players who get along with you and mesh well with each other (e.g. shared experiences and shared interests).
    - Understand that leaders influence platoon cohesion over time. Leaders build positive cohesion in the ways they communicate with and approach teammates.
    - Although friendship may help team cohesion initially, it could also get in the way of providing useful feedback toward achieving platoon goals.

Step 4: Once platoons are created, leaders can develop a plan for how they will structure their platoons and move toward success this season. Leaders could consider the following questions and use notebooks to record their answers:

- What will be the name of your platoon?
- What will be the mission statement or code of the platoon?
- What roles and responsibilities will each leader of the platoon have across the year?
- What roles and responsibilities will each platoon member have across the year?
- How will you communicate with the platoon across the year?
- What initial and on-going meetings will you hold with your platoon?
- What will be the goals of these meetings?
- What initiatives and strategies will your platoon engage this year to earn points?
- What might get in the way of earning points and/or platoon cohesion?
- How will issues or concerns be voiced within the platoon?
- How will issues or concerns be resolved within the platoon?

Instagram, SnapChat, Tiktok, Twitter, etc...

Background:

Social Media has become an integral part of life for many people around the world. On a team, social media can be used to connect people and celebrate competitive victories, day-to-day development, off-season conditioning, academic awards, and great things team members are doing on campus and in the community. Despite its many positives, social media can also carry possible draw-backs or dangers. When used incorrectly, social media can cause serious long-standing, negative outcomes for young people. As a leader on the team, it is important to understand how to use social media effectively to promote individual and programmatic success.

Objectives:

1. Identify pros and cons of social media usage on teams
2. Compile a list of norms/rules related to social media usage on the team
3. Discuss social media etiquette and posting content that promotes individual and programmatic success

Materials:

- Laptops or devices to engage with social media (optional)
- Spiral notebooks
- Writing utensils
- White board or chalkboard

Leadership Council Check-ins (optional):

- Address any team issues that have come-up since last meeting
- Discuss any mentee issues that have come-up since last meeting
- Troubleshoot Platoon issues that have come-up since last meeting

Activities:

Step 1: Discuss ways the team can use social media to celebrate progress: in the sport, in the classroom, and in the community. Develop a list of norms/rules for the team related to social media use in this area that can be implemented within the team.

- What are some ways we can use social media to celebrate team progress in the sport?
- What are some ways we can use social media to celebrate team progress in the classroom?
- What are some ways we can use social media to celebrate team progress in the community?

- What are some things we want to avoid when using social media to celebrate progress?
    - Examples: only celebrating wins in the sport, only celebrating certain players, negative comments on posts…
- How can we implement these norms/rules within the team and with those that follow our social media pages?

Step 2: Discuss ways the team can use social media to advertise for upcoming games and fundraise. Develop a list of norms/rules for the team related to social media use in these areas that can be implemented within the team.

- What are some ways we can use social media to advertise the program?
- What are some ways we can use social media to fundraise?
- What are some things we want to avoid when using social media for advertising and fundraising?
    - Examples: spending too much time on advertising and fundraising and not enough time on celebrating players, losing people's interest with too much fundraising, negative comments on posts…
- How can we implement these norms/rules within the team and with those that follow our social media pages?

Step 3: Discuss ways the team can use social media to support individual player recruitment. Develop a list of norms/rules for the team related to social media use in this area that can be implemented within the team.

- How can we use social media to promote individual player recruitment?
    - Highlight or training videos
    - Links to players' individual pages
- What are some things we want to avoid when using team social media for recruitment?
    - Examples: spending too much time on recruitment and managing negative comments on posts…
- How can we implement the above norms/rules within the team and with those that follow our social media pages?

Other considerations for individual player's social media pages for recruitment:

- Follow college coaches at programs you would like to attend
- Direct message coaches about your interest in being evaluated for their team
- Showcase athletic abilities by posting mini highlights and training videos
- Post highlights in other sports to show athletic ability and versatility
- Consult with current coaches about your interest in collegiate athletics so that they can offer more support in the recruitment process

- Review the NCAA and NJCAA guides and handbooks for recruiting: http://fs.ncaa.org/Docs/eligibility_center/Student_Resources/CBSA.pdf, https://www.njcaa.org/governance/handbook/index

Step 4: Discuss basic social media etiquette with players and ensure they understand that what they post now can impact them for many years to come.

- Are you making a good impression with this post?
- Will coaches, parents, teachers, and teammates think highly of you with this post?
- If you are posting personal accolades, are you thanking your teammates or others in your life that contributed to these successes?
- How many personal accolades are you posting in comparison to team successes?
- Is your post respectful of opponents?
    - Those who talk badly about opponents, shine a negative light on themselves and the team.
- Is your post braggadocious?
    - A coach once said upon being hired, *"They are gonna have to put another number on the scoreboard for how much we are going to score."* The media brought it up everytime his team lost.
- Is your post spelled correctly, using proper grammar?
    - This can be very embarrassing and detract from your message if it is not.
- Does your post contain any of the following? *If so, you should refrain from posting it.*
    - Referencing others outside the team that are not relevant to recruiting or programmatic initiatives
    - Sharing links, pictures, or video of nudity or sexually suggestive content
    - Sharing links, pictures, or video about alcohol, vaping, or drug use
    - Sharing links, pictures, or video about weapons
    - Sharing links, pictures, or video about risky behaviors (e.g. driving fast or other dangerous activities)
    - Sharing links, pictures, or video about politics, religion, or other controversial topics

Approaches to Leadership

Background:

Being a successful leader means being able to influence people in the right direction. The best way to influence your teammates is to show that you are invested in the goals of the program. You do this by caring about each other and doing what it takes to get the job done. Leaders "talk the talk *and* walk the walk." Leaders hold themself accountable and hold their teammates accountable even when it may be difficult or uncomfortable. Leaders care for themselves just as much as they care for their teammates.

Objectives:

1. Identify characteristics and actions of a good leader
2. Understand the difference between transactional and transformational leadership
3. Describe ways to be a transformational leader on the team

Materials:

- Spiral notebooks
- Writing utensils
- White board or chalkboard
- Copies of *Leadership Types* worksheet

Leadership Council Check-ins (optional):

- Address any team issues that have come-up since last meeting
- Discuss any mentee issues that have come-up since last meeting
- Troubleshoot Platoon issues that have come-up since last meeting

Activities:

Step 1: Write the following questions on the board and discuss players' responses as a group, pointing out similarities and differences.

- Why is this team important to you?
- Why do you want to be a leader on the team?

Step 2: Ask the players to look back on the time when they were new to the program. Have them write down the initials of an older player that they felt was an <u>ineffective leader</u>. Ask them to answer questions related to why this player was <u>ineffective</u>.

- What did they do that was ineffective?
- What did they say that was ineffective?

- How did they make you feel as a player?
- How did their actions impact your investment in the team?

Step 3: Now have them write down the initials of an older player that they felt was an <u>effective</u> <u>leader</u>. Ask them to answer questions related to why they thought this player was <u>effective</u>. Discuss their responses as a group, pointing out similarities and differences in their answers.

- What did they do that was effective?
- What did they say that was effective?
- How did they make you feel as a player?
- How did their actions impact your investment in the team?

Step 4: In pairs, have players think of examples of transformational leaders from movies or media. Ask them to answer the below questions and share their answers with the large group.

- Who was the leader?
- At what time and context did the leader live?
- How did the leader communicate with their group?
- How did the leader behave within their group?
- How did the leader build trust within the group?
- How did the leader inspire the group?

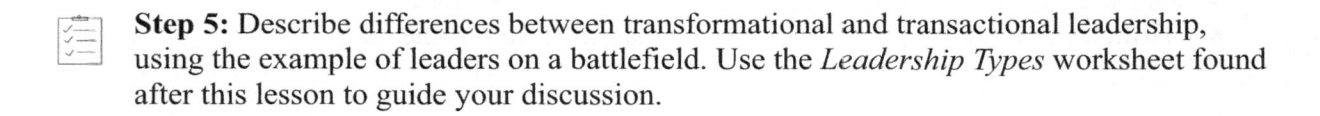

Step 5: Describe differences between transformational and transactional leadership, using the example of leaders on a battlefield. Use the *Leadership Types* worksheet found after this lesson to guide your discussion.

Step 6: Ask players to consider the following questions over the course of the next week. They can write down some ideas to share with the group at the next Leadership Council meeting.

- What can I do to build more trust with the other members of the team?
- How can I show more passion so that others want to follow me?
- What things can I do to leave a positive legacy amongst my younger teammates?

Leadership Types

Transactional Leaders   **Transformational Leaders**

Underline <u>Transactional</u> or <u>Transformational</u> for each statement…

- Encourages soldiers to keep fighting by never giving-up themselves
  Transactional or *Transformational*

- Sees themself as more important than the troop
  Transactional or *Transformational*

- Honors the sacrifices made by soldiers
  Transactional or *Transformational*

- Fails to consult with soldiers about battle plans and avoids their feedback
  Transactional or *Transformational*

- Celebrates joys and acknowledges grief with their soldiers
  Transactional or *Transformational*

- Shares responsibility for winning or losing a battle
  Transactional or *Transformational*

- Sees themselves and their soldiers as equally important
  Transactional or *Transformational*

- Asks soldiers about battle plans and implement their feedback
  Transactional or *Transformational*

 Transactional Leaders	 Transformational Leaders

Underline <u>Transactional</u> or <u>Transformational</u> for each statement…

- Protects their own safety at the cost of others
  Transactional or *Transformational*

- Is uncaring if their soldiers get hurt on the field
  Transactional or *Transformational*

- Encourages soldiers to keep fighting by threats of punishment
  Transactional or *Transformational*

- Takes credit when the battle is won
  Transactional or *Transformational*

- Makes sacrifices to protect others on the field
  Transactional or *Transformational*

- Protects their own safety and the safety of others
  Transactional or *Transformational*

- Blames and punishes soldiers when the battle is lost
  Transactional or *Transformational*

- Ignores the sacrifices made by soldiers
  Transactional or *Transformational*

Troubleshooting Leadership Issues with Teammates

Background:

One of the most important jobs of a leader is to ensure there is unity within the team. Leaders are "bridge builders" not "wall builders." What they do sets the tone for how the rest of the team functions and interacts with each other. This becomes even more important when conflict arises within teams and athletes look to team leaders for guidance. Sometimes conflict happens between leaders which causes detriment to these players and the whole team. It is crucial for leaders to be able to navigate conflict effectively so that they can model this to their teammates.

Objectives:

1. Identify individual and collective worries and concerns on the team
2. Describe individual and collective hopes and contributions on the team
3. Discuss ways to address team concerns using team strengths

Materials:

- Post-it notes
- Spiral notebooks
- Writing utensils
- White board or chalkboard
- Copies of *Identifying Risks and Resources* worksheets (Strengths and Challenges)
- Copies of *Understanding Strengths to Help Challenges* worksheet

Leadership Council Check-ins (optional):

- Address any team issues that have come-up since last meeting
- Discuss any mentee issues that have come-up since last meeting
- Troubleshoot Platoon issues that have come-up since last meeting

Activities:

Step 1: Gauge athletes' sense of the team dynamics. Give them 4 Post-it notes each and a writing utensil. Let them know this is an anonymous exercise so they can be as truthful as possible.

- On the 1st Post-it note, they write one thing they <u>worry about as a teammate</u>.
- On the 2nd Post-it note, they write one thing they <u>hope for as a teammate</u>.
- On the 3rd Post-it note, they write one thing they are <u>missing from the team</u>.
- On the 4th Post-it note, they write one thing they can <u>contribute to the team</u>.

Step 2: Collect the post-it notes and read them by category. Have someone record the major concerns and strengths that come-up in the discussion on the white board or chalkboard.

Step 3: Coaches should use the list of concerns and strengths to guide discussion across the following questions.

- What are the top 3 concerns? Why do we think these came-up?
- What are the top 3 strengths? Why do we think these came-up?
- How can we use the strengths to address each concern?

Step 4: Coaches should provide athletes with *Identifying Risks and Resources* worksheets and *Understanding Strengths to Help Challenges* worksheet to help guide discussion. Coaches could also have players complete these as homework before the next Leadership Council meeting.

Identifying Risks and Resources

In this activity, you will brainstorm specific strengths and resources you have across the individual, family, team, university, and community levels. Examples for **Individual** could be things like "strong" and "motivated." Examples for **Family** could be things like "caring" and "supportive." Examples for **Team** could be things like "patient" and "pushes me." Examples for **School & Community** could be things like "safe" and "cares about athletics."

Identifying Strengths

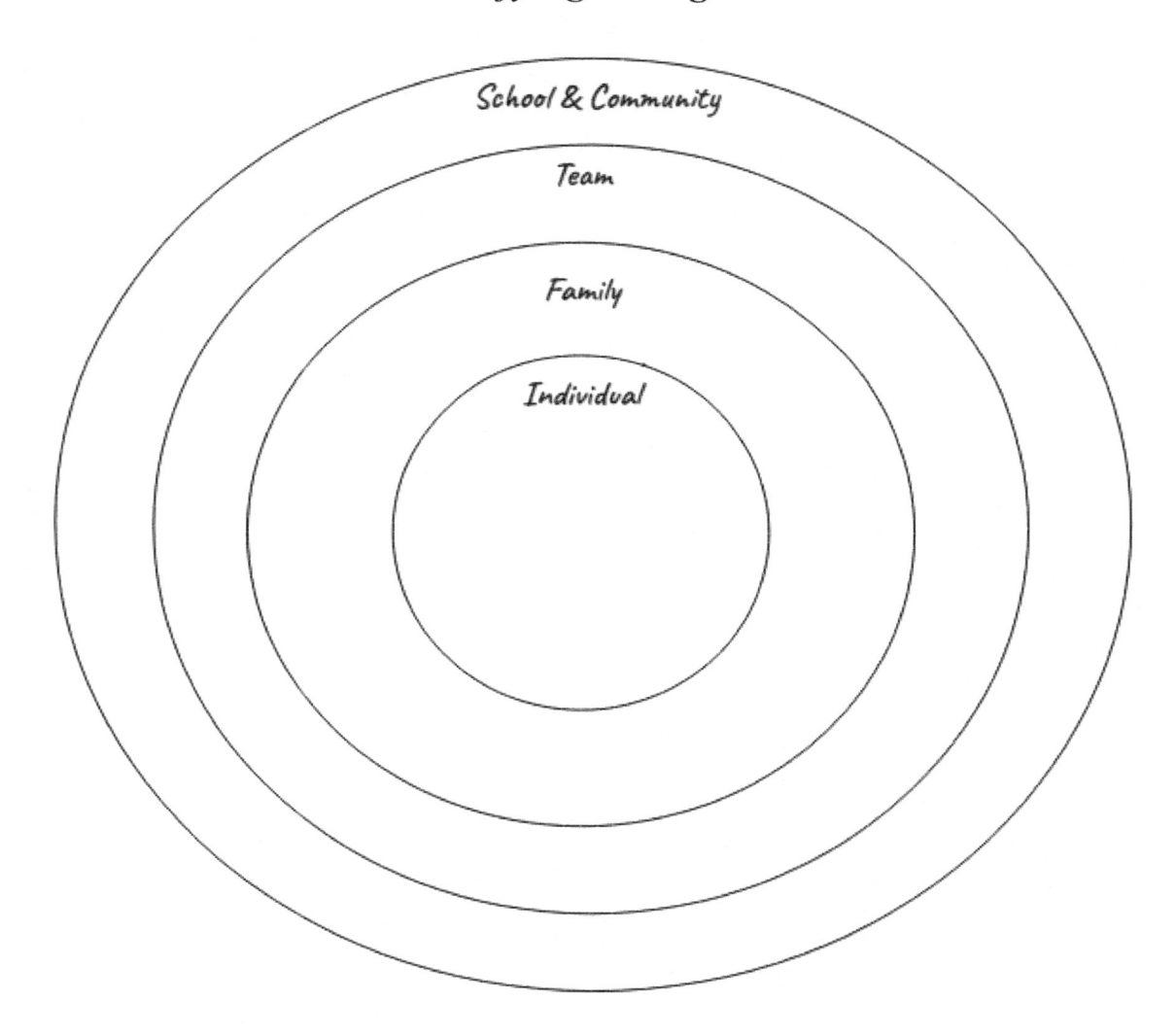

(Concentric circles labeled from outside in: School & Community, Team, Family, Individual)

Identifying Risks and Resources

In this activity, you will brainstorm specific challenges you have across the individual, family, team, university, and community levels. Examples for **Individual** could be things like "get down on myself" and "get frustrated." Examples for **Family** could be things like "busy" and "stressed." Examples for **Team** could be things like "demanding" and "some conflicts." Examples for **School & Community** could be things like "unsafe" and "doesn't care about athletics."

Identifying Challenges

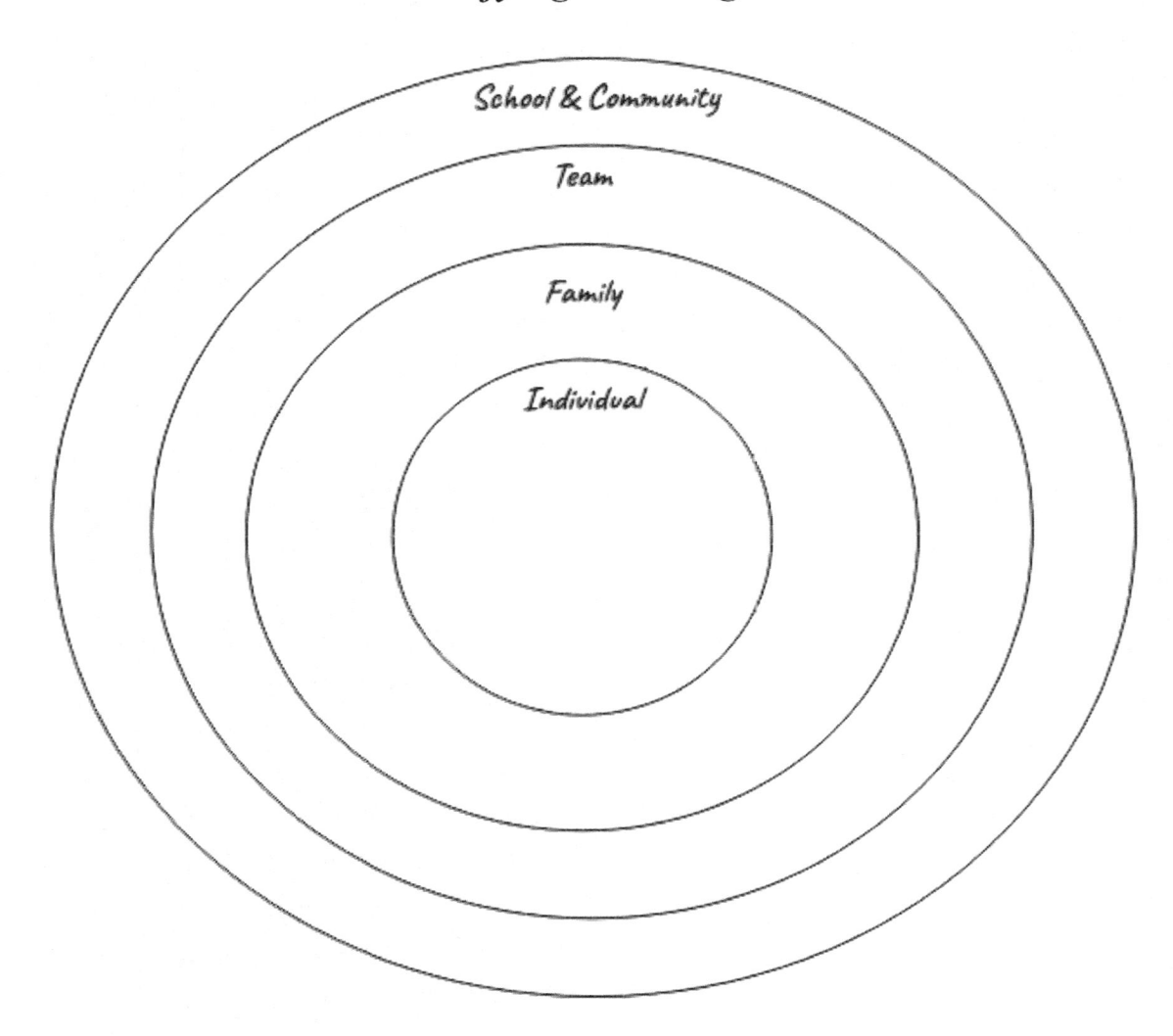

- School & Community
- Team
- Family
- Individual

Using Strengths to Help Challenges

In this activity you will use your strengths to address and overcome your challenges. See the example to help you complete the exercise.

Challenges	Strengths
Individual Level: • I get down on myself easily.	**Individual Level:** • I am motivated to keep going even when I'm upset.
Family Level: • Sometimes my family is too busy to come to all my games.	**Family Level:** • My family works hard to support me.
Team Level: • Sometimes it feels like coaches are too demanding.	**Team Level:** • When I work hard, that motivates other players to work hard, too, and we all do better.
School & Community Level: • Our sport doesn't get enough funding compared to others.	**School & Community Level:** • Even though they can't give us more money, the community and students support us as fans.

Goal Setting

Background:

Being able to set goals and create plans toward achieving them is an essential skill for team leaders to have. Leaders need to understand how to set P.U.R.P.O.S.E. driven goals so that they can help their teammates to do the same. Coaches also rely on leaders to voice teammates' needs and concerns in the goal setting process so that every member of the program has a stake and investment in the direction of the team.

Objectives:

1. Identify elements of P.U.R.P.O.S.E. driven goals
2. Understand how P.U.R.P.O.S.E. driven goals move individuals and teams forward
3. Reflect upon personal and programmatic P.U.R.P.O.S.E. driven goals

Materials:

- Spiral notebooks
- Writing utensils
- White board or chalkboard
- Copies of *P.U.R.P.O.S.E. Driven Goals*
- Copies of *Goal Setting* worksheet

Leadership Council Check-ins (optional):

- Address any team issues that have come-up since last meeting
- Discuss any mentee issues that have come-up since last meeting
- Troubleshoot Platoon issues that have come-up since last meeting

Activities:

Step 1: Present P.U.R.P.O.S.E. driven goals, explaining each area of the acronym.

- **Prioritize the program's mission**
- **Unite individuals within a shared destiny**
- **Reflect risks and resilience**
- **(have) Plans**
- **(are) Open to feedback**
- **See and celebrate progress**
- **Evaluate progress and redirect action**

Step 2: Discuss your **Program's mission statement** and the concept of **Shared Destiny** within teams. Have athletes discuss what shared destiny means to them and the importance of reliance on one another.

- What does it mean to rely on someone?
- What does it mean to be someone others can rely on?
- What is the difference between individual goals and team goals?
- What are individual goals that can detract from the team?
- What are individual goals that can support the team?

Step 3: Discuss how goals need to be **Open to feedback** and why this is important.

- Why might it be important for goals to be mutually agreed upon in a team?
- What happens when coaches or individual players make team goals without consulting the team?

Step 4: Discuss how coaches and teammates must work together to **See and Celebrate** goal progress. Write athletes' answers on the board.

- What motivates you toward a goal when you feel stuck?
- How can we motivate each other through adversity?

Step 5: Describe **Evaluating Progress** and **redirecting action** toward goals.

- How do you know you are moving successfully toward a goal?
- Why is it important to be flexible and able to adjust goals?
- What might get in the way of achieving goals that could be out of our control?
- In these situations, what can we do to redirect progress and keep moving the team forward?

Step 6: Spend time on the **Plan** portion of goal setting and ask athletes to answer the following questions in their notebooks or *Goal Setting* worksheet pertaining to individual goals they have for themselves this season.

- What is the goal?
- Who is going to do it?
- When will they do it?
- Where will they do it?
- Why is the goal important?
- How will they meet the goal?

P.U.R.P.O.S.E. Driven Goals:

Prioritize the program's mission
Goals should put the mission of the team first. If the mission of the team is to try your best, then each player should have a goal of trying their best!

Unite individuals within a shared destiny
Goals should help players see that they have to work together to be successful. They need to be good for individual players and good for the whole team!

Reflect risks and resilience
Goals should take into account the strengths and growing-areas of each player and of the team as a whole. If one player is struggling, a team goal should be to help that player get better!

(have) **P**lans
Goals need to have plans to make them happen. A goal plan answers these questions: Whose goal is it? What do they want to achieve? When do they want to achieve it? Where will it be achieved? Why is the goal important? How will they achieve the goal?

(are) **O**pen to feedback
Goals and plans should be open to feedback because everyone on the team needs to agree on the goal. If players don't agree on goals, they probably won't be able to achieve them as a team.

See and celebrate progress
Coaches and teammates should see and celebrate times when players are moving toward goals. When we celebrate progress, it helps us to feel good and keep trying!

Evaluate progress and redirect action
Sometimes things get in the way of achieving goals that are outside of our control like injuries, illnesses, or family and friendship issues. At these times, we can update goals to fit our situations and needs. Doing this helps us stay motivated and moving toward success.

Goal Setting

Who?	
What?	
When?	
Where?	
Why?	
How?	

Mental Health Issues and Getting Support

Background:

In order to successfully achieve goals, athletes and coaches must acknowledge how psychology influences performance. Team leaders need to understand how to identify and address possible mental health concerns within themselves and their teammates to help move themselves and the team forward. Leaders also need to be able to reach out for support from coaches, programmatic staff, and mental health providers toward this goal.

Objectives:

1. Identify common mental health concerns impacting the lives of high school athletes
2. Describe the connections between emotions, thoughts, and behaviors
3. Discuss the acronym O.P.E.N. as an approach to managing difficult emotions

Materials:

- Post-it notes
- Spiral notebooks
- Writing utensils
- White board or chalkboard
- Copies of *Being O.P.E.N.* worksheet

Leadership Council Check-ins (optional):

- Address any team issues that have come-up since last meeting
- Discuss any mentee issues that have come-up since last meeting
- Troubleshoot Platoon issues that have come-up since last meeting

Activities:

Step 1: Hand out 4 Post-it notes to each athlete. Ask them to record their answers to the following questions on Post-it notes. Let them know this is an anonymous exercise so they can be as truthful as possible.

- <u>1st Post-it note</u>: What is one mental health concern that high school athletes deal with within themselves (e.g. anxiety, depression, identity issues)?
- <u>2nd Post-it note</u>: What is one mental health concern that high school athletes deal with within their families (e.g. parental conflict, parental divorce, death of loved ones)?
- <u>3rd Post-it note</u>: What is one mental health concern that high school athletes deal with within their friendships/relationships (e.g. conflict with friends, break-ups)?

- <u>4th Post-it note</u>: What is one mental health concern that high school athletes deal with within their teams (e.g. feeling unaccepted by teammates, feeling underappreciated by coaches)?

Step 2: Collect the Post-it notes and read them by category. Have someone record similarities and differences on the white board or chalkboard.

Step 3: Use the following script to describe how cognitions, emotions, and behaviors fit together to shape the ways we navigate mental health concerns.

> *All of the mental health challenges we just discussed are in some way connected to the way we think, feel, and behave. When we have conflict with parents or friends we may feel sad, angry, or anxious–thinking negatively about ourselves or others. These thoughts and feelings lead us to behave in ways that may not be the most beneficial to us in the short and long term (e.g. saying mean things or acting out). In the same way, when we feel unaccepted or underappreciated within the team, we could also feel down, frustrated, and worried–again, thinking negative thoughts about ourselves and others. These feelings and thoughts could lead us to be less motivated to do our best on the team or quit altogether. Using the acronym, O.P.E.N., we can help ourselves manage challenging emotions that arise within and beyond the team.*

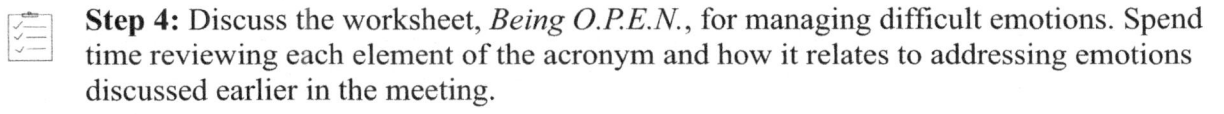

Step 4: Discuss the worksheet, *Being O.P.E.N.*, for managing difficult emotions. Spend time reviewing each element of the acronym and how it relates to addressing emotions discussed earlier in the meeting.

- *<u>O</u>pen yourself to the feeling*
    - How does fighting or avoiding negative emotions get in the way of resolving them?

- *<u>P</u>ractice patience with yourself*
    - Why is being patient with yourself and your feelings important?
    - What can we learn from sadness?
    - What can we learn from anger?
    - What can we learn from worry?

- *<u>E</u>xpress the feeling*
    - Why is expressing and releasing emotions important?
    - What are some ways to express feelings that work for you?
    - How can we help each other to express emotions?

- *Never give up*
    - How can you remind yourself to keep being open to emotions?
    - How can we remind each other to keep being open to emotions?

Step 5: Reinforce the importance of seeking social support to manage difficult emotions and mental health concerns. Have them track specific answers in their notebook.

- Who can you go to for extra support in managing mental health concerns in your family (e.g. older siblings, parents, extended family)?
- Who can you go to for extra support in managing mental health concerns in your friend group (e.g. best friends, romantic relationship)?
- Who can you go to for extra support in managing mental health concerns in the team (e.g. teammates, coaches)?
- Who can you go to for extra support in managing mental health concerns related to academics (e.g. teammates, coaches, teachers, counselors, administrators)?
- Who can you go to for extra support in managing mental health concerns in your community (e.g. counselors, psychologists, hospitals)?

Being O.P.E.N.

*O*pen yourself to the feeling

You have to open yourself to feelings before you can resolve them. If you try to avoid feelings or fight them off, you prevent yourself from doing the things you need to do to make yourself and the team better. Remember that accepting feelings does not mean that you allow yourself to be run by them. It's actually the opposite. When we listen and learn from emotions we get better at controlling them.

*P*ractice patience with yourself

It is important to be patient with ourselves when it comes to emotions. Feelings are not our enemies. They are more like friends that give us important messages. Anger tells us when we have been harmed. Worry tells us to protect ourselves. Sadness tells us that we have lost something or someone that is important to us.

*E*xpress the feelings

By expressing our emotions, we gain better control of them. Some people express their emotions by talking to others about them, writing about them, letting themself cry, or doing some other activity to express them. If we don't express our feelings, they build-up and get in the way of our wellbeing, relationships, and goals.

*N*ever give up

Emotions will always be with us because they serve a purpose. Learning how to manage emotions may be difficult if we have not been taught to listen or express them. It is important to keep encouraging ourselves and each other to better manage emotions because practice makes everyone better.

Communication Filters

Background:

Healthy communication is crucial to any well-functioning team. When leaders give and receive feedback on the team they need to understand their own communication filters. Communication filters influence the words we say, how we say them, and the ways we hear messages. If leaders can "clear" their filters and help teammates to do the same, the whole team can become better communicators.

Objectives:

1. Identify elements of communication filters
2. Describe ways to clear personal communication filters
3. Practice clearing personal filters to more effectively communicate

Materials:

- Spiral notebooks
- Writing utensils
- White board or chalkboard
- Copies of *Communication Filter*
- Copies of *Filters and How We Communicate*
- Copies of *Filters and How We Receive Communication*
- Copies of *Clearing the Filter to Better Communicate*
- Copies of *Clearing the Filter to Better Receive Communication*

Leadership Council Check-ins (optional):

- Address any team issues that have come-up since last meeting
- Discuss any mentee issues that have come-up since last meeting
- Troubleshoot Platoon issues that have come-up since last meeting

Activities:

Remember to be sensitive to athletes' sharing in these activities because their history, past relationships, and values may be triggering to reflect upon. Remind athletes that they <u>do not</u> need to share specific details about their experiences that may be sensitive.

Step 1: Give each athlete a copy of the *Communication Filter*. Explain the *Communication Filter* to players and each element that impacts it:

- **History**
  (e.g. immigration, poverty, grief, identities, ability issues…)
- **Past Relationships**
  (e.g. relationships with caregivers, friends, teammates, coaches…)

- **Values**
  (e.g. cultural values like being macho or being passive, respect, religion...)

Step 2: Give each athlete a copy of *Filters and How We Communicate*. Read directions and have athletes complete these worksheets individually. Once they are done, have them discuss their reflections in pairs.

Step 3: Discuss overall reflections in the large group, highlighting similarities and differences. Record themes on the white board or chalkboard.

Step 4: Give each athlete a copy of *Filters and How We Receive Communication*. Read directions and have athletes complete these worksheets individually. Once they are done, ask them to discuss their reflections in pairs.

Step 5: Discuss overall reflections in the large group, highlighting similarities and differences. Record themes on the white board or chalkboard.

Step 6: (Optional) Give each athlete copies of *Clearing the Filter to Better Communicate* and *Clearing the Filter to Better Receive Communication* worksheets. Ask athletes to complete them for homework before the next meeting.

Communication Filters

History
Past Relationships
Values

Filters and How We Communicate

Everytime we communicate the actual words we say and how we say them go through a filter. Our filters are made-up of our histories, experiences in past relationships, and values. All these things sometimes get in the way of us communicating effectively. In this activity you will be given an opportunity to reflect on your personal filter and how this can obstruct communication.

What in your <u>history</u> impacts the way you communicate?

Example: *When I was younger, I had a stutter that made me really self-conscious about being understood. I would choose not to communicate what I was thinking or feeling because it was easier to stay quiet. I think sometimes this still impacts me today. I worry that I will come across as unclear so I only speak when I have to.*

___

What in your <u>past relationships</u> impacts the way you communicate?

Example: *My parents are pretty strict and seem to not listen to me or want my opinion on things. Because of this, I always try to speak my mind with others. Sometimes this impacts my communication because people tell me that I can come across angry or stubborn when I'm not trying to be.*

___

What in your <u>values</u> impacts the way you communicate?

Example: *In my culture, we have a strong value of respecting elders. People have told me that this helps me be humble and listen to people in authority, like coaches. I like this about myself, but a part of me feels like it can get in the way of speaking my mind when I need to.*

___

Clearing the Filter to Better Communicate

Now that you know more about yourself and your communication filter, you can practice clearing your filter and communicating differently. Review the below examples and write about how you can better communicate in each scenario.

📱 You are worried about a teammate who has posted some stuff on social media about being depressed and not wanting to be alive anymore. You've tried to talk with them and be extra caring, but you are still worried. You hesitate to say anything to coaches because you don't want the teammate to be upset or get into trouble. You had a friend go through something similar in middle school who ended the friendship over you telling a teacher about the situation. Knowing how your filter can be clouded, what are you going to do to clear it and communicate more effectively in this situation?

This is definitely a situation where I should talk with coaches. I need to realize that getting my teammate the help they need shows how much I care about them even if they can't see it now. When people are so depressed they question the point of living, they are not able to make clear decisions about what may be best for them and their safety. That's why others need to step-in and help.

👥 You are frustrated that a member of the team is not pulling their weight and you really want to talk to them about it. You hesitate because you are new to the team and worry that you haven't built a strong enough relationship with the other person. They may take the feedback negatively and make it even harder for you to adjust on the team. Knowing how your filter can be clouded, what are you going to do to clear it and communicate more effectively in this situation?

_____
_____
_____
_____
_____

⚖️ You are upset that your coach has chosen to put you as second string again, after a player that you feel doesn't try as hard as you do. It makes you angry and a little hopeless to think that you've invested so much effort in the team and making yourself better, but the coach doesn't see it. You want to talk to them about it but hesitate because you worry they will get angry and for sure not play you. Knowing how your filter can be clouded, what are you going to do to clear it and communicate more effectively in this situation?

_____
_____
_____
_____
_____

Filters and How We Receive Communication

Everytime we receive communication, the actual words people say and how they say them go through a filter. Our filters are made-up of our histories, experiences in past relationships, and values. All these things sometimes get in the way of us hearing messages clearly. In this activity you will be given an opportunity to reflect on your personal filter and how this can obstruct your ability to receive communication.

What in your <u>history</u> impacts the way you receive communication?

Example: *My family immigrated to the U.S. before I was born. I have to translate for my parents all the time. People get frustrated with my parents because they don't know the language. I think this makes me worry about what people think about me when I communicate.*

_____
_____
_____
_____

What in your <u>past relationships</u> impacts the way you receive communication?

Example: *I remember my parents getting divorced when I was younger. I had to go back and forth between my parents' houses and always felt the pressure to make them happy. I think I'm like that with other people, too. I try so hard to make other people happy, that I don't think about what makes me happy.*

_____
_____
_____
_____

What in your <u>values</u> impacts the way you receive communication?

Example: *As a man in my culture, I've been taught to be tough. I think this has helped me get through some hard times in my life, but it may be something that holds me back. It's difficult for me to acknowledge when I've made a mistake and this prevents me from getting better. I also think people get frustrated by this and it makes them less likely to give me feedback.*

_____
_____
_____
_____

Clearing the Filter to Better Receive Communication

Now that you know more about yourself and your communication filter, you can practice clearing your filter and receiving communication differently. Review the below examples and write about how you can better receive communication in each scenario.

📱 Your teammate just ghosted you when you had a plan to meet-up this weekend. This is your first year on the team and they are pretty much the only one you've hung out with so far. You've been ghosted in the past and the person really didn't have a good reason. They just didn't seem to care as much as you did about the relationship. Knowing how your filter can be clouded, what are you going to do to clear it and receive communication more effectively in this situation?

Maybe this friend is different from the other one. Maybe I might be reading too much into them not responding. They could have had something come-up and they couldn't message me or forgot to. Just because something happens with one friend, it doesn't have to mean that it will happen again. Instead of avoiding the situation, I might open a conversation about ways we can meet-up in the future.

📣 Coach yelled at you in practice for making the same mistake again. She said, "You should be playing better than this!" You don't understand why you keep getting it wrong and feel embarrassed and frustrated with yourself. You know that she is just trying to help, but the more she yells the more you get in your head. Knowing how your filter can be clouded, what are you going to do to clear it and receive communication more effectively in this situation?

_____
_____
_____
_____
_____

👥 You hear that another player on the team is talking badly about you. They are a junior and you are a sophomore in the same position. You have taken their starting spot at the last scrimmage because Coach wanted to see what you could do. This other player is saying stuff about how you're not really a good athlete and other things about you. You feel angry and not sure what to do. Knowing how your filter can be clouded, what are you going to do to clear it and receive communication more effectively in this situation?

_____
_____
_____
_____
_____

Being H.U.M.B.L.E.

Background:

Giving feedback and receiving it can be challenging for people because most of us don't like to be told we are doing something wrong. As leaders on this team, however, it is important that you all are able to do this often and effectively to move the team forward. The good news is there are specific skills we can practice to help you give and receive feedback.

Objectives:

1. Describe common challenges to giving feedback and receiving it
2. Understand the acronym H.U.M.B.L.E. to improve communication
3. Practice strategies to more effectively give and receive feedback

Materials:

- Spiral notebooks
- Writing utensils
- White board or chalkboard
- Copies of *Being H.U.M.B.L.E.*
- Copies of *How do We Hold Each Other Accountable?*

Leadership Council Check-ins (optional):

- Address any team issues that have come-up since last meeting
- Discuss any mentee issues that have come-up since last meeting
- Troubleshoot Platoon issues that have come-up since last meeting

Activities:

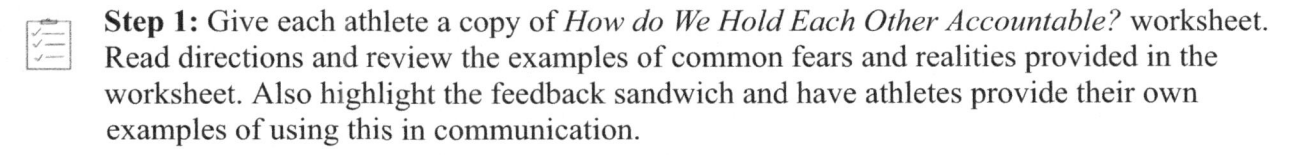

Step 1: Give each athlete a copy of *How do We Hold Each Other Accountable?* worksheet. Read directions and review the examples of common fears and realities provided in the worksheet. Also highlight the feedback sandwich and have athletes provide their own examples of using this in communication.

- **Fear:** "If I check someone they will…"
- **Reality:** We can't control how someone feels or what they will do, but…
- **Feedback Sandwich:** 1 positive, the feedback, and 1 encourager…

Step 2: Have athletes complete the remainder of the worksheet individually and share their answers with a partner. Discuss reflections in the large group related to overall similarities and differences. Record themes on the white board or chalkboard.

Step 3: Give each athlete a copy of *Being H.U.M.B.L.E.* worksheet. Describe each element within the acronym, making sure to gauge athletes' understanding. Ask for examples of what each element looks like and does not look like on the team.

- *<u>H</u>old yourself accountable*
- *<u>U</u>nderstand where the feedback is coming from*
- *<u>M</u>anage your emotions and behaviors*
- *<u>B</u>e thankful for the feedback*
- *<u>L</u>earn ways to get better*
- *<u>E</u>xecute ways to get better*

Step 4: Ask athletes to create skits in pairs or small groups related to giving feedback within the team. Have them use the feedback sandwich and H.U.M.B.L.E. in their skits. Athletes will act out their skits for each other at the end of the meeting.

Step 5: You might also consider having team leaders collaborate on a group skit to act out for the whole team. This could be done alongside leaders facilitating a team-wide discussion related to giving and receiving feedback.

Being H.U.M.B.L.E.

*H*old yourself accountable.
Many people automatically become defensive when they hear that they've made a mistake. It is important to recognize this and push past it to take personal responsibility. We can't commit to making ourselves better if we don't take ownership of our mistakes.

*U*nderstand where the feedback is coming from
It's easier to accept feedback when we remember that it is given to us by people who care. Members of the team hold each other accountable because we are mutually invested in individual and programmatic success.

*M*anage your emotions and behaviors
When people face their mistakes they often feel frustrated, worried, and disheartened. These feelings are normal and actually a testament to your investment in the team. You feel this way because you care about doing well. That being said, you have to find ways to recognize and release these emotions so that they do not cloud your ability to own the feedback and implement it. Consider using the acronym O.P.E.N. to help you recognize and release emotions.

*B*e thankful for the feedback
Expressing gratitude for feedback helps you, the person giving it, and the team as a whole. When we view feedback with gratitude we change the way we see it. Receiving feedback becomes less of a threat and more like a gift that helps us get better.

*L*earn ways to get better
What went wrong? When and Where did it happen? Why did it happen? Who else was involved? How can I and others improve? Maybe you only make the mistakes in games and not practice or when you are mentally distracted and not calm. Maybe the mistakes happen when you are engaging a specific teammate and not with other members of the team. If you can determine that mistakes happen in a specific context or with specific people, then you can more accurately determine ways to improve. Asking these questions also helps us to quiet negative self-talk that we might slip into when emotionally overwhelmed. If you are feeling upset over some feedback, you might have negative self-talk like, "I'm bad at everything!" or "I'm such a failure." When you take the time to really listen to the feedback and learn specific ways to get better, you can engage in positive self-talk like, "If I could do it the other day, I know it's possible!"

*E*xecute ways to get better
By moving through the above areas you've properly prepared yourself to implement the feedback. Now it's time to do it! When you start to execute strategies to get better, it is important to check-in with teammates and coaches about your progress. Asking them to give you feedback on how you are doing, is crucial to your on-going development as well as the overall success of the team.

How Do We Hold Each Other Accountable?

In this activity, we will challenge common fears related to holding people accountable and give you a chance to come-up with your own responses to fears you have about checking your teammates. Addressing our fears helps us become more confident in holding each other accountable throughout the season.

1. **Fear: *"If I check someone for doing something wrong they will be angry at me."***
   Reality: Yep, some people may get angry when someone calls them out. We can't really control how someone will react to feedback, but we can control how we approach the situation. If we check someone in anger and use a mean tone of voice, then they are much more likely to become angry. But if we approach the situation calmly and patiently, they are less likely to respond in anger.

2. **Fear: *"If I check someone for doing something wrong they will be sad or embarrassed."***
   Reality: Yep, just like the fear of someone being angry, we can't control how someone will react to holding them accountable. It is actually a good thing that you are concerned for your teammate and don't want them to feel bad. That shows you care. However, to really show you care about someone you have to be honest with them and give them feedback that will help them in the long run. So, if you're worried about making them feel bad or embarrassed you can talk to them one-on-one away from the team and consider using the feedback sandwich.

Say what they're doing right		"Good hustle, Jean!"
Say what they need to work on		"Next time, make sure that you look to see who is more open before you pass."
Say something encouraging		"You got this!"

3. **Fear: *"If I check someone for doing something wrong they will not want to be my friend."***
   Reality: Yep, just like we can't control how people feel, we can't control how they will behave after we hold them accountable. They may feel angry and embarrassed and be colder to you in practice and out of practice. They may avoid you or express their frustration with you to other teammates or friends. These are actually normal reactions for people when they get called out. We all need time and space to blow off steam or process what people tell us so that we can fully accept and implement feedback. If you've approached the situation with positivity, respect, calmness, and patience, then your teammate will likely hear and appreciate the feedback when they are done processing. Remember, that coaches are here to support you as well. If there is tension within the team, coaches need to know about it so that we can help you build positive relationships with each other.

4. **Fear:** *"If I check someone for doing something wrong they will check me back."*
   Reality: Yep, that's what we want to happen! It is normal for you to feel angry, bad, or embarrassed when you hear that you are doing something wrong or could be doing something better. You have these reactions because you are really invested in the season and want to do your best. Despite your discomfort, teammates and coaches need to hold you accountable because they care about you and want you to get better. We need to normalize holding each other accountable in our program. If checking each other is common, then the challenging emotions associated with it will likely get smaller over time.

5. **Fear:** *"If I check someone for doing something wrong…*
   _____

   Reality:
   _____
   _____
   _____
   _____

6. **Fear:** *"If a teammate checks me for something I did wrong…*
   _____

   Reality:
   _____
   _____
   _____
   _____

Communication B.A.S.I.C.S.

Background:

Communication B.A.S.I.C.S. provide us with strategies and considerations that can guide the ways we see and approach everyday communication. In using the B.A.S.I.C.S. model, people take the time to reflect upon their emotions and reactions to messages as well as people's roles and responsibilities in relationships. Then, people use the model to set specific goals and plans for communication that include sharing their feelings about the situation, using clear and concise language, and infusing respect into their approach.

Objectives:

1. Identify elements of communication B.A.S.I.C.S.
2. Describe ways to apply these elements to communication in everyday situations
3. Practice applying communication B.A.S.I.C.S. on the team

Materials:

- Spiral notebooks
- Writing utensils
- White board or chalkboard
- Copies of *Communication B.A.S.I.C.S.*

Leadership Council Check-ins (optional):

- Address any team issues that have come-up since last meeting
- Discuss any mentee issues that have come-up since last meeting
- Troubleshoot Platoon issues that have come-up since last meeting

Activities:

Step 1: Give each athlete a copy of *Communication B.A.S.I.C.S.* Explain each letter of the acronym and how this can be applied to improving overall communication within and apart from the team.

- ***Be H.U.M.B.L.E. and O.P.E.N.*** *(these are covered in previous lessons)*
    - Why are these two acronyms useful in basic communication?

- ***Attend to context***
    - Why is it important to know who you are talking to and each of your communication filters?

- *<u>S</u>et goals and make a plan*
    - Why is it important to have goals for communication and a plan?

- *<u>I</u>-statements*
    - Why is it important to start with how you feel when communicating?

- *<u>C</u>ommunicate clearly and concisely*
    - What happens when communication is unclear?

- *<u>S</u>how respect*
    - Why would respect be important to hold in communication?

Step 2: Discuss ways athletes can implement these concepts in everyday life. Provide the following examples and have them discuss how they could use the model to resolve the communication in pairs. Ask athletes to share their thoughts with the large group and record themes on the board.

- A friend has been talking badly about you with other friends and you want to talk to them about it.
- Your cousin is making risky choices and you want to talk to them about making better decisions.
- Your parent/caregiver is blaming you for something you didn't do and you want to talk to them about the situation.

Step 3: Discuss ways athletes can implement communication B.A.S.I.C.S. on the team. Provide the following examples and have them describe how they could use the model to resolve the communication in pairs. Address athletes' overall thoughts in the large group.

- Their teammate keeps complaining about the team and coaches and it is starting to bring down the team.
- They would like to try a new position or technique and want to talk to coaches about it.
- They are feeling worried about something at home or at school and want to talk to coaches about it.

Step 4: Have athletes write about a current situation in their own lives that they would like to use the B.A.S.I.C.S. model to help them resolve. You can ask them to share with the group if they are willing, but let them know they are not required to do so.

Communication B.A.S.I.C.S.

*B*e H.U.M.B.L.E. and O.P.E.N.
It's important to be **H.U.M.B.L.E.** and **O.P.E.N.** when you approach communication. These are especially helpful when you are receiving feedback and want to better understand and manage your emotions surrounding the communication.

*A*ttend to context
One must attend to the context of communication in order to respond effectively. Helpful context questions: *Who are you and who are you talking to? What are both of your roles and responsibilities in this situation? What is the communication about? How are your communication filters impacting the ways you both express yourselves and receive messages?*

*S*et goals and make a plan
You should organize your thoughts, how you want to communicate them, and in what context. Sometimes we might have the goal of just expressing our feelings and concerns and it would best be done outside of practice time. Other times we might need to approach the other person during practice so we can give them feedback about their sport related performance.

I-statements
I-statements are phrases that people use to more effectively communicate. They start with owning how you feel. Then they let the other person know how you see them in the situation. Finally, they end in a request for change. Example: *"I feel frustrated when I give you feedback and it doesn't seem to be implemented. Can we talk more about what is happening in this situation so we can get on the same page?"*

*C*ommunicate clearly and concisely
Many times people get caught-up in their emotions or non-relevant details and their message gets lost. It is important to stick to your goals in the situation and use emotions and details that help you to achieve those goals.

*S*how respect
You show respect to yourself by staying true to your values and goals in the communication. You show respect to others by being patient, calm, caring, and understanding.

Diversity and Inclusion in Teams

Background:

Diversity means that every person has unique experiences, abilities, identities, and cultural backgrounds that shape the ways they see themselves, others, and the world. Leaders strive to make every teammate feel valued and successful in the program. This is not always easy because people with different experiences, abilities, identities, and cultural backgrounds may experience challenges in life and in the program that impact their ability to be successful. Our job as a team is to help identify possible obstacles to inclusion and find ways to overcome them using our collective strengths and resilience.

Objectives:

1. Identify elements of diversity within ourselves and each other
2. Describe ways in which these may impact ours' or others' inclusion on the team
3. Discuss avenues toward using strengths and resilience to increase inclusion

Materials:

- *Coaches may review Chapter 3 activities to help structure their discussion*
- Spiral notebooks
- Writing utensils
- White board or chalkboard

Leadership Council Check-ins (optional):

- Address any team issues that have come-up since last meeting
- Discuss any mentee issues that have come-up since last meeting
- Troubleshoot Platoon issues that have come-up since last meeting

Activities:

Step 1: Read the following questions to athletes and have them track their answers privately in their notebooks. Remind them that they do not have to share their specific answers with anyone. This activity is to get them thinking about diversity and how it impacts everyone.

- **Think of one area you are different from most other athletes on the team** (Examples: cultural background or identities, language, finances, neighborhood, athletic ability, academic ability…)

- **Answer the following questions based on this area of difference:**
    - Have you ever been: made fun of, called bad names, had assumptions made about you, been singled out, or had threats of violence made toward you because of this difference?
    - Do people avoid talking about your difference when it does matter to you?
    - Have you ever felt like less of a person because of your difference?
    - Have you ever wished that you were not different in this way?
    - Do you ever feel worried, stressed, hopeless, frustrated, guilty, or embarrassed about your difference?
    - In what ways does your difference impact you on the team?

Step 2: After they complete the assessment, you may discuss their **general reactions** to the questions. *If athletes have more questions or concerns related to this activity, this would be a great opportunity for you to meet with them one-on-one to discuss ways you can support their inclusion on the team.*

- What was it like to think about these things?
- Have you thought about them before?
- Why are these questions important to ask?
- What can we learn from these questions?

Step 3: Write the following three questions on the white board or chalkboard. Have athletes discuss answers to the questions in pairs.

- What are some areas of diversity that we see on our team?
    - Examples: gender, race, physical or academic ability, access to resources.

- What might get in the way of some teammates being included or successful on the team?
    - Examples: biases, lack of resources, physical challenges, academic issues.

- What might help these teammates feel more included and successful?
    - Examples: caring for each other, holding each other accountable, giving reminders or extra help, offering to study and do homework together, and helping in other ways.

Step 4: In the large group, have partners discuss their answers to each question. Record themes on the board. Make sure to take a picture of the board before you erase it so that you can reference it as a team later.

Sport Psychology and Mental Performance

Background:

Sport psychology is a field of psychological research, theory, and practice related to understanding athletic performance and helping athletes, coaches, and teams work better together. Mental performance is a subset of sport psychology related to athletes' abilities to: focus on what they need to, be emotionally and cognitively flexible, and persist through physical and psychological challenges. It is essential that leaders have foundational knowledge surrounding mental performance as it impacts them and their teammates.

Objectives:

1. Identify aspects that detract from mental focus and motivation
2. Understand the basics of mental imagery to improve focus
3. Transform negative self-talk into positive self-talk to improve motivation

Materials:

- Spiral notebooks
- Writing utensils
- White board or chalkboard
- One copy of the *Imagery Script*
- Copies of *Negative & Positive Self-talk*

Leadership Council Check-ins (optional):

- Address any team issues that have come-up since last meeting
- Discuss any mentee issues that have come-up since last meeting
- Troubleshoot Platoon issues that have come-up since last meeting

Activities:

This meeting may need to be split into 2 different lessons if timing is an issue. If the lesson is split, complete Steps 1, 2 & 3 in one lesson and Steps 4 & 5 in another lesson.

Step 1: Discuss **mental focus** and why it is important to physical performance. Ask athletes the below questions and record their responses on the board.

- What does it look like to be focused during practice and games?
- What gets in the way of focus at practice and games?
- How can we help ourselves and each other re-focus?

Step 2: Introduce **imagery** as a way to improve mental focus and performance.

- Mental imagery is a way of visualizing in your mind what you want to achieve in real life. Many top athletes across sports use mental imagery to combat anxiety, boost confidence, and improve focus and performance.

- Athletes visualize themselves performing different techniques, moving their body effectively, overcoming challenges, and achieving goals using imagery.

- It is theorized that visualization trains your brain (and body) to see mental rehearsal as real-world practice. Thinking about being successful increases one's ability to actually be successful.

- Imagery can happen at practice, at home, or during competition. It should become part of routines athletes do to prepare themselves to achieve their short and long-term goals.

- Athletes can find imagery scripts on-line or even create their own that is tailored to what they want to think about and the goals they would like to achieve.

- Effective visualizations focus on process and outcomes as well as create a space in the mind that engages as many senses as possible (e.g. vision, hearing, touch, kinetic, smell, and even taste).

- When athletes first start using imagery it may be challenging to maintain focus or build a highly detailed visualization in their head. They also might have difficulties imagining themselves successfully completing a movement if they've faced physical challenges or other emotions or thoughts get in the way.

- In these moments, it is really important for athletes to keep redirecting their mind back to the visualization. Everytime one turns their mind and imagines success, they train themselves to be more in control of their thoughts. Overtime, imagery will become easier and they will start to see improvements in confidence and performance.

Step 3: Read the *Imagery Script* to players. They can close their eyes and/or you can dim the lights in the meeting room. If they do not want to close their eyes you can have them focus on one spot on the wall or floor. Make sure to read slowly pausing throughout so that athletes can formulate the images in their mind. After you complete the script, make sure there is enough time to process their experience in the activity.

- What were the images that came to your mind?
- What were the sights, sounds, feels, smells…?

- Who was around you and what were they doing?
- What were some of the thoughts that came to your mind?
- What was it like to breathe in a different way?
- If you were to practice this on your own, what would you add?
    - Visualizing yourself performing a skill or carrying out a play

Stop the lesson, here, if you run out of time. Complete Steps 4 & 5 in another lesson.

Step 4: Discuss the importance of motivation amidst physical, emotional, and mental challenges. Ask athletes the questions below and have them share their answers with a partner. After this, ask partners to present their answers to the group.

- Why is persistence important on the team?
- What stands in the way of persistence?
- What motivates you as a player?
- How can you motivate your teammates?

Step 5: Discuss the differences between positive self-talk and negative self-talk as they relate to persistence through adversity. Give athletes copies of the *Negative & Positive Self-talk* worksheet to complete on their own.

- Negative self-talk is talking to yourself in mean or maladaptive ways.
  Example: "*I suck at this! I'll never get it right.*"
    - Negative self-talk tears us down and zaps our motivation to continue because we think we can't do it or it is pointless to try.
    - What are other examples of negative self-talk?

- Positive self-talk is talking to yourself in kind and adaptive ways.
  Example: "*You can do it, you've done it before!*"
    - Positive self-talk builds us up and increases our motivation to continue because we think we can do it and we should try.
    - What are other examples of positive self-talk?

- Now that athletes know the difference, ask them to practice changing negative self-talk to positive. Have athletes come-up with positive reframes to the below examples in the large group. Record their answers on the board.
    - Change "*I won't ever get this right!*" to _____
    - Change "*I am such a failure.*" to _____
    - Change "*No one believes in me.*" to _____
    - Change "*Why do I even try?*" to _____

Imagery Script

"We are going to do an imagery exercise right now. I will read some things I want you to visualize in your mind. Then when we are done, I will ask you some questions about what it was like. You can close your eyes or you can focus on a spot on the floor or wall while I read. If you have a hard time concentrating on the image in your mind, that is okay. Just try your best.

Let's start by focusing on your breath. Breathe in slowly and breathe out slowly. Focus on the feeling of filling your lungs with air. Notice the rise and fall of your chest as you breathe. (Pause)

Now, bring to mind an image of yourself in a competitive sport situation. Where are you? What time of day is it? Is it sunny, warm, rainy, or cold? Focus on what you see around you. Who is with you? Are your teammates or coaches there? (Pause)

Focus on what you hear. Is anyone talking, laughing, or yelling? What are they saying? How do you feel when they are talking to you? (Pause)

What do you smell or feel around you? If you are outside, is it the smell and feel of grass, water, wind, or sun? If you are inside, is it the hardness of the court or floor and smell of the gym? (Pause)

Notice what you feel in your body. Focus on how your muscles feel at that moment. Are they relaxed or tense? Maybe your heart is racing and you're breathing fast. Maybe your stomach feels a bit uneasy. (Pause)

Notice what thoughts or emotions run through you at this moment. Focus on feeling confident and calm. (Pause)

In your mind, imagine your team around you. What are your teammates saying and doing that make you feel confident? What are coaches saying and doing that make you feel strong? (Pause)

If worry or fear start to creep in, acknowledge them. What are they saying to you? (Pause)

Remember that worry exists because you care about doing well. You are so invested in getting better for yourself and for the team. That's what makes you successful. (Pause)

After you listen to the worry, let it go. Do this by drawing your attention to your breathing. Breathe in confidence. (Pause) Breathe out fear. (Pause) Breath in strength. (Pause) Breathe out worry. (Pause) Do this a couple more times. (Pause)

Notice how your body feels more calm and relaxed in your mind and in this moment. (Pause) Remember, you can always come back to this moment. Anytime you feel the worry and fear creep in, you can listen to it, (Pause) learn from it, (Pause) and let it go.

Now, when you are feeling ready, open your eyes and bring your mind back to this room.

Negative & Positive Self-talk

Negative Self-talk	**Positive Self-talk**
"I am going to make a mistake." ⇨ _____ ⇨ _____ ⇨	_____ _____ _____
"I will never get better!" ⇨ _____ ⇨ _____ ⇨	_____ _____ _____
"My team doesn't care about me." ⇨ _____ ⇨ _____ ⇨	_____ _____ _____

Navigating Injury

Background:

Navigating injury can be tough for the overall team and individual athletes. When athletes get injured they often struggle with emotional challenges related to being unable to engage their athletic identity and support the team in ways they are accustomed. Their teams also face challenges in reorganizing and picking-up the slack for missing athletes. It is important for leaders on teams to understand common challenges associated with injury and ways to effectively address them.

Objectives:

1. Identify common challenging emotions related to injury
2. Describe ways emotions impact cognitions and behaviors related to injury
3. Implement the acronym O.P.E.N. to resolve difficult emotions related to injury

Materials:

- Post-it notes
- Spiral notebooks
- Writing utensils
- White board or chalkboard

Leadership Council Check-ins (optional):

- Address any team issues that have come-up since last meeting
- Discuss any mentee issues that have come-up since last meeting
- Troubleshoot Platoon issues that have come-up since last meeting

Activities:

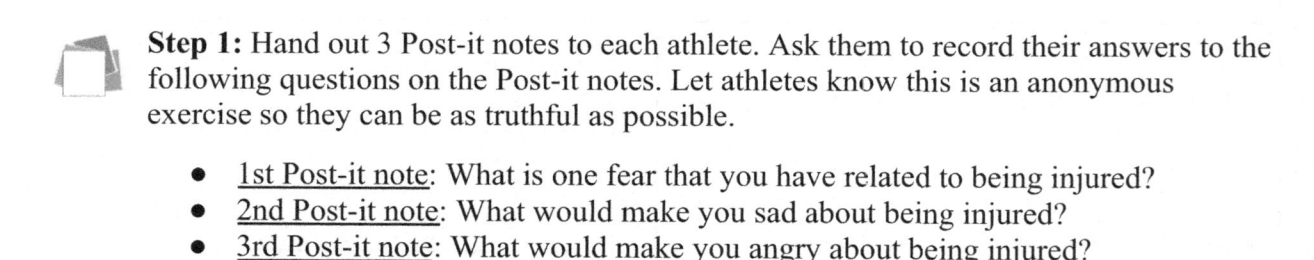

Step 1: Hand out 3 Post-it notes to each athlete. Ask them to record their answers to the following questions on the Post-it notes. Let athletes know this is an anonymous exercise so they can be as truthful as possible.

- <u>1st Post-it note</u>: What is one fear that you have related to being injured?
- <u>2nd Post-it note</u>: What would make you sad about being injured?
- <u>3rd Post-it note</u>: What would make you angry about being injured?

Step 2: Collect the Post-it notes and read them by category. Have someone record similarities and differences on the white board or chalkboard.

Step 3: Discuss how cognitions, emotions, and behaviors fit together to shape the ways we navigate concerns related to injury. Read the following:

When facing injury we can experience fear, sadness, anger, or other emotions. We can also have thoughts related to these feelings that can lead us to behave in ways that may not be the most beneficial to us or others in the short and long term. For example, if we are afraid of injury, this can cloud our ability to focus on the moment and do our best...which at times can actually lead to being injured. In the same way, if we are angry or sad that we did get injured, this may negatively impact our ability to do the things we need to do to rehabilitate. Further, these same challenging thoughts and emotions may also zap our motivation to contribute to the team in other ways. Using the acronym O.P.E.N., we can help ourselves manage challenging emotions related to injury.

Step 4: Revisit the acronym, O.P.E.N., for managing difficult emotions. Spend time reviewing each element of the acronym and how it relates to addressing emotions around injury.

- ***Open yourself to the feeling***
    - How does fighting or avoiding negative emotions related to injury get in the way of doing our best?

- ***Practice patience with yourself***
    - Why is being patient with yourself and your feelings about injury important?
    - What can we learn from worry around injury?
    - What can we learn from sadness around injury?
    - What can we learn from anger around injury?

- ***Express the feeling***
    - Why is expressing and releasing emotions about injury important?
    - What are some ways to express feelings about injury that work for you?
    - How can we help each other to express feelings about injury?

- ***Never give up***
    - How can you remind yourself to keep being open to and expressive of emotions about injury?
    - How can we remind each other to keep being open to and expressive of emotions about injury?

Step 5: Reinforce the importance of seeking social support to manage emotions and challenging thoughts related to injury as well as engage strategies to physically rehabilitate. Encourage athletes to record their answers in their notebooks.

- Who can you go to for extra support in managing emotions and thoughts related to injury:
    - Family?
    - Friend group?
    - Team?
    - School?
    - Community?

- Who can you go to for extra support in staying on track toward physical rehabilitation when injured:
    - Family?
    - Friend group?
    - Team?
    - School?
    - Community?

Looking toward the Future

Background:

It's important for athletes to reflect upon their personal values and set P.U.R.P.O.S.E. driven goals for life after high school. Personally reflecting on their values and setting related goals can help keep athletes motivated and on-track for successful and fulfilling futures. Discussions about college, vocational schools, military service, and the possibility of playing at the next level are essential discussions for high school athletes to have with the support of coaches.

Objectives:

1. Understand common risk factors in adjustment to life after graduation
2. Reflect upon personal values and how these intersect with life directions and decisions
3. Formulate P.U.R.P.O.S.E. driven goals for life after graduation

Materials:

- Spiral notebooks
- Writing utensils
- White board or chalkboard
- Copies of *P.U.R.P.O.S.E. Driven Goals for After Graduation*
- Copies of *Clarify Purpose and Direct Action toward Goals* worksheet

Leadership Council Check-ins (optional):

- Address any team issues that have come-up since last meeting
- Discuss any mentee issues that have come-up since last meeting
- Troubleshoot Platoon issues that have come-up since last meeting

Activities:

Step 1: Discuss common worries and adjustment issues faced by high school athletes looking toward graduation. Gauge athletes' views of each concern and how they may be personally impacted. Athletes can answer questions and take notes in their notebooks.

- What are the benefits of going into <u>college or vocational school</u>?
    - What college or vocational school should I apply to?
    - What do I need to do in high school to get into college or vocational school?
    - Will I need a scholarship or financial aid to attend these schools?
        - If so, how do I apply and obtain it?

- How far are these schools from my home and family?
- How will this college or vocational school help me to achieve my long-term career goals?

- What are the benefits of going into the military?
    - What branch of the military would best suit me?
    - What do I need to do in high school to get into the branch that I want to get into?
    - How will going into the military help me to achieve my long-term career goals?

- High school athletes with a desire to play at the collegiate level should consider:
    - Division:
        - What division would best fit my current and prospective athletic ability?
        - What division would allow me to enjoy my time in college the most?
        - What division will allow me to play the most?
    - Academics:
        - What academic programs/majors does the school offer and do these coincide with my career interests?
        - What is the graduation rate of student-athletes?
        - What careers are graduating student-athletes pursuing and how successful are they at pursuing them?
    - Financial needs:
        - Will I need a scholarship or financial aid to attend these schools?
        - Is the program that wants to recruit me able and willing to provide me with a scholarship?
        - If so, what amount are they able to give me and how does this compare with other schools?
        - What other monetary benefits do players receive in the program apart from scholarships (e.g. NIL opportunities, financial literacy programs)?
    - Proximity to family:
        - How far are these schools from my home and family?
        - How often will I be able to visit my home and family?
    - Quality of the program:
        - What is the current state of team cohesion within the athletic program I hope to join?
        - How do coaches get along with players?
        - Have there been recent coaching changes or changes planned in the near future?
        - How do players get along with each other?
        - How many players have transferred to other programs in the past year?

- Programmatic resources:
    - What type of programmatic resources are available to student-athletes on campus?
    - How does the program help student-athletes achieve school-sport-life balance?
        - Academic support, mental health support, sports medicine support, specialized housing, state-of-the-art training facilities, student-athlete organizations, etc.
- Walking-on:
    - If I am not offered financial assistance to my dream school and athletic program, am I willing to still attend?
    - Am I willing to try-out for the athletic program if I am not recruited for a spot on the team?
    - What will it be like if I am not able to earn a spot on the team?
    - How will I cope with the disappointment of not earning a spot?

- Independent of the road they take, high school athletes should start <u>planning for life after sport</u>, considering these questions:

    - What will life be like without the team?
    - What other purpose and goals can I set for myself to keep me motivated?
    - Who can I count on in my life to keep me on track after graduation?
    - How can I structure my life to keep me moving toward goals?
    - How can I feel good about myself and my trajectory apart from being an athlete?

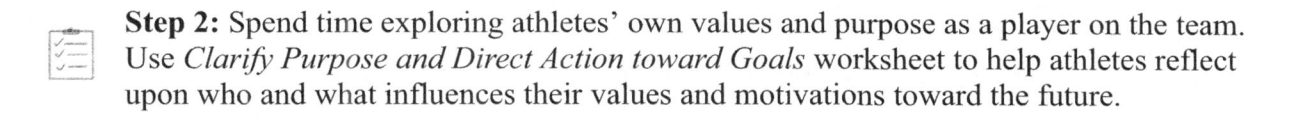

Step 2: Spend time exploring athletes' own values and purpose as a player on the team. Use *Clarify Purpose and Direct Action toward Goals* worksheet to help athletes reflect upon who and what influences their values and motivations toward the future.

Step 3: Discuss athletes' reflections on the worksheet and record themes on the board.
- Who were the people you wrote about?
- Why did you write about them?
- What values did they teach you that you still hold today?
- How did you use these values to answer questions about your future?

Step 4: Discuss *P.U.R.P.O.S.E. Driven Goals for After Graduation* worksheet, explaining each area of the acronym as it applies to life after college.

- **Prioritize your personal mission statement**
    - How do we translate values into a personal mission?

- **Unite individuals within a shared destiny**
    - How will your goals affect those around you?
    - Who else is invested in your goals?

- **Reflect risks and resilience**
    - What stands in the way of your goals now?
    - What obstacles could you face in achieving goals in the future?
    - What strengths do you have within yourself, your family, your team, your school, and your community that can help you overcome obstacles?

- **(have) Plans**
    - What do you want to achieve?
    - When do you want to achieve it?
    - Where will it be achieved?
    - Why is the goal important?
    - How will you achieve it?

- **(are) Open to feedback**
    - For those that are invested in your goal, do they also have a say in it?
    - When and how will you draw the line between what you want to do and what other people want you to do?

- **See and celebrate progress**
    - How will you celebrate progress toward your goal?
    - Who can help you do this?

- **Evaluate progress and redirect action**
    - How will you know you are making progress toward your goal?
    - How will you know when you need to adjust the goal or your plans to achieve it?
    - Who can help you do this?

P.U.R.P.O.S.E. Driven Goals for After Graduation:

Prioritize your personal mission statement
Goals should reflect your values and mission in life. If you value being a good person and challenging yourself, then your goals should help you to do those two things.

Unite individuals within a shared destiny
Goals should take into account both individual desires as well as the needs of loved ones and your community. Many professional athletes, for example, strive to use their positions to help build-up their neighborhoods and cities. Similarly, many former high school athletes go on to be teachers or coaches, inspiring and supporting countless young people.

Reflect risks and resilience
Goals should take into account your personal strengths and growing-areas as well as contextual challenges and resources. Your specific experiences, abilities, identities, and cultural background should inform your goals and the plans you make to achieve them.

(have) Plans
Goals need to have plans to make them happen. A goal plan answers these questions: Whose goal is it? What do they want to achieve? When do they want to achieve it? Where will it be achieved? Why is the goal important? How will they achieve the goal?

(are) Open to feedback
Goals and plans should be open to feedback because we need others to give us outside perspectives on things we might miss. This is even more important when loved ones are emotionally and financially invested in the goals and plans we make.

See and celebrate progress
Celebrating progress toward goals is what keeps people motivated to keep going. Building in small and large rewards along the way helps to avoid burn-out, procrastination, and giving-up.

Evaluate progress and redirect action
Evaluating progress toward goals and redirecting action when issues arise that drastically inhibit success is crucial for long-term goal attainment. When people are able to adjust their progress toward goals, they decrease their propensity toward frustration and hopelessness as well as prevent giving-up on their pursuits altogether.

Clarify Purpose and Direct Action toward Goals

Reflecting on the values we hold and where they came from helps us to clarify our purpose in life and the goals we would like to pursue in the future.

🎯 Who are the most influential people in your life as a young person?

_____
_____
_____

🎯 Why are they so important to you?

_____
_____
_____

🎯 What values do you learn from these people?

_____
_____
_____

🎯 As an adult, what values do you want to pass on to others?

_____
_____
_____

Using your values, answer the following questions about your future career:

What is something you would enjoy doing as a career that connects with your values?

_____

_____

How will this career positively influence yourself, loved ones, and the community?

_____

_____

What type of college, vocational school, military training, etc. will help you pursue this career?

_____

_____

What kinds of obstacles might you face in pursuing this career now and after graduation?

_____

_____

How could you use your strengths to overcome these obstacles?

_____

_____

References

Abrego, L. J. (2011). Legal consciousness of undocumented Latinos: Fear and stigma as barriers to claims‑making for first‑and 1.5‑generation immigrants. *Law & Society Review*, *45*(2), 337-370.

Alessi, E. J., Greenfield, B., Manning, D., & Dank, M. (2021). Victimization and resilience among sexual and gender minority homeless youth engaging in survival sex. *Journal of interpersonal violence*, *36*(23-24), 11236-11259.

Anglemyer, A., Horvath, T., & Rutherford, G. (2014). The accessibility of firearms and risk for suicide and homicide victimization among household members: a systematic review and meta-analysis. *Annals of internal medicine*, *160*(2), 101-110.

Ayón, C. (2018). Unpacking immigrant health: Policy, stress, and demographics. *Race and Social Problems*, *10*, 171-173. Alberts, A., Elkind, D., & Ginsberg, S. (2007). The personal fable and risk-taking in early adolescence. *Journal of youth and adolescence*, *36*, 71-76.

Bacon K. L., Stuver S. O., Cozier Y. C., Palmer J. R., Rosenberg L., Ruiz-Narváez E. A. (2017). Perceived racism and incident diabetes in the Black Women's Health Study. *Diabetologia*, 60(11), 2221–2225. https://doi.org/10.1007/s00125-017-4400-6

Banwell, J., & Kerr, G. (2016). Coaches' Perspectives on Their Roles in Facilitating the Personal Development of Student-Athletes. *Canadian Journal of Higher Education*, *46*(1), 1-18.

Barnum, M. (2023, November 9). *Schools face a funding cliff. how bad will the fall be?*. Chalkbeat. https://www.chalkbeat.org/2023/9/13/23871838/schools-funding-cliff-federal-covid-relief-esser-money-budget-cuts/

Baugh, C. M., Kiernan, P. T., Kroshus, E., Daneshvar, D. H., Montenigro, P. H., McKee, A. C., & Stern, R. A. (2015). Frequency of head-impact–related outcomes by position in NCAA division I collegiate football players. *Journal of Neurotrauma*, *32*(5), 314-326.

Beamon, K. (2014). Racism and stereotyping on campus: Experiences of African American male student-athletes. *The Journal of Negro Education*, *83*(2), 121-134.

Beamon, K. K. (2008). " Used Goods": Former African American College Student-Athletes' Perception of Exploitation by Division I Universities. *The Journal of Negro Education*, 352-364.

Blakemore, S. J. (2012). Development of the social brain in adolescence. *Journal of the Royal Society of Medicine*, *105*(3), 111-116.

Boden, B. P., Breit, I., Beachler, J. A., Williams, A., & Mueller, F. O. (2013). Fatalities in high school and college football players. *The American Journal of Sports Medicine*, *41*(5), 1108-1116.

Bridge, J. A., Ruch, D. A., Sheftall, A. H., Hahm, H. C., O'Keefe, V. M., Fontanella, C. A., Brock, G., Campo, J. V., & Horowitz, L. M. (2023). Youth Suicide During the First Year of the COVID-19 Pandemic. *Pediatrics (Evanston)*, *151*(3), 1-. https://doi.org/10.1542/peds.2022-058375

Bureau of Labor Statistics. (2021) https://www.bls.gov/opub/reports/race-and-ethnicity/2021/home.htm#:~:text=Survey%20(CPS).-,Among%20adult%20men%20(20%20years%20and%20older)%20in%20the%20largest,Hispanic%20men%20was%206.1%20percent.

Butcher, F., Galanek, J. D., Kretschmar, J. M., & Flannery, D. J. (2015). The impact of neighborhood disorganization on neighborhood exposure to violence, trauma symptoms, and social relationships among at-risk youth. *Social Science & Medicine, 146,* 300–306.

Centers for Disease Control and Prevention. (2023, October 25). *Preventing youth violence, CDC*. Centers for Disease Control and Prevention. https://www.cdc.gov/violenceprevention/youthviolence/fastfact.html#:~:text=Homicide%20is%20the%20third%20leading,assault%2Drelated%20injuries%20each%20day.

Centers for Disease Control and Prevention. (2023b, October 5). *Summary of initial findings from CDC-funded Firearm Injury Prevention Research |violence prevention|injury Center|CDC*. Centers for Disease Control and Prevention. https://www.cdc.gov/violenceprevention/firearms/firearm-research-findings.html

Centers for Disease Control and Prevention. (2023c, June 15). Products - data briefs - number 471 - June 2023. Centers for Disease Control and Prevention. https://www.cdc.gov/nchs/products/databriefs/db471.htm#:~:text=Vital%20Statistics%20System-,Suicide%20rates%20for%20people%20aged%2010%E2%80%9324%20increased%20from%202007,11.0)%20(Figure%201).

Centers for Disease Control and Prevention. (2023d, May 9). *Disparities in suicide*. Centers for Disease Control and Prevention. https://www.cdc.gov/suicide/facts/disparities-in-suicide.html#:~:text=Suicide%20rates%20vary%20by%20race%20and%20ethnicity&text=Non%2DHispanic%20AI%2FAN%20people,34%20is%2082.1%20per%20100%2C000.

Centers for Disease Control and Prevention. (2022, October 21). *Suicide, suicide attempt, or self-harm clusters*. Centers for Disease Control and Prevention. https://www.cdc.gov/suicide/resources/suicide-clusters.html

Centers for Disease Control and Prevention, National Center for Health Statistics. (2021). National Vital Statistics System, Mortality 2018-2021 on CDC WONDER Online Database, Data are from the Multiple Cause of Death Files, 2018-2021, as compiled from data provided by the 57 vital statistics jurisdictions through the Vital Statistics Cooperative Program. http://wonder.cdc.gov/ucd-icd10-expanded.html

Chan, A., Pullen Sansfaçon, A., & Saewyc, E. (2023). Experiences of discrimination or violence and health outcomes among Black, Indigenous and People of Colour trans and/or nonbinary youth. *Journal of Advanced Nursing, 79*(5), 2004–2013. https://doi.org/10.1111/jan.15534

Coard, S. I. (2022). Race, discrimination, and racism as "growing points" for consideration: attachment theory and research with African American families. *Attachment & Human Development, 24*(3), 373–383. https://doi.org/10.1080/14616734.2021.1976931

Cochran, B. N., Stewart, A. J., Ginzler, J. A., & Cauce, A. M. (2002). Challenges faced by homeless sexual minorities: Comparison of gay, lesbian, bisexual, and transgender homeless adolescents with their heterosexual counterparts. *American Journal of Public Health, 92*(5), 773-777.

Conway, C. A., Roy, K., Hurtado Choque, G. A., & Lewin, A. (2020). Family separation and parent–child relationships among Latinx immigrant youth. *Journal of Latinx Psychology, 8*(4), 300–316. https://doi.org/10.1037/lat0000153

Corsano, P., Musetti, A., Caricati, L., & Magnani, B. (2017). Keeping secrets from friends: Exploring the effects of friendship quality, loneliness and self-esteem on secrecy. *Journal of Adolescence, 58*, 24-32.

Crosby, S. D. (2016). Trauma-informed approaches to juvenile justice: A critical race perspective. *Juvenile and Family Court Journal, 67*(1), 5-18.

David, J. L., Powless, M. D., Hyman, J. E., Purnell, D. M., Steinfeldt, J. A., & Fisher, S. (2018). College Student Athletes and Social Media: The Psychological Impacts of Twitter Use. *International Journal of Sport Communication, 11*(2), 163-186. Retrieved Oct 24, 2023, from https://doi.org/10.1123/ijsc.2018-0044

Deal, C., Doshi, R. D., & Gonzales, G. (2023). Gender minority youth experiencing homelessness and corresponding health disparities. *Journal of Adolescent Health, 72*(5), 763-769.

Deal, C., & Gonzales, G. (2023). Homelessness among sexual minority youth. *Pediatrics, 152*(6), e2023062227.

De Arellano, M. A., Andrews III, A. R., Reid-Quiñones, K., Vasquez, D., Doherty, L. S., Danielson, C. K., & Rheingold, A. (2018). Immigration trauma among Hispanic youth: Missed by trauma assessments and predictive of depression and PTSD symptoms. *Journal of Latina/o Psychology, 6*(3), 159.

Deutsch, A., Crockett, L., Wolff, J., & Russell, S. (2012). Parent and peer pathways to adolescent delinquency: variations by ethnicity and neighborhood context. *Journal of Youth & Adolescence, 41*(8), 1078–1094. https://doi.org/10.1007/s10964-012-9754

Dixon, M. A., & Bruening, J. E. (2007). Work–family conflict in coaching I: A top-down perspective. *Journal of Sport Management, 21*(3), 377-406.

Doran, G.T. (1981) There's a SMART Way to Write Management's Goals and Objectives. Journal of Management Review, 70, 35-36.

Dragomir, R. R., & Tadros, E. (2020). Exploring the impacts of racial disparity within the American juvenile justice system. *Juvenile and Family Court Journal, 71*(2), 61-73.

Elkind, D. (1981). Understanding the young adolescent. In *The life cycle: Readings in human development* (pp. 167-176). Columbia University Press.

English D., Lambert S. F., Tynes B. M., Bowleg L., Zea M. C., Howard L. C. (2020). Daily multidimensional racial discrimination among Black U.S. American adolescents. *Journal of Applied Developmental Psychology*, 66, Article 101068. https://doi.org/10.1016/j.appdev.2019.101068

Erikson, E. H. (1963). *Childhood and society*. WW Norton & Company.

Farella Guzzo, M., & Gobbi, G. (2023). Parental death during adolescence: A review of the literature. *OMEGA-Journal of Death and Dying, 87*(4), 1207-1237.

Forde A. T., Sims M., Muntner P., Lewis T., Onwuka A., Moore K., Diez Roux A. V. (2020). Discrimination and hypertension risk Among African Americans in the Jackson Heart Study. *Hypertension*, 76(3), 715–723. https://doi.org/10.1161/HYPERTENSIONAHA.119.14492

Frey, L. M., & Fulginiti, A. (2017). Talking about suicide may not be enough: family reaction as a mediator between disclosure and interpersonal needs. *Journal of Mental Health (Abingdon, England), 26*(4), 366–372. https://doi.org/10.1080/09638237.2017.1340592

Fulginiti, L. C. (2008). Fatal footsteps: Murder of undocumented border crossers in Maricopa County, Arizona. *Journal of Forensic Sciences, 53*(1), 41-45.

Gatti, U., Tremblay, R. E., & Vitaro, F. (2009). Iatrogenic effect of juvenile justice. *Journal of Child Psychology and Psychiatry, 50*(8), 991-998.

Ghani, U., Farooq, O., Alam, S., Khan, M. J., Rahim, O., & Rahim, S. (2023). Sudden Cardiac Death in Athletes: Consensuses and Controversies. *Curēus (Palo Alto, CA), 15*(6), e39873–e39873. https://doi.org/10.7759/cureus.39873

González-Valero, G., Zurita-Ortega, F., Lindell-Postigo, D., Conde-Pipó, J., Grosz, W. R., & Badicu, G. (2020). Analysis of self-concept in adolescents before and during COVID-19 lockdown: Differences by gender and sports activity. *Sustainability, 12*(18), 7792.

Golash-Boza, T., & Hondagneu-Sotelo, P. (2013). Latino immigrant men and the deportation crisis: A gendered racial removal program. *Latino Studies, 11*, 271-292.

Gorse, M. (2022). Risk and protective factors to LGBTQ+ youth suicide: A review of the literature. *Child and Adolescent Social Work Journal, 39*(1), 17-28.

Gould, D., Carson, S., Fifer, A., Lauer, L., & Benham, R. (2009). Stakeholders' perceptions of social-emotional and life skill development issues characterizing contemporary high school sports. *Journal of Coaching Education, 2*(1), 20-44.

Gould, M., Jamieson, P., & Romer, D. (2003). Media contagion and suicide among the young. *American Behavioral Scientist, 46*(9), 1269-1284.

Graham, J. A., & Dixon, M. A. (2014). Coaching fathers in conflict: A review of the tensions surrounding the work-family interface. *Journal of Sport Management*, *28*(4), 447-456.

Griffin, P. (1994). Homophobia in sport: Addressing the needs of lesbian and gay high school athletes. *High School Journal*, 77, 80–87.

Grossman, D. C., Mueller, B. A., Riedy, C., Dowd, M. D., Villaveces, A., Prodzinski, J., ... & Harruff, R. (2005). Gun storage practices and risk of youth suicide and unintentional firearm injuries. *Jama*, *293*(6), 707-714.

Herring, C., & Henderson, L. (2016). Wealth inequality in black and white: Cultural and structural sources of the racial wealth gap. *Race and Social Problems*, *8*, 4-17.

Hicks, K., Harrison, L., & Smith, M. (2016). Not just an athlete: The impact of high school coaches on the educational pursuit of first-year African American college football players. *Journal for the Study of Sports and Athletes in Education*, *10*(1), 33-47.

Hurwich-Reiss, E., & Gudiño, OG (2016). Acculturation stress and behavior problems among Latino adolescents: The impact of family factors. *Journal of Latina/o Psychology*, *4*(4), 218.

Hsu, C. J., Meierbachtol, A., George, S. Z., & Chmielewski, T. L. (2017). Fear of reinjury in athletes: implications for rehabilitation. *Sports Health*, *9*(2), 162-167.

Imran, N., Zeshan, M., & Pervaiz, Z. (2020). Mental health considerations for children & adolescents in COVID-19 Pandemic. *Pakistan Journal of Medical Sciences*, *36*(COVID19-S4), S67.

Kaltman, S., Hurtado de Mendoza, A., Gonzales, F. A., Serrano, A., & Guarnaccia, P. J. (2011). Contextualizing the trauma experience of women immigrants from Central America, South America, and Mexico. *Journal of Traumatic Stress*, *24*(6), 635-642.

Kaukiainen, A., Salmivalli, C., Lagerspetz, K., Tamminen, M., Vauras, M., Maki, H., & Poskiparta, E. (2002). Learning difficulties, social intelligence, and self-concept: Connections to bully-victim problems. *Scandinavian Journal of Psychology,* 43, 269-278.

Kerr, G., Willson, E., & Stirling, A. (2019). Prevalence of maltreatment among current and former national team athletes. *Partnership with AthletesCAN*, 1-51.

Koutavas, A., Yera, C., Collyer, S., Curran, M., Harris, D., & Wimer, C. (2023) What Would 2022 Child Poverty Rates Have Looked Like if an Expanded Child Tax Credit Had Still Been in Place? *Poverty and Social Policy Brief 7*(3).

Lafrenière, M. A. K., Jowett, S., Vallerand, R. J., & Carbonneau, N. (2011). Passion for coaching and the quality of the coach–athlete relationship: The mediating role of coaching behaviors. *Psychology of sport and exercise*, *12*(2), 144-152.

Leachman, M., Masterson, K., & Figueroa, E. (2017). A punishing decade for school funding. *Center on Budget and Policy Priorities*, *29*, 1-17.

Logan, K., Lloyd, R. S., Schafer-Kalkhoff, T., Khoury, J. C., Ehrlich, S., Dolan, L. M., ... & Myer, G. D. (2020). Youth sports participation and health status in early adulthood: A 12-year follow-up. *Preventive medicine reports*, *19*, 101107.

Marketplace (2023). https://www.marketplace.org/2023/08/24/school-districts-end-of-federal-pandemic-funding/

Marques de Miranda, D. M., da Silva Athanasio, B., Oliveira, A. C. S., & Simoes-e-Silva, A. C. (2020). How is COVID-19 pandemic impacting mental health of children and adolescents?. *International journal of disaster risk reduction*, *51*, 101845.

Meeus, W., Iedema, J., Helsen, M., & Vollebergh, W. (1999). Patterns of adolescent identity development: Review of literature and longitudinal analysis. *Developmental review*, *19*(4), 419-461.

Mez, J., Daneshvar, D. H., Abdolmohammadi, B., Chua, A. S., Alosco, M. L., Kiernan, P. T., ... & McKee, A. C. (2020). Duration of American football play and chronic traumatic encephalopathy. *Annals of Neurology, 87*(1), 116-131.

Mez, J., Daneshvar, D. H., Kiernan, P. T., Abdolmohammadi, B., Alvarez, V. E., Huber, B. R., ... & McKee, A. C. (2017). Clinicopathological evaluation of chronic traumatic encephalopathy in players of American football. *Jama, 318*(4), 360-370.

Musetti, A., Eboli, G., Cavallini, F., & Corsano, P. (2019). Social relationships, self-esteem, and loneliness in adolescents with learning disabilities. *Clinical Neuropsychiatry, 16*(4), 165.

NAEP Report Card (2023a) NAEP Report Card: Mathematics. https://www.nationsreportcard.gov/mathematics/nation/achievement/?grade=8

NAEP Report Card (2023b) NAEP Report Card: Reading. https://www.nationsreportcard.gov/reading/nation/achievement/?grade=8

National Center for Education Statistics (2023a) Status Dropout Rates. https://nces.ed.gov/programs/coe/indicator/coj/status-dropout-rates

National Center for Education Statistics (2023b) Undergraduate Enrollment. https://nces.ed.gov/programs/coe/indicator/cha/undergrad-enrollment

National Conference of State Legislators. (2023) State Minimum Wages. https://www.ncsl.org/labor-and-employment/state-minimum-wages#:~:text=Summary,wage%20below%20%247.25%20per%20hour.

National School Board Association. (2020). Black students in the condition of Education 2020. https://www.nsba.org/Perspectives/2020/black-students-condition-education

Ocampo, R. (in press) The Warrior Mentality: A New Framework for Coaching Diverse Teams.

Osterweis, M., Solomon, F., & Green, M. (1984). *Bereavement: Reactions, consequences, and care*. National Academies Press.

Panchal, U., Salazar de Pablo, G., Franco, M., Moreno, C., Parellada, M., Arango, C., & Fusar-Poli, P. (2023). The impact of COVID-19 lockdown on child and adolescent mental health: Systematic review. *European Child & Adolescent Psychiatry, 32*(7), 1151-1177.

Park, A. L., Furie, K., & Wong, S. E. (2023). Stronger athlete identity is a risk factor for more severe depressive symptoms after musculoskeletal injury in pediatric athletes: A systematic review. *Current Reviews in Musculoskeletal Medicine, 16*(5), 220-228.

Payscale. (2019) Racial Wage Gap for Men. https://www.payscale.com/research-and-insights/racial-wage-gap-for-men/

Perry, N. B., Dollar, J. M., Calkins, S. D., Keane, S. P., & Shanahan, L. (2018). Childhood self-regulation as a mechanism through which early overcontrolling parenting is associated with adjustment in preadolescence. *Developmental psychology, 54*(8), 1542.

Phoenix Union High School District (2021) https://az01001825.schoolwires.net/cms/lib/AZ01001825/Centricity/Domain/109/SCH%20F%20Salary%20Schedule%20-%202021-22%20SY.pdf

Qiao, N., & Bell, T. M. (2017). Indigenous adolescents' suicidal behaviors and risk factors: evidence from the National Youth Risk Behavior Survey. *Journal of Immigrant and Minority Health, 19*, 590-597.

Richardson, J. B. (2012). Beyond the playing field: Coaches as social capital for inner-city adolescent African-American males. *Journal of African American Studies*, *16*, 171-194.

Rio Grande Sun (2022). Espanola Upgrades Coaches' Salaries. https://www.riograndesun.com/sports/espa-ola-upgrades-coaches-salaries/article_22e506b6-f192-11ec-82f5-c7b5e7a1ca3d.html

Rogol, A. D., Roemmich, J. N., & Clark, P. A. (2002). Growth at puberty. *Journal of adolescent health*, *31*(6), 192-200.

Romer, D., Jamieson, P. E., & Jamieson, K. H. (2006). Are news reports of suicide contagious? A stringent test in six US cities. *Journal of Communication*, *56*(2), 253-270.

Ruddock-Hudson, M., O'Halloran, P., & Murphy, G. (2012). Exploring psychological reactions to injury in the Australian Football League (AFL). *Journal of Applied Sport Psychology, 24*(4), 375–390. https://doi.org/10.1080/10413200.2011.654172

Ryan, R. M., & Kuczkowski, R. (1994). The imaginary audience, self-consciousness, and public individuation in adolescence. *Journal of Personality*, *62*(2), 219-238.

Ryan, T. D., & Sagas, M. (2011). Coaching and family: The beneficial effects of multiple role membership. *Team Performance Management: An International Journal*, *17*(3/4), 168-186.

Saffici, C. (2015). Teaching & coaching: The challenges and conflicts of dual roles. *The Sport Journal*. https://doi.org/10.17682/sportjournal/2015.005

Sakdiyakorn, M., Golubovskaya, M., & Solnet, D. (2021). Understanding Generation Z through collective consciousness: Impacts for hospitality work and employment. *International Journal of Hospitality Management*, *94*, 102822.

Salhi, C., Azrael, D., & Miller, M. (2021). Parent and adolescent reports of adolescent access to household firearms in the United States. *JAMA network open*, *4*(3), e210989-e210989.

Sánchez, B., Hurd, N. M., Neblett, E. W., & Vaclavik, D. (2018). Mentoring for Black male youth: A systematic review of the research. *Adolescent Research Review*, *3*, 259-278.

Santiago, C. D., Wadsworth, M. E., & Stump, J. (2011). Socioeconomic status, neighborhood disadvantage, and poverty-related stress: Prospective effects on psychological syndromes among diverse low-income families. *Journal of Economic Psychology*, *32*(2), 218-230.

Schenewark, J., & Dixon, M. (2012). A dual model of work-family conflict and enrichment in collegiate coaches. *Journal of Issues in Intercollegiate Athletics, 5*, 15-39.

Schwartz, P. D., Maynard, A. M., & Uzelac, S. M. (2008). Adolescent egocentrism: a contemporary view. *Adolescence*, *43*(171).

Sewell A. A. (2017). The illness associations of police violence: Differential relationships by ethnoracial composition. *Sociological Forum*, 32(S1), 975–997. https://doi.org/10.1111/socf.12361

Sheats, K. J., Irving, S. M., Mercy, J. A., Simon, T. R., Crosby, A. E., Ford, D. C., ... & Morgan, R. E. (2018). Violence-related disparities experienced by black youth and young adults: Opportunities for prevention. *American Journal of Preventive Medicine*, *55*(4), 462-469.

Shering, S. (2024). 120,000 gun safes recalled after safety features fail; 6-year-old reportedly opens safe. https://publications.aap.org/aapnews/news/28368/120-000-gun-safes-recalled-after-safety-features?autologincheck=redirected

Sibrava N. J., Bjornsson A. S., Pérez Benítez A., Moitra E., Weisberg R. B., Keller M. B. (2019). Posttraumatic stress disorder in African American and Latinx adults: Clinical course and the role of racial and ethnic discrimination. *The American Psychologist*, 74(1), 101–116. https://doi.org/10.1037/amp0000339

Simonetto, D., Hannem, S., & Thomson, E. F. (2022). From field to family: The ripple effects of sports‑related violence. *Power Played: A Critical Criminology of Sport*, 201-219.

Soto J. A., Dawson-Andoh N. A., BeLue R. (2011). The relationship between perceived discrimination and Generalized Anxiety Disorder among African Americans, Afro Caribbeans, and non-Hispanic Whites. *Journal of Anxiety Disorders*, 25(2), 258–265. https://doi.org/10.1016/j.janxdis.2010.09.011

Slutzky, C. B., & Simpkins, S. D. (2009). The link between children's sport participation and self-esteem: Exploring the mediating role of sport self-concept. *Psychology of Sport and Exercise*, 10(3), 381-389.

Smith, D. L. (2008). Disability, gender and intimate partner violence: Relationships from the behavioral risk factor surveillance system. *Sexuality and Disability*, 26, 15-28.

Stone, D.M., Holland, K.M., Bartholow, B., Crosby, A.E., Davis, S., and Wilkins, N. (2017). Preventing suicide: A technical package of policies, programs, and practices.

Svanelöv, E., Wallén, E. F., Enarsson, P., & Stier, J. (2020). 'Everybody with disability should be included': A qualitative interview study of athletes' experiences of disability sports participation analysed with ideas of able-mindedness. *Scandinavian Journal of Disability Research*, 22(1).

The Board of Governors of the Federal Reserve System. (2023) Greater Wealth, Great Uncertainty: Changes in Racial Inequality in the Survey of Consumer Finances.
https://www.federalreserve.gov/econres/notes/feds-notes/greater-wealth-greater-uncertainty-changes-in-racial-inequality-in-the-survey-of-consumer-finances-20231018.html

The Institute for Diversity and Ethics in Sport (2022). The 2022 DI FBS Leadership College Racial and Gender Report Card: The lack of diversity within collegiate athletic leadership continues.
https://www.tidesport.org/_files/ugd/c01324_28927dc8a8cf4c2db2c444cc8334fc6e.pdf

The Washington Post. (2022) *How the NFL Blocks Black Coaches*.
https://www.washingtonpost.com/sports/interactive/2022/nfl-black-head-coaches/

Tracey, J. (2003). The emotional response to the injury and rehabilitation process. *Journal of Applied Sport Psychology*, 15(4), 279–293. https://doi.org/10.1080/714044197

Trevor Project (2023). https://www.thetrevorproject.org/

U.S. Department of Education. (2022). *U.S. Department of Education announces over $220 million dollars in investments from government, private, and public sectors to support student recovery*.
https://www.ed.gov/news/press-releases/us-department-education-announces-over-220-million-dollars-investments-government-private-and-public-sectors-support-student-recovery

U.S. Census Bureau. (2023, September 12). *Poverty in the United States: 2022*. Census.gov.
https://www.census.gov/library/publications/2023/demo/p60-280.html#:~:text=Highlights-,Official%20Poverty%20Measure,and%20Table%20A%2D1

Van Itallie, T. B. (2019). Traumatic brain injury (TBI) in collision sports: Possible mechanisms of transformation into chronic traumatic encephalopathy (CTE). *Metabolism*, 100, 153943.

Van Leijenhorst, L., Zanolie, K., Van Meel, C. S., Westenberg, P. M., Rombouts, S. A., & Crone, E. A. (2010). What motivates the adolescent? Brain regions mediating reward sensitivity across adolescence. *Cerebral cortex*, 20(1), 61-69.

Ventresca, M., & Henne, K. (2022). Is CTE a defense for murder? Critical insights into violence, crime, and brain trauma in sports. *Power Played*, 177–200. https://doi.org/10.59962/9780774867818-008

Vogel, E. A., Rose, J. P., Roberts, L. R., & Eckles, K. (2014). Social comparison, social media, and self-esteem. *Psychology of Popular Media Culture,* 3(4), 206–222. https://doi.org/10.1037/ppm0000047

Washington-Childs, A. E. (2017). The NFL's problem with off-field violence: How CTE exposes athletes to criminality and CTE's potential as a criminal defense. *Virginia Sports & Entertainment Law Journal*, 17, 244.

Wilhite, B., & Shank, J. (2009). In praise of sport: Promoting sport participation as a mechanism of health among persons with a disability. *Disability and Health Journal*, 2(3), 116–127. https://doi.org/10.1016/j.dhjo.2009.01.002

Wilson, P. E., & Clayton, G. H. (2010). Sports and disability. *PM & R : The Journal of Injury, Function, and Rehabilitation*, 2(3), S46–S56. https://doi.org/10.1016/j.pmrj.2010.02.002

Witt, P. A. (2018). Why children/youth drop out of sports. *Journal of Park and Recreation Administration*, 36(3), 191–199. https://doi.org/10.18666/jpra-2018-v36-i3-8618

Yarcheski, A., & Mahon, N. E. (2016). Meta-analyses of predictors of hope in adolescents. *Western journal of nursing research*, 38(3), 345-368.

Made in the USA
Columbia, SC
07 July 2024